YOUR HISTORY IS NOT OUR STORY

Christian Heritage Rediscovered

The Series, as the name suggests, is meant to focus on Christian Faith & Living vis-à-vis topics like Literature & Poetry, Indigenous Philosophizing, Ethical response towards Agriculture, Health & Healing, Science & Technology, Ecofeminist Theology, Sociological approach towards Human Rights, Law & Politics, Arts, History of Ideas, Ancient Civilizations, Cultural Contiguity, Religious Cosmologies & Mysticism, Footsteps of famous Theologians, World Peace & Harmony, Global Capitalism, Network Marketing, Cybertheology, Population & Demographics, Epigraphic Studies, Contextualized Education, and many others. We welcome a Mss. on any topic/s mentioned, whether they are original works, scholarly monographs, collections of conference papers, revised dissertations, or translations of historical documents. Through the Series we, the Publishers, are striving to put forward published works that may help Institutions, Academic Bodies, Researchers, Scholars and the World at large in furthering their respective knowledge and understanding on the concerned subject. We welcome your comments on our efforts and further suggestions on how we can foster the upcoming thoughtful theologically grounded books.

Christian Heritage Rediscovered - 79

YOUR HISTORY IS NOT OUR STORY

Re-imaging Colonial Historiography of Tribals and Christianity in North East India

Walotemjen
&
Songram Basumatary

CWI
Christian World Imprints

This volume is a compilation of the articles written by Lt. Dr. Walotemjen and Rev. Dr. Songram Basumatary of Gurukul Lutheran Theological College & Research Institute, Chennai, India, compiled and edited by Rev. Dr. Songram Basumatary. Though the articles by Lt. Dr. Walotemjen, included/published herein, appear posthumously, these bear moral right to be identified as his original writings.

Compiled and Edited by: Songram Basumatary

First Published in 2019 by

Christian World Imprints
Christian Publishing & Books from India
H-12 Bali Nagar, **New Delhi-110015**
info@christianworldimprints.com
www.ChristianWorldImprints.com
Phone: +91 11 25465925

ISBN: 978-93-5148-352-6 (HB)
ISBN: 978-93-5148-353-3 (PB)

Printed in India.

Dedicated to

The Beloved parents,
A. Senti Jamir and T. Meyila Pongen

Contents

Preface

The title of this book, "YOUR HISTORY IS NOT OUR STORY" is used as a tribute to Lt. Dr. Walotemjen Jamir, a short-lived budding Indian Church Historian who was very much concerned and burdened with the question of misrepresented image in the historiography of Subaltern communities as a whole and the tribes of North East India in specific. The 'Your History' here is used to refer the history written by the dominant historiographers; and the 'Our Story' to refer the real life or lived-life stories of people on whom history is written about.

Dr. Walotemjen Jamir was born on 19th August, 1974 in Mokokchung, Nagaland, India, and while in service at Gurukul Lutheran Theological College & Research Institute, Chennai, he unexpectedly passed away at the age of 44. He was born to his parents A. Senti Jamir and T. Meyila Pongen who are very devout evangelical Christians. Among the five children born to them, Dr. Walotemjen was the second one. But after his older brother's death at the age of just 21, Dr. Walotemjen became like a first child in the family on whom rests the certain special desires of parents to be fulfilled as per the traditional Naga society. And being a devout evangelical Christian, it was his parents' desire that one of their children is dedicated for ministry of the Lord.

Dr. Walotemjen did his schooling in Don Bosco School, Tuli, Nagaland; Senior Secondary education in Mountain View Christian College, Kohima, Nagaland; and B.A. from North Eastern Hills University (NEHU), Shillong. It was like spirit leading him to fulfil the desires of his parents, while he was in college, whenever he comes home he used to tell his parents that he would like to study theology after his graduation.

The desire of his parents and the dream of his own came into reality in God's opportuned time. Right after the completion of B.A. in 1996, he pursued Bachelor in Divinity studies at Clark Theological College, Mokokchung, Nagaland; and after being awarded B.D. degree in 2000, he joined for Master of Theology in History of Christianity, at FFRRC, Mar Thoma Theological Seminary, Kottayam,

Kerala in 2003 and earned the M.Th. degree in the year 2005; and with the inspiration and wholehearted support of his parents and his only one sister, Dr. Imosongla Jamir, he continued Doctor of Theology studies in 2007 in the same Seminary and awarded the Doctor of Theology in History of Christianity by the Senate of Serampore College (University) on 8th February 2014.

In between and after the theological studies, he served the Church and few theological institutions in various capacities. In 2000, he was ordained as a Youth Pastor at Yimyu Baptist Church, Mokokchung, and served the Church till 2003. After the M.Th. studies, he worked as an Academic Dean at Withee Bible College, Dimapur, Nagaland, as well as lecturer at Bethel Bible College, Guntur, A.P. And right after completing his D. Th., he was appointed as Assistant Professor at Gurukul in 2011. Since then, he has been serving Gurukul in various capacities such as HoD of the History of Christianity, Dean of Martin Luther Library, Head of Dalit/Tribal/Adivasi Studies, etc. and was also appointed as Dean of Graduate Studies just before his sudden death. While in Gurukul, he got married with Temjentola Ozukum on 8th October 2015 and blessed with a son – Lensur Jamir on 26th August 2017. But, very unfortunate that while College was just reopening for new academic session (2018-2019), he suddenly fell ill and admitted in Apollo Hospital, Chennai on 11th June 2018, and died of multiple organ failure on 15th July 2018.

Dr. Walotemjen has left multiple fond memories in the hearts of many Senate of Serampore College (University) theological fraternities in general and the Gurukul community in particular. As a person, he will be remembered for his affable and humane image filled with humour and joy in his hearts and in his words. Doubtlessly, his commitment, integrity, sincerity both in daily life and academic life remain as footprint to be followed by many. More so, academically his bibliophilism and the persistent and uncomplicated critical thinking and articulation with conscience and a sense of responsibility are something inspirational. He was truly concerned and burdened with various issues the subaltern communities are facing. One of his topmost priorities that needs to be challenged in order to have a dignified identity and human life among the Dalit/Tribal/Adivasi in general and NEI tribes in specific is reimaging the historiography about them. For, according to him, the history written by the dominant historians are not the true story of the people. To a Dalit, a history of Dalit is not his/her story. To a Tribal, a history of Tribal is not his/her story. To a woman, history is his-tory, not her story.

His seven articles along with six of mine included in this volume are the replicas of that challenge. For, history is not only written on a particular event, but it is written from the story of people. As history of any kind is written based on the available sources, the event, story and story-teller are part and parcel of writing history. However, what happened and still what is happening in the writings of history of people at the margins is that the historians are not part of the event, story or the story-teller.What is the space of the people in the history? Are they mere objects of history-writing or they are subjects as well? These are some of the serious questions Dr. Walotemjen wrestled with and challenged in his writings.

He argued that the author of the history is people themselves on whom the history is written. Of course, the author of the history for him should not necessarily be from within the people about whom the history is written, but at least represented truly. The issues in the present historiography is like story is on someone, story-teller is somebody else, and the history writer is yet another one. For example, the colonizers, anthropologists and missionaries described who the tribals are and told the story about them according to their perceptions and subjective views. And based on their reports or narratives, the history is written. In the process, there has never been an objective history written about them. The true story of the people is never told and written. What has come about in the history is subjective representation of historiographer from outside. Perhaps, a complete mismatched in depicting who they are and who they are not.

There are always two sides to history. The first is the narrative history that records the events and the second is analytic history that analyse the meaning of the events. The source of narrative history is event, and it is mostly written based on the reports, stories, written documents and other historical evidences of the event created or discovered after the events. The objective of such histories has to do with what occurred in the past, what lesson one can learn for what is happening today, and what insight one may draw for what is going to happen tomorrow. Here, the questions on set are: "Based on what sources the history written?"; "With what objective was it written?" and "What insight or lesson one can draw or learn from such history?"

It is evident that history on the people at the margins are written as descriptive and prescriptive in nature in order to suit the convenience of the dominants. Perhaps, it is a common fact that history is written by the winners about the losers, not the losers writing about the winners or about themselves. The losing side has less or no chance at all presenting their stories. The history is mostly written to appropriate the dominant people's anti-native agenda without recognizing the lived-stories of people and deep realities of events.

What has gone wrong with the history of people at the margins like Dalits, Tribals of India and the various tribes of NEI is exactly this. Neither the history written objectively, nor their stories considered as the primary sources of writing their history. The historians who wrote history about them are not the historians of people and the public. Their history is not written from the pragmatic prism. It is less or no analytic, but more descriptive and prescriptive. It is certainly not people's history, but the history of events where people are treated as objects. Therefore, as interpretation of the lives and events of people of the past has a tremendous influence on the present, such history has done a colossal damage to their image. And as historical analysis and the written history are commonly used as tools by various agencies, the distorted history of Tribals in India in general, and NEI in particular are utilized at maximum to keep them at the margins of mainstream society.

Therefore, the objective of this book is to bring out to light the very fact of dehumanizing image projected about the people's at the margins, especially the North East Indian tribes and make an attempt to reimage the history written with colonial and missionary prisms about them. The first and the second chapters are a quick look at the background of North East India and a mutual mistaken perception and tension between what is called mainland India and the North East India. The third to seven chapters are all about the issues raised above. The first one on the set is on the "Hegemonic Colonial Historiography over the History of NEI Tribes" where the author highlights the strangeness of the history of NEI tribes. The second and the third on the set, i.e., chapter four and five explore the possibility of reconstructing Tribal Historiography with their own resources with strong emphasis on oral history. The six is an attempt to recover and reconstruct the true story of women and write the feminist historiography.

From chapters seven to nine are analysis on the theories and motives of conversion movements among the Dalits and Tribals in India and in Nagaland among the Ao Nagas; the positive and negative impacts of Christianity upon Tribes of NEI. Finally, the chapters ten to thirteen talk about the dynamics between Christianity and Administrators and how Christianity brought about Tribal Awakening in North East India and various ethno-political movements based on the question of identity, and lastly the role of Christianity in NEI in public sphere today.

As a compiler and editor of the book as well as co-author, I take my pleasure to extend heartfelt gratitude to the institution where Dr.Walotemjen and I got space and opportunity to reflect and work on the basic critical questions raised in this book. I also thank the family members of Dr.Walotemjen, especially his wife, Temjentola Ozukum and sister Dr. Imosongla Jamir, the Asst. Professor in the Dept. of Tourism, Hotel, Hospitality and Heritage Studies, Jamia Millia Islamia (A Central University), New Delhi for their complete trust and opportunity given to me in bringing out the book. I also thank Mr. Sudhanshu Kanda, the Christian World Imprints, for his great help in publishing the book within a very short period of time.

May the spirit of Dr. Walotemjen rest in peace in eternity and his family members and all the readers of this book be blessed on earth!

Songram Basumatary
Compiler & Editor
06.03.2019

Chapter 1

Bird's Eye View of the North East India

North-East India?

North-East India (NEI) is the uncritically-constructed and commonly-used name of "seven sister" states of the Indian Union – Arunachal Pradesh, Assam, Manipur, Meghalaya, Mizoram, Nagaland and Tripura. Perhaps, the reorganisation of the region into autonomous political units was the initial impetus that necessitated the coinage of this new neologism.[1] The National Integration Policy makers felt necessity to bunch together the geographical entity, the social setting, economy, politics and aspirations of the ethnic groups of the region into one unit. With such political and noble economic aim in view, the North East Council (NEC) was formed in 1972 by the order of the President of India as the region's apex funding and development agency. Since then, the Indian intelligentsia, the bureaucracy as well as the media began to use "North-East India" as a name for eight states including Sikkim.[2] As a matter of fact, some of the serious questions relating to this neologism are: Is NEI one geo-political unit? Is it not a complex ethnic equated region? Who are the Northeasterners? Can one get a clear picture of the region and people by this name? Is this politically legitimised policy of bunching together a help anyway?

[1] For a detailed discussion on this issue, see Sujit Choudhury, "The North-East: A Concept Re-examined," in *Dynamics of Identity and Intergroup Relations in North-East India*, ed. Kailash S. Aggarwal (Shimla: IIAS, 1999), 90-97.

[2] Sikkim has recently been formally bracketed under "North-East" after it has been included into the North Eastern Council (NEC).

The turn of the events in the political history of NEI in recent decades is the reactions against the outcomes of clubbing the region together, and an attempt to look at it as a single entity and stereotyping of the region as troubled zones of Indian Union. This political legitimisation, indeed, has swallowed the ethnic groups of the region into "Indian minorities" in the political process. It has helped to ignore the distinct identities, and the specific concerns, grievances and aspirations of various tribes related to their rich traditions, religions, history, customs and cultures. Therefore, often it is resented that "the concept of North-east and the regional reorganisation of this multi-ethnic setting has done colossal damage in social, political and economic parameters."[3]

The Land and People

Geographically, NEI lies between 22° and 29° North Latitude and 89° and 97° East Longitude. It is surrounded by 99% international boundaries with Bhutan and Tibet (China) in the North and North-East, Myanmar in the South and South-East and Bangladesh in the South-West. It is connected with the rest of India by a narrow corridor commonly called: "Chicken's Neck" between Nepal in the North and Bangladesh in the South near Siliguri, (North Bengal) approximately measuring 20/22 KM. Therefore, the oft-repeated cliché by many authors of the region is that the region is land-locked.

The region covers only 2,56,083 square kilometres,[4] bounded with difficult mountain terrain and river intersected green valleys. Topographically, the region is divided into five physiographic blocks namely, the Assam Himalayas, the Brahmaputra Valley, the Shillong Plateau, the Barak/Surma Valley and South-Eastern hilly region. Since the largest portion of the area is mountainous, the majority of the people inhabit the four plains areas – the Brahmaputra Valley, the Barak/Surma Valley (in Assam and Manipur), the Tripura Plains and the Manipur Plateau.[5] Geo-politically it is divided into two regions – hills and plains. Climatically, the region presents three types of climate – the humid tropical climate in Assam plains and Tripura; the pleasant sub-Alpine type in Meghalaya, the high altitude tectonic valleys of Nagaland and the typical Alpine cold climate prevalent in the lesser and higher Himalaya regions of Arunachal Pradesh. Such a geographical location with difficult terrain and poor means of communication, promoted the growth of a distinct culture and practices, which were different from those of the plains.[6]

---

[3] U.A. Shimray, "Socio-Political Unrest in the Region Called North-East India," *EPW* XXXIX/42 (October 16-22, 2004): 4637.

[4] *Basic Statistics of NER 2006*, available at: http://databank.nedfi.com

[5] Cf. N. K. Das, *Ethnic Identity, Ethnicity and Social Stratification in North East India* (New Delhi: Inter-India Publications, 1989), 28.

[6] Perhaps, in reality, the mountains served the region two ways – on the one hand it shielded as defensive ramparts, safe from foreign invasions but on the other hand it shielded from development

With regard to the people, tracing the development of human history of the unrecorded past of the region has been a daunting task to the historians, archaeologists and social anthropologists. At times, NEI has even been ignored by archaeologists. The founder of Indian Archaeology, Lord Cunningham, who surveyed the entire length and breadth of India, did not venture to set foot in the region. If we glance at the archaeological Atlas of India during that time, we find the whole NEI blank. Dhavalikar terms this region as *terra incognita.*[7] Though there are remarkable archaeological activities in different parts of the country during post-independence India, this region of the country has not yet received due attention. Despite the region being attracted by researchers of related disciplines to her geographical location, geo-archaeological features, ethnic composition and many other such considerations, a concrete archaeological evidence is still very meagre till today. The modern archaeological methods of exploration and excavation could uncover only very little about the region. Even the study and research in archaeology on the region relatively is very new and recent one. With regard to anthropology, though there are strong criticisms levelled against them,[8] we have to rely heavily on the writings of British colonial anthropologists.

Nevertheless, an analysis of the history, anthropology and archaeological findings on ancient culture presently available, and presenting them, particularly to the historians and theological community, may help the contemporary native history writers and theologians with regard to the stories of historical and cultural continuities and discontinuities. Therefore, an attempt is made here to review some of the earlier studies done by the archaeologists and social anthropologists in order to initiate a discussion about something explicit about the issue of historiography and theology in the region.

Among the earliest archaeological literature on the region is G.E. Westmacott's article – "Description of Ancient Temples and Ruins at Chardwar in Assam" published in the *Journal of the Asiatic Society of Bengal* in 1835, following which, some army personnel as well as some civilians undertook similar ventures.[9] However, it was only in 1867, that Sir John Lubbock from University of London in his article – "The Stone Age, Stone Tools in Upper Assam", for the first time reported about the evidence of prehistoric culture from the region that appeared

---

as well by solitary confinement.

[7] Cf. M.K. Dhavalikar, "Archaeology of Gauhati," *Bulletin of the Deccan College, P & R Institute* (1973): 137.

[8] For instance, Pathy comments that: "Anthropology, like all other social sciences, is historically and socially conditioned. [It] originated in the colonial milieu to meet primarily the administrative problems that arose in the process of expansion and consolidation of colonialism. Therefore, for a long time, it continued to reflect the interest of the colonial empires". Jaganath Pathy, "Imperialism, Anthropology and the Third World," *EPW* 16/14 (April 4, 1981): 623.

[9] Cf. Gautam Sengupta and Jai Prakash Singh, "Introduction," in *Archaeology of North-East India*, ed. Gautam Sengupta and Jai Prakash Singh (New Delhi: Har-Anand Publications, 1991), xii.

in June 22 issue of *Atheneum.*[10] Since then, there were sporadic reports of finding polished stone tools in different parts of the region in journals and periodicals published in India and abroad.[11] The first systematic study on the prehistoric culture of the region appeared in an article "Prehistory of Assam" in *Man in India* only in 1928 by John Hutton, then Deputy Commissioner of the Naga Hills.[12] Different relics unearthed so far in various sites of the region give some glimpses of Paleolithic,[13] Microlithic, Hoabinhian and Neolithic[14] cultural pasts.[15] Yet, till now, the greatest hurdle is to ascertain a clear picture of the prehistoric people of the region and their cultures. To determine at what point of time the early people first settled in NEI, there is a need of further excavations and systematic explorations.

However, in terms of populace, it is crystal clear that the region is the homeland of large tribes who belong to different ethnic and linguistic backgrounds. Ethnologically, the region is called as melting pot of many branches of the human race, cultures, language, religion and historical backgrounds. This suggest that the region has been "one of the greatest routes of migration of [hu]mankind."[16] Waves

---

[10] J. Lubbock, "The Stone Age, Stone Tools in Upper Assam," *Athenaeum* (June 22, 1867): 822.

[11] For instance, see E.H. Steel, "Celts Found Among the Namsang Nagas," *Proceedings of the Asiatic Society of Bengal* (1870): 267-68.; Lt. Barron, "Note on Stone Implements from the Naga Hills," *Journal of the Royal Anthropological Institute* 1 (1872): 62-63; H.H. Godwin-Austin, "A Celt Found in the Khasi Hills at Shillong," *Proceedings of the Asiatic Society of Bengal* (1875): 158.; H.C. Dasgupta, "On Two-shouldered Stone Implements from Assam," *Journal of the Asiatic Society of Bengal* 9 (1913): 291-93.; S.C. Brown, "Grooved Stone Hammers from Assam, etc.," *Journal of the Asiatic Society of Bengal* 10/4 (1914): 107-9.; R.D. Banerjee, "Neolithic Implements from the Abor Country," *Annual Report of the Archaeological Survey of India* 102 (1924-25): 102.; J.H. Hutton, "Two Celts from the Naga Hills," *Man* 24/15 (1924): 20-22.; G.D. Walker, "Garo Manufacturing of Bark Cloth," *Man* 75/5 (1931): 15-16.

[12] J. H. Hutton, "Prehistory of Assam," *Man in India* 8/4 (Dec.1928): 228-32.

[13] For the first time, Bopardikar of the Archaeological Survey of India discovered Palaeoliths in Daphamum area of Lohit District of Arunachal Pradesh. Cf. B.P. Bopardikar, "Prehistoric Investigation Daphabhum Scientific Survey Expedition (NEFA)," in *Archaeological Congress and Seminar* (Nagpur: Nagpur University, 1972), 1-8.

[14] The first remarkable archaeological discovery site of the region is Daojali Hading of the North Cachar Hills District of Assam. The excavators found stone tools, mullers, pestles, grinding stone or hewns, cord-marked pottery, bone fragments and a piece of tortoise shell that shows region's linkage with South East Asian cultures in the Neolithic period. Cf. M.C. Goswami and A.C. Bhagabati, "A Preliminary Report on a Collection of Neolithic Tool Types from West Assam," *Man in India* 39/4 (1959): 312-24.; M.C. Goswami and T.C. Sharma, "A Brief Report on the Investigation into Prehistoric Archaeology in the N.C. Hills," *Journal of Gauhati University* 13/2 (1963): 63-66.

[15] For detail on this, see T. B. Subba and G.C. Ghosh, eds., *The Anthropology of North-East India* (New Delhi: Orient Longman, 2003), 14-25.

[16] J. H. Mills, *Assam Review* (March, 1928), 24. As cited in Swarna Lata Baruah, *A Comprehensive History of Assam* (New Delhi: Munshiram Manoharlal Publishers Pvt. Ltd., 1985), 3.

of people belonging to different ethnic groups flocked into this region from time immemorial. As the stories go, groups of tribes-people migrated from one place to other in search of fertile land in order to make their home. Thus, the region has been a veritable meeting point of diverse ethnic groups as they came in spurts from everywhere. As a result there is an inter-mingling of races and in its fall-out, it is difficult to ascertain the roots of the various groups. In the plains, there is a concomitant inter-mixing of people and in the hills, isolation. The North-Eastern tribes, mainly in the hills are in some important respects different from their far more numerous counterparts in Middle India. They constitute local majorities within recognised territories where their distinctive cultures have long flourished in relative isolation.

Most of the tribes and non-tribes are immigrants[17] who entered the region in successive waves either from the neighbouring countries or from the Indo-Gangetic plain.[18] It is generally contended that the tribes of the NEI, apart from some of the dominant plain people, are mainly from the Mongoloid stock. According to M. Hussain,

> Almost all the tribals are held to be the remnants of primitive or ancient Mongolian migrants to this region. They established themselves in their present homeland in the remotest past. Needless to say, the tribals are undoubtedly the original natives of Assam [NEI]. Even in the non-tribal dominated Brahmaputra Valley today, it was the Bodo-Kachari tribals who created the first culture and civilisation and in a real sense they are the first natives of the valley.[19]

But due to lack of the exact dates of the migrations, it is very difficult to ascertain who settled first in the region. Whosoever may be the earliest settlers of the region, the general assumption is that the Tibeto-Burmans of the Indo-Chinese stock poured into the region since 2000 BC onwards. The original home of these Mongoloid people was the upper courses of the Yangtse-Kiang and the Hoang-Ho in North-West China.[20] Historically speaking, the Kiratas/Bodo-Kocharis are among the earliest known inhabitants. According to some scholars, the Bodos or Bodo-Kacharis, the early migrants of Mongoloid stock from China, could be the

---

[17] As per the findings of the Anthropological Survey of India, in fact, all tribal people in India have been migrants. Almost all the tribal groups have oral traditions and historical accounts of their migration. Cf. K.S. Singh, *The Scheduled Tribes: People of India*, National Series, vol. III, Anthropological Survey of India (Delhi: OUP, 1994), 7.

[18] Cf. B.B. Goswami, "The Tribes of Assam: A Few Comments on their Societal and Cultural Ties with the Non-Tribes," in *Tribal Situation in India*, ed. K.S. Singh (Shimla: IIAS, 1972), 271.

[19] Monirul Hussain, "Tribal Question in Assam," *EPW* XXVII/20 & 21 (May 16, 1992): 1047.

[20] For details, see Baruah, *A Comprehensive History of Assam...*, 66-67.

original autochthons of Assam.[21] The Bodo tribes occupying the plains, gradually built up a distinctive culture of their own.[22] It seems that subsequent to the arrival of the various tribes of Tibeto-Burmans there must have been a mingling of races, languages and cultures in then Assam. Considering the some of the custom and cultural traits of some tribes, it is also evident that the Negroids and the Austro-Asiatics preceded them. In that matter, the Dravidians also possibly preceded the Mongoloids. The Negrito elements allied to the Papuans and the Andamanese form one of the earliest strains in the population of the hills, particularly among the Nagas. Both ethnography and material culture of the tribes point to the existence of such a strain.[23] Some of the physical and cultural features indicate similarities with the Papuan and Melanesian physical features and Negroid cult. For instance, physical features like woolly hair found among some Ao, Rengma, Phom, Konyak Nagas and Nishis, and reverence for the ficus and practice of hanging combs of bees and wasp in the entrance of the houses of some Nagas are similar with the Negroid cult.[24] The last stock of people flocking to the region were the Alphines[25] and the Aryans.[26]

Due to such geographical features and racial compositions, NEI is regarded as a distinct geo-ethnic unit. The region today is an ethnic minefield. There is no exact figure of tribes and linguistic groups. The estimated number varies from scholar to scholar.[27] K. S. Singh in his book, *The Scheduled Tribes* lists

[21] Cf. Edward Gait, *A History of Assam* (Guwahati: LBS Publications, 1983 [1926]), 236.; Singh, K.S. *The Scheduled Tribes: People of India* National Series III, Anthropological Survey of India (Delhi: OUP, 1994).; Hussain: 1047.

[22] Kanaklal Barua, "Pre-historic Culture in Assam", in Kanaklal Barua, *Studies in the Early History of Assam: A Collection of Papers Published in Research Journals on Aspects of the History and Culture of Assam*, ed. M. Neog (Gauhati/Jorhat: Assam Sahitya Sabha, 1973), 207-220 (218-220). [This article appeared in two parts in *JARS*, VII/1 (April 1939), 6-18 & VII/2 (July 1939), 35-41]

[23] Cf. Ibid., 66.

[24] For details, see P.C. Choudhury, *The History of Civilization of the People of Assam to the Twelfth Century A.D.* (Gauhati: Gauhati University, 1966), 79ff.

[25] For detail study on the presence and influence of Alphines in NEI, see "Alphines in Eastern India," Ibid., 121-131.; M. Neog, "Introduction," and "History behind a Phonetic Difficulty," in Barua, xviii-xix & 192-97.

[26] Cf. Baruah, 65-68.

[27] In his incomplete survey, Rakshat Puri identified just 42 major tribes. Cf. Rakshat Puri, "Towards Security in the North-East: Transportation and Nationalism," in *Tribal Situation in India*, ed. K.S. Singh (1972), 99-100. According to E. H. Pakyntein's note, as per the list of Scheduled Tribes in the Indian Constitution, SC and ST lists Modification Order, 1956, out of 414 main Indian tribes, 83 tribes are in NEI [Assam -35, Manipur -29 and Tripura – 19] excluding Nagaland and Arunachal Pradesh (these two states were not been scheduled that time) and non-tribal linguistic groups. For a detailed list, see E. H. Pakyntein, "Tribal Communities in India," in *Tribal Awakening*, ed. M.M. Thomas and R.W. Taylor (Bangalore: CSRS, 1965), 3-4 & 19-29. While studying on migration and classifications of the various groups in the NEI, Stephen Fuchs names over 60 representative tribes. Cf. "The Races of North East India," *International Missionary Review* 12/3&4

total 461 Scheduled Tribes of India, out of which 150 are of NEI.[28] But there are numerous communities and groups and sub-groups in NEI accounting about 400 with 257 recognised dialects.[29] Downs estimates the number of languages spoken in the region to be of 50 major language groups and 150 minor groups.[30] The great majority of them are of Mongoloid racial stock. They speak languages of different divisions and sub-divisions of the Tibeto-Burman linguistic family basically divided into three groups, namely, Bodo, Naga and Kuki-Chin. The Bodo language is spoken largely in the plains of Assam as well as Tripura. The later two groups are predominant in Nagaland and Manipur. Only the Khasi and Jaintia (Pnar) tribes of Meghalaya speak Mon-Khmer language which belongs to Austro-Asiatic language family. The language belonging to Siamese-Chinese group is spoken by the Phakials, Khamtees and a few number of Ahom.

A Brief Sketch of the Political History

The political history of ancient Assam is steeped in myths with just little evidence in the form of archaeological corroboration. Though the interpenetrative characters place in relief the migration of people from different stocks, as discussed above, it is difficult to ascertain the groups of migration and even the route of migration due to lack of written historical records.[31] As per the written records available, the region has politically traversed a long road from pre-colonial, colonial, post-colonial and finally an internal-colonialism. Different groups of rulers established their kingdom in course of history. The history of ancient Assam is said to be roughly covering the period from the days of the Epics[32] to the early part of the

(Sept.-Dec.1990), 160-72. In 1967, George Gillespie identified 52 language groups within a single denominations, the CBCNEI, "Baptists in Babel," unpublished manuscript referred by F.S. Downs. Cf. note 2 in F. S. Downs, *History of Christianity in India: Northeast India in the Nineteenth and Twentieth Centuries*, Vol. 5, Part 5 (Bangalore: The Church History Association of India, 1992), 2.

[28] K.S. Singh, *The Scheduled Tribes: People of India*, 1212-1228.

[29] For an exhaustive survey on this, see H. M. Bareh, *Encyclopaedia of North-East India*, vol. I-VIII (New Delhi: Mittal Publication, 2001).

[30] Cf. Downs, 2.

[31] Because, it is only with the coming of the *Ahoms*, a procedure of keeping records of all events of the time began. The political events of the period, such as, warfare, diplomatic correspondence, working of the administration, including the appointment and dismissal of ministers, officers etc. are recorded in the documents called *Buranjis* (chronicles). Cf. Baruah, *A Comprehensive History of Assam…*, 43-44.

[32] Records of the foundation of the city of *Pragjyotisha*, the ancient name of Assam, by Amurtaraja and its location in the Varaha mountain is found in the Ramayana [*Adikanda*, XXXV; *Kiskindhya-kanda*, XIII]. Similarly in the Mahabharata there are references to the city and country of *Pragjyotisha*, to its rulers Naraka and Bhagadatta and to the *Chinas*, *Kiratas* and other people as constituting the army of Bhagadatta, who very gallantly fought the Pandavas in the Mahabharatta war [*Sabha Parva* XXVI-XXX; *Aswamedha Parva*, IXXV, IXXVI; *Udyoga Parva*, XVIII; *Drona Parva*, XXVI-XXXX; *Bhisma Parva* & *Karna Parva*, V]. Cf. Ibid., 32.

13th century,[33] but little is known about the history of Assam before the rise of the *Varmanas* in the 4th century CE[34] which is considered to be the starting point of the authentic political history of Assam.[35] First, there were traditional rulers during early history then followed by *Varmanas*, *Palas*, *Koches*, *Ahoms*, and finally the British.

The modern history of NEI, roughly dates from the advent of British traders and the decline of its monarchical kingdoms.[36] It is with the formal inauguration of the British rule in 1826 that the modern period began in the history of Assam, which covered the period till India's independence.[37] The consolidation of colonial rule, however, took a long time. Highlighting the separate and distinct identities of the tribes of different areas, various administrative decisions were taken and thus the different units of the region came under British rule at different points of time. For instance, the Assam plain was occupied in 1826 itself, followed by Cachar in 1830, the Khasi Hills in 1833, the Naga Hills in 1835,[38] the Garo Hills in 1872-733 and the Lushai Hills in 1890s.[39]

Pre-British Assam was largely confined to the Brahmaputra plains under the control of the *Ahoms* who did not have any real sovereignty over the hills and their tribal inhabitants. Non-tribal rulers were content to leave the tribals in the surrounding hills alone, save certain formal ceremonial and trade relations. Yet the *Ahoms* largely succeeded in maintaining cordial relations with the tribes

[33] In 1228 AD, Assam was invaded by *Ahoms* which is marked as the beginning of the medieval history of Assam. Cf. Gait, *A History of Assam*, 1 & 73.; Baruah, *A Comprehensive History of Assam...*, 36.

[34] Some of the Chinese sources accounts that the Ancient Assam had commercial and cultural contacts with China from the very early times since the *Varmana* dynasty. The accounts of Shung Shu (CE 420-79) record the sending of two embassies from India to China, of which one was sent by Yu-Chai of the Kapili valley who has been identified with the King Kalyanavarman (c. 420-40) of the *Varmana* dynasty. In later centuries also, there are mentions of kings like Avantivarman. Cf. Baruah, *A Comprehensive History of Assam...*, 35.

[35] Ibid., 28.

[36] Presidential address by H.L. Gupta at the Sixth Session of North East India Historical Association held at Agartala in 1985. As referred by B. K. Roy Burman, "Prefatory Introduction," in A. Mackenzie, *The North-East Frontier of India* (New Delhi: Mittal Publications, 2005 [1884]), 6. [A photographic reproduction of the original publication in 1884 under the title *History of the Relations of the Government with the Hill Tribes of the North-East Frontier of Bengal.*]

[37] Politically, Assam was passed on to the hands of the British rule by the Treaty of Yandabu on 24th February, 1826 and finally she has identified herself completely with the mainstream of Indian culture since the revolt of 1857. Cf. Baruah, 3.

[38] But Ao area was included to the Naga Hills only on 24 December, 1888 as sub-division with its headquarter at Mokokchung. Cf. H. K. Barpujari, *Problem of the Hill Tribes: North-East Frontier, 1873-1962* (Gauhati: Spectrum Publications, 1981), 84.

[39] Cf. Robert Reid, *The Lushai Hills* (Calcutta: Firma KLM Pvt. Ltd., 1942), 19ff.; Robert Reid, *History of the Frontier Areas Bordering on Assam from 1883-1941* (Shillong: n.p., 1942), 303.; Barpujari, 89ff.

through policies of great tact and diplomacy for about 600 years, from the 13th century to the advent of British.[40] In a way, unlike the present-day attribution as "Disturbed Areas", the hill tribes were mostly undisturbed during pre-colonial period. Perhaps due to fear of the fierce tribes and remoteness of the villages, the Sanskritic cultures of Assam could not penetrate into the hill regions. Secondly, sociologically speaking, it was Christianity that helped the hill tribes to preserve their identity in the face of the threat of assimilation into the Hindu society.[41] Meantime British administration also discouraged further Sanskritisation; rather it encouraged the maintenance of distinct tribal/ethnic identities. The tribes of the plains being in unprotected open boundaries, assimilated to the Sanskritic culture and religion.

Today, it is commonly claimed by the "insiders",[42] mainly by the hill tribes, that prior to the advent of colonial rule, the hill areas were neither a part of the then Assam nor of the rest of India. Historically speaking, it is true indeed. Though the different tribes living in the North-Eastern hill region had some trade relations with the neighbouring people of the valley, the hill tribes were neither a part of India nor of Assam, politically. Each of the major tribes had a kind of "village state" as their own political organisation, which they managed, according to their customs and traditions. Before the advent of British, most of the tribes in the region lacked political or legal institutions transcending the level of their villages. The villages were the kingdoms or states and the village chiefs were the rulers. They maintained their own distinct tribal culture, tradition, taboos, social system which was quite different from the people of the valley. The racial and cultural difference of the hill tribes with plains generally made them distinct and different. For instance, the governor of Assam, Sir Robert Neil Reid in the early 1940s said that "they are not Indian in any sense of the word, neither in origin, nor in language, nor in appearance, nor in habits, nor in outlook, and it is only by historical accident that they have been tacked to an Indian province."[43]

---

[40] Cf. P.N. Luthra, "North-east Frontier Agency Tribes: Impact of Ahom and British Policy," *EPW* VI/23 (June 5, 1971): 1144 ff.

[41] For critical discussion on this, see F.S. Downs, "Identity: The Integrative Principle," *Journal of Social Science and Humanities of North Eastern Hills University* 9/3 (1991): 7-18. This article can be found in *Asia Journal of Theology* 6/2 (Oct. 1992): 238-249; *Journal of Tribal Studies* I/1 (Dec. 1997): 30-50.

[42] Local people of the region are commonly termed as "insiders" and the migrants from mainland India and Bangladesh are called "outsiders".

[43] Cited in Imdad Hussain, "ASSAM: Unification and Roots of Division," in *Reorganisation of Northeast India Since 1947*, ed. B. Datta Ray and S.P. Agrawal (New Delhi: Concept Publishing Company, 1996), 16.

Even before Reid, there were two commissioners namely, N.E. Parry[44] and J.H. Hutton[45] who had similar views. Both of them separately submitted memoranda to the Indian Statutory Commission (1928) suggesting the formation of a North Eastern Frontier Province comprising of many backward tracts of Assam and Burma. Particularly, in his memorandum, Hutton particularly showed how the hill people neither racially, historically, culturally, nor linguistically had any affinity with the people of the Assam plains, while their administration was wholly on different lines.[46] Further it is stressed that "the backward tracts should be excluded from the province of Assam in the new Constitution. These areas have nothing in common with the rest of the Province...the present artificial union should be ended."[47] One of the members during the debate in the Simon Commission remarked that: "If I read the signs and portents of the time correctly, I feel most sure that the hill districts will be separated sooner or later and I hope within about five or six years."[48] Similarly, one of the Assamese *Swarajists* also once said that "before long Assam Valley will have to see its own way to disjoin itself from the hill districts."[49]

Looking at such signs of the time, actually, Sir Andrew Clow wanted the Tribal Areas to be grouped together in a State-like structure to negotiate with the Government of India through their own representation. He cautioned that: "...it is only by giving the tribes the right to put them forward as their spokesmen (*sic*) that they can be heard. If unsuitable arrangements are imposed from above on tribesmen (*sic*), who have not been heard, there will be bitter discontent and unrest on this frontier."[50] He even criticised Reid's administration that there was too much of a tendency to treat the tribals as subjects "for reservation and study rather than as objects of our help and guidance."[51] He made a criticism of British policy as being too chary of extending their administration and too slow in building up self-government institution among tribal people.

---

[44] He was Deputy Commissioner of Garo Hills and later Superintendent of Lushai Hills District.

[45] The Deputy Commissioner of Naga Hills District who introduced the "Crown Colony Scheme".

[46] *Memorandum of the Government of Assam to the Indian Statutory Commissioner,* vol. XIV, 111-122. As referred in David R. Syiemlieh, "The Future of the Hills of North-East India 1928-1947: Some British Views," in *Reorganisation of Northeast India Since 1947,* ed. B. Datta Ray and S.P. Agrawal (New Delhi: Concept Publishing Company, 1996), 25.

[47] *Memorandum to Simon Commission by Assam Government.* As cited in Hussain, "ASSAM: Unification and Roots of Division," 21.

[48] As cited in Ibid., 22.

[49] As cited in Ibid.

[50] *Cambridge South Asia Archive,* Pawsey Papers, Box 1, No.5, Clow to Pawsey, 24 April 1947. As referred in Syiemlieh, 31.

[51] *Cambridge South Asia Archive,* Pawsey Papers, Box 1, No.5, Clow to Pawsey, 24 April 1947. As referred in Ibid.

On the other hand, they had much fear about the hill tribes that by any means tried to discourage the outrages by implementing measures of retribution. While dealing with the Lushais in their expedition, J.W. Edgar, the D.C. of Cachar in 1869 remarked:

> The injuries they have done to us were so injurious, the gain to them so very great, and the difficulties they found so small, that if they are allowed to get off with impunity and without making reparation, I fear they will be encouraged to commit outrages upon us on a far larger scale hereafter, and that the other tribes on our border, seeing the success of the Lushais, might be tempted to follow their example.[52]

The advent of the British in the 19th century incorporated the region into the Indian Empire though much of the extensive tribal territory it encompassed was kept isolated as a matter of deliberate policy and lightly administered by what has been termed a "government of men (*sic*)."[53] The region has been systematically undermined disconnected from the historical connection it had with the rest of India during pre-colonial period by the policy of progressive segregation of the region particularly the tribal populations by categorising them as "non-regulated", "backward", or "excluded" areas that were administered with separate provisions unlike the administrative pattern prevailing in the rest of British India. To make the policy more effective, an Inner Line Regulation was introduced in 1873[54] that prohibited access to the categorised areas to all outsiders without permission. It is interesting to note that just few years before the introduction of the regulation even "Passports were issued for the Angamis visiting the plains and to prevent inter-tribal feuds, a system of Residentiary Delegates was stationed at the headquarters from various communities and to whom stipends were granted for acting as interpreters or *dobhasies* of their respective clans."[55]

However, the hill tribes were not completely independent. They were either under British India or subjects to the Burmese and Manipur. Beadon, the Secretary of the Government of Bengal in his report (24 April, 1865) explained that "the Angami Nagas are independent only in the sense that the British Government had refrained from reducing them to practical subjection and has left them, except at occasional intervals, entirely to themselves; but they have never

[52] *Foreign Political Proceedings-A*, December, 1869, No. 245. As cited in H. K. Barpujari, *Problem of the Hill Tribes: North-East Frontier, 1843-1972* (Gauhati: United Publishers, 1976), 141.

[53] For detail studies on this, see A.C. Sinha, *North-Eastern Frontier of India: Structural Imperatives and Aspects of Change* (New Delhi: Indus Publishing Co., 1994).

[54] For a detailed study on the background and implications of Inner Line Regulation, see Barpujari, *Problem of the Hill Tribes: North-East Frontier, 1873-1962*, 1-27.

[55] *Bengal Judicial Proceedings*, April 1867, Nos. 17-9; Dec., 1968, Nos. 93-5; Jan., 1869, No 81. As cited in Barpujari, *Problem of the Hill Tribes: North-East Frontier, 1843-1972*, 109.

enjoyed or acquired political or territorial independence."[56] Even in the Inner Line regulation, according to Mackenzie, the purpose was stated as "under the orders of the government of India the 'Inner Line' is defined merely for purposes of jurisdiction. It does not decide the sovereignty of the territory beyond."[57]

The British excluded the various hill tracts but did not give them an independent status. There was indeed an economic motif behind such policy, as we see John Hutton's separate note saying, "The hills are unprofitable possessions." Certainly the hills – the backward tracts were neglected because of non-productivity whereas the oil, coal, timber and tea rich plain of Assam was grabbed because of its productivity. Since the hill areas were always in deficit, provincial administrators of Assam after 1914 were not eager to assume responsibility. This definitely points to the fact that these areas were disjoined due to the extra headache of expenditure. Even later on, the memorandum of the Assam Government submitted to the Simon Commission in July, 1928 states that "neither the Government nor the political parties of Assam were interested in tagging the hills districts with the constitutional Government of Assam."[58] Consequently, though there was resistance to such an exclusion,[59] the British succeeded in excluding the Naga, Lushai and the North Cachar Hills and the Balipara and Sadiya Frontier Tracts from the Assam Legislature.

Actually, first of all, one must understand that such a policy was the outcome of genuine and sincere thinking and of dire necessity[60] because there were various causes leading to the ethnic unrest.[61] The objective of the policy of minimum interference was to stop the increasingly frequent raids upon the plains by the

---

[56] *Foreign Political Proceedings –A*, June, 1886, Nos. 37-39. As cited in Ibid., 101.

[57] Mackenzie, *The North-East Frontier…*, 89.

[58] S. K. Chaube, *Hills Politics in North East India* (Calcutta: Orient Longman, 1973), 22.

[59] For instance, J. J. M. Nichols-Roy wrote: "I wrote strongly against that exclusion. I was able to convince the Assam Government Sir Lawrie Hammond to make the British portion of the Khasi and Jaintia Hills, the Garo Hills and the Mikir Hills to be partially excluded areas". As cited in Imdad Hussain, "ASSAM: Unification and Roots of Division," in *Reorganisation of Northeast India Since 1947* ed. B. Datta Ray and S.P. Agrawal (New Delhi: Concept Publishing Company, 1996), 22.

[60] Cf. V. K. Anand, *Nagaland in Transition* (New Delhi: Associated Publishing House, 1967), 18.

[61] Cf. B.C. Chakravorty identifies eight probable causes. Firstly, tribes set upon the war path as a result of a trivial insult or misunderstanding. Secondly, it was due to the intrigues of Burmese or Bhutanese officials. Thirdly, it was due to the refusal of the British to recognise the rights given to the hill tribes by the Ahom Kings to collect revenue from the plains areas below the *duars* (passes). Fourthly, it was due to the unsettling effects of tribal migration and conflict caused by arrival of new groups in already-settled areas. Fifthly, it was caused by the government prohibition of traditional practices like head-hunting or slavery or human sacrifice. Sixthly, it was due to old inter-tribal or inter-village feuds. Seventhly, it was due to the government's efforts to collect revenue or requisition of forced labour – or anticipation of such action. Finally, it was an old custom of tribal tradition almost as a part of their culture to raid the plains. Cf. B.C. Chakravorty, *British Relations with the Hill Tribes of Assam Since 1858* (Calcutta, 1964), 166-68.

hill tribes. Since they were not content to confine their hostile activities to their own territories, the British rule could not leave them alone. Gait suggests that the purpose of British policy like Inner Line was to end the quarrels and serious disturbances caused by unrestricted intercourse between British subjects in Assam and the wild tribes living across the frontiers.[62]

Secondly, along with administrative changes, the British administration tried to protect the hills tribes from exploitation by crafty people of the plains. They tried to ensure that no encroachments were made into tribal areas and they aimed to protect rights, privileges, customs, traditions, and way of life of the tribes. It is viewed that "had such action not been taken, the consequences would have been serious. The tribes would have probably become extinct, either because of poor economic condition due to exploitation, or deadly feuds would have taken place against the plainsmen(*sic*) and against themselves."[63] Moreover, unlike the tribals of plains, by the policy of Inner Line Regulation, which is still in operation in Arunachal Pradesh, Nagaland and Mizoram, the hill tribes were able to take possession of their land and preserve their cultural traditions. According to Downs,

> Whatever may have been the original purpose of the Inner Line, in the course of time it came to function as a means of protecting the tribes from exploitation at the hands of outsiders. It helped [to] preserve tribal land and identity, but in the process reinforced the barriers already separating the hills people from their plains neighbours.[64]

Lastly, it was also to define limits to the adventurous exponents of forward policy and let the tribes manage their affairs by themselves as well as to establish personal influence for good among the chiefs and the tribes.[65]

Therefore, as the people of those days, who lived in their present, the British administration perhaps appeared to be their messiah. Barpujari in his article, "East-India Company: Saviour of Assam"[66] elaborates in detail about the "Messianic" role played by British administration in rescuing the tribes of Assam from terror as the neighbouring vigorous and warlike race of Burmese Shan invaded the Brahmaputra Valley in the eighth century after Christ.[67] The Burmese took advantage of the weak monarchies, divided ruling houses, self-centred ambitions,

---

[62] Cf. Gait, *A History of Assam*, 316.

[63] Subba and Ghosh, eds., 59.

[64] Downs, *History of Christianity in India: Northeast India in the Nineteenth and Twentieth Centuries*, 22-23.

[65] For detail documents of Inner Line Regulation, 1873, see B.B. Kumar, *Reorganization of North East India (Facts and Documents)* (New Delhi: Omsons Publications, 1996), 83-86.

[66] Cf. H. K. Barpujari, *Assam in the Days of the Company (1826-1858)* (Gauhati: Spectrum Publications, 1980 [1963]), 11-12.

[67] Cf. Mackenzie, *The North-East Frontier*..., 2.

unscrupulous and faction-ridden nobility, internecine struggles for power and incessant tribal insurrections in the region and dislodged the ruling dynasties of Manipur and Assam and posed a serious threat to Cachar and Bengal.[68] According to Barpujari, "the dreadful atrocities perpetuated on the helpless Assamese by these inhuman invaders could better be imagined than described."[69] It is said that during the Burmese invasion, devastation, murder and desecration were the order of the day. The gruesome atrocity on the part of the Burmese is narrated by J. Butler as follows:

> All who were suspected of being inimical to the reign of terror were seized and bound by Burmese executioners, who cut off the lobes of the poor victims' ears and choice portions of the body, such as the points of the shoulders, and actually ate the raw flesh before the living sufferers: they then inhumanly inflicted gashes on the body, that the mutilated might die slowly, and finally closed the tragedy by disembowelling the wretched victims." "Some they flayed alive, others they burnt in oil and others again they drove in crowds into village *Namgars* (prayer houses), which they then set on fire.... No consideration whatsoever was shown to age, sex or rank." It was dangerous for a beautiful woman to meet a Burmese even on the public road. Even Brahmins were made to carry loads of beef, pork and wine.[70]

At such an hour of peril, the British had emerged as the deliverer of the people of Assam.[71] They emancipated thousands of Assamese slaves. They resettled the refugees in their original homelands.[72] It is contended that "had not been there a timely arrival of the British as its saviour, perhaps, the valley of the Brahmaputra would have been converted into a Burmese province or parcelled out amongst the hillmen (*sic*) of the North and the South."[73]

However, the divisive and exclusive impact of British colonial policies cannot be overlooked. Ever since the British occupied the region, they proceeded to establish a degree of political and administrative dominion over the tribes and they are the ones who first branded the vast plain-hill complex in the region. Though they adopted the policy of the *Ahoms* in keeping peaceful relation between the plains by introducing commercial contact, they did not have much interest in the hill regions because there were not much exploitable economic gains.

---

[68] Cf. B. K. Roy Burman, "Prefatory Introduction," in Ibid., 6.

[69] Barpujari, *Assam in the Days of the Company (1826-1858)*, 10-11.

[70] *Travels and Adventures in the Province of Assam*, London, 1855. As cited in Ibid., 11. Also see S.K. Bhuyan, *Anglo-Assamese Relations (1771-1826)* (Gauhati, 1974 [1949], 508-10.

[71] Cf. H. K. Barpujari, *Assam in the Days of the Company (1826-1858)*, 12.

[72] Cf. H. K. Barpujari, *Problem of the Hill Tribes: North-East Frontier, 1822-1942* (Gauhati: Lawyer's Book Stall, 1970), 110 ff.

[73] Ibid., 20. [paraphrased]

To see things at their worse, the introduction of Inner Line in 1873, whatever the good motive behind it, virtually cut off the prospect of increasing relations between the hill tribes and the largely non-tribal plain people.[74] It has created "a frontier within a frontier" and accentuated a political and cultural schism between the tribes of the hills and the populace of the plains. According to B.B. Kumar,

> Their policy of gradual segregation of the tribals and non-tribals, hills and the plains; segregation of the tribal population by introduction of the "Inner Line Regulation", creation of "non-regulated", "backward" and "excluded" areas/tracts was able to break centuries of historical, cultural, social and religious continuum and connectedness. The colonial theories/myths – the myth of race, core-fringe conflict, isolation – colonial misinterpretation of history and culture further deepened the impact.[75]

It also internally perpetuated an isolationist tendency among the people of the hills. The general policy of administration followed with regard to the tribal areas in the hills created a major cultural and communication gap between the hills tribes and plains-tribes.

Another extraordinary disaster were the repercussions of the partition of East Pakistan (Bangladesh) which completely confused the existing complexity of ethnicity. It created physical and psychological severity, disrupted communications and market. Because prior to partition, the economic and politics were largely dictated from Bengal and all communications were through the present Bangladesh, the region was utterly cut-off from water, road and rail routes. The cumulative impact of the partition is rhetorically described by B.G. Verghese in the following words:

> The physical and psychological severity of the blow was not fully appreciated elsewhere in the country and the disruption in the communications and markets was not repaired soon enough nor infrastructure developed to match the new needs completed as expeditiously as necessary. Isolated and traumatised, the Northeast turned inward. A succession of insurgencies and movements to seek separation or autonomy, assert identity or exclude foreigners and outsiders aggravated the hiatus, with the rest of the country coming to think of the Northeast with disinterest as a far-away place, perpetually troubled. Beset with its own internal problems and complexes, the Northeast fell behind economically and despite its inherent wealth

---

[74] Cf. M. Alemchiba, *A Brief Historical Account of Nagaland* (Kohima: Naga Institute of Culture, 1970), 150-51.

[75] B.B. Kumar, "Ethnicity and Insurgency in India's North-East," in *Problems of Ethnicity in the North-East India*, ed. B.B. Kumar (New Delhi: Concept Publishing Company for Astha Bharati, 2007), 18.

remains at the bottom of the heap as a conglomeration of seemingly impecunious special category state.[76]

The ethno-political situations in the region after the Independence of India has its legacy in such a historical background of colonial rule. The heightened and growing emphasis on a separate identity by ethnic groups in the recent years is the result of such a policy. The so-called preservationist or protective policy[77] turned to be a pretext for the exclusion and separation from the mainland India and proliferation of conflicts throughout the region.

Further, despite conferment of autonomy and Statehood, the separateness nursed during colonial India has survived in the region, which is expressive in different ethno-identity movements prevalent in the region. As the British left the situation of the region unsettled, the Government of India proved to be the successor of British. After the independence, the establishment of District boundaries affected most of the tribal groups and created multi-ethnic Districts that brought dislocation of numerous ethnic groups from one place to other. With the transformation of Administrative Districts into political entities, inter-District borders created political problems and today the inter-ethnic conflicts over the issue of habitats.[78] Though under the provision of the Sixth Schedule of the Constitution[79] and its objective to develop hitherto backward areas and bring them the benefits of modern education and technology without doing harm to their traditional ways, the effort to bring the hills people within the mainstream of national life stirred up fears and, in some cases, hostility. Various tribes both in hills and plains began to agitate for recognition leading to separatist movements. In the mid-1950s such movements commonly known as Naga Insurgency[80] began

[76] B. G. Verghese, *India's Northeast Resurgent: Ethnicity, Insurgency, Governance, Development* (Delhi: Konark Publishers Pvt. Ltd., 2004 [1996]), 336-337.

[77] The British refrained from any deliberate or systematic effort to introduce change in the pattern of tribal society. They established strong and stable government in the plains, while they did not meddle in the tribal affairs. Even they conceded that tribal people were the owners of their land. They took pains to enforce the principle that forest trees and the produce were tribal property. One can see even asking permission from the local owner if they required timber. This had a deep and permanent effect on the tribal mind. The tribal freedom to manage their own affairs, to enjoy the right of total possession of the land and plantations, and the uninterruption within their area, were fully maintained. This looking good gesture of British in fact attracted the tribals and by which they accepted the fact that they are superior authority and invited them for mediation between warring groups or in matters of land disputes or in murder cases or if the property of a person was seized by another. This consequently helped the British to be masters and the hill tribes subjects. Cf. Luthra, "North-east Frontier Agency Tribes…, 1149.

[78] Cf. B. Pakem, ed. *Nationality, Ethnicity and Cultural Identity in North East India* (New Delhi, Guwahati: Omsons Publications, 1990), 20.

[79] For detail discussion on this, see Chaube, *Hills Politics…*, 91-104.

[80] For an in-depth scholarly study on Naga Insurgency, see M. Horam, *Naga Insurgency: The Last Thirty Years* (New Delhi: Cosmo Publications, 1988).

and after a decade the Mizo Insurgency and following their footsteps, there has been numerous movements for separation. Such political atmosphere kept the region excluded from the process of modernisation and development activities consequently leading to be domination of economic profile of the region by plains.

Socio-Economic and Religio-Cultural Life

In the seclusion of the hills and, in most cases, untouched by historic civilisations, the tribal groups persisted in the traditional forms of economy, social organisations, rituals and belief systems until recent times. They inherited the legacy of British administration on economy. With their elaborate economic policy, the British exploited the masses. Economically speaking, they never did much for the well-being of the indigenous people. Robinson says that

> The great body of the cultivators are, in fact, mere servants of the merchants, who engage them to pay their rent for them, whilst they in turn agree to surrender all the produce of their land to him.... If the produce be more than the debts, the farmer keeps the surplus.... If on the other hand, he should be very unfortunate in his harvest, the poor cultivator's little all is sold by the merchant, and with his family he is turned out upon the cold unfeeling world, to beg his bread or to perish.[81]

With regards to the richness of resources and the culture of people of the region, one of the mission reports says that

> With their vast forests, with soil exceedingly rich...with coal, iron, gold...precious stones, with cheap means of transportation afforded by their rivers, untold wealth and power are within the grasp of the inhabitants of this country. The people are good-natured and indolent with no connection of their peculiar opportunities and no ambition to seize them even if they know of them.[82]

In fact, the region is rich in natural resources. Due to such rich natural resources, *Ahoms* called the region "*Mun-dung-sun-kham*" (country, full, garden, gold), meaning the country full of golden gardens.[83] But due to various reasons, the region is still backward and the majority of the people particularly in the hilltops and rural plains are in utter poverty.

---

[81] William Robinson, *A Descriptive account of Assam* (Calcutta, Delhi, 1841 [1975]), 218.

[82] R.D. Grant, *Report on the Committee on Mission in Assam*, 1891; *The Baptist Missionary Magazine*, 1892. As cited in Barpujari, *Assam in the Days of the Company (1826-1858)*, 283.

[83] Cf. Gait, *A History of Assam*, 75.; Baruah, *A Comprehensive History of Assam...*, 223.; C. Becker, *History of the Catholic Missions in North East India, 1890-1915*, ed. G. Stadler and S. Karotemprel, trans., G. Stadler and S. Karotemprel (Calcutta: Firma KLM Pvt. Ltd., 1980), 35.

Coming to the religio-cultural life, though the various tribes of the region did not have a nation or state or systematically organised social institutions, they had myths and legends of their origins; the stories of roots about their coming from, and had their own belief systems, customs, rites and rituals. Most of the tribes of both the hills and the plains had their own traditional religion with certain common beliefs in a Supreme Being, other supernatural beings perceived as spirits, human life and natural world and the religious rites and rituals connected with. Their religion and life-world was inter-connected with spiritual beings, nature and all other living beings. It was so much so inter-connected that there are so many stories of God marrying human beings.

Prior to the British, the impact of Hinduism was felt somewhat superficially among some tribes like Akas, the Miris and the Jayantias, but Buddhism was deep rooted among some of the tribes of present Bhutan and Arunachal Pradesh such as the Bhutias, the Monpas and the Khamtees. The Nagas "appear to acknowledge a divine power to be the Maker of the world and the dispenser of all events."[84] Some other tribes like Nishis, the Mishmis and the Hill Miris had a notion of a Supreme Being but they never worshipped. Since all of them were inhabiting the lofty mountains, roaring rivers, deep valleys and dense forests, they had certain beliefs in spirits. Krick narrates that "If a stone rolls from the mountain, if a leaf drops from a tree, it must be a spirit of a stroll; if winds blow through the forests, the gods were indulging some healthy exercise, if winds shake the trees and howl through the valley, the *deos* or the spirits were quarrelling."[85]

However, the religious life of the various tribes had gone through tremendous changes in course of history. A major shift had taken place after the British administration entered into the region. A large number of people in the plains of Assam, Manipur and Arunachal Pradesh have accepted Hinduism, both Brahmanical and Vaishnavism, whereas the great majority of the hill tribes embraced Christianity.

Actually, prior to the coming of Christianity, the Brahmins from Northern India succeeded in assimilating into Hinduism almost all the tribes of the plains[86] including the powerful *Ahoms* who ruled Assam for over six hundred years and

---

[84] W. A. Robinson, *Descriptive Account of Assam* (Calcutta, 1841), 395 ff. Cf. Barpujari, *Problem of the Hill Tribes: North-East Frontier, 1822-1942*, 11.

[85] N.M. Krick, "An Account of an Expedition amongst the Abors in 1853," *JASB*. IX (1913), 120. As cited in Robinson, *Descriptive Account of Assam*, 12.

[86] Particularly the Bodos of Assam and Garo Hills of Meghalaya were greatly affected. Cf. R. N. Mosahary, "Aryanisation and Hinduisation of the Bodos," in *Proceedings of the North East India History Association, Tenth Session* (Shillong: NEIHA, 1989), 165-179.; D.N. Majumdar, "A Study of Tribe-Caste Continuum and the Process of Sanskritization among the Bodo-Speaking Tribes of the Garo Hills," in *Tribal Situation in India*, ed. K.S. Singh (Shimla: IIAS, 1972), 263-70.

who in course of time not only adopted the Hindu religion, discarding their own, but also forgot their own Shan language and adopted Assamese.[87]

In fact, it happened so that though the Aryans were the last immigrants to the region, surprisingly they became the most dominant group who influenced almost all realms of life – political, economical, socio-cultural and religious life of the region for centuries. One of the strategies due to fear of the warring tribes is that they incorporated and adopted myths and cults of the non-Aryans. The prevalent religious elements among the non-Aryans such as fetishism, animism, cult of fertility, human sacrifice, ancestor worship etc. were accommodated into Hinduism, which was not the case with Christianity. Such an accommodative policy, according to Baruah, was a help in organising civil society and the making of great culture of ancient Assam.[88] The wave of community feeling grew with the emergence of Neo-Vaishnavism and "as a result of the propagation of Neo-Vaishnavism, heterogeneous faiths and creeds that prevailed in the land gradually disappeared and a common and simple religion based on the strict monotheism and on ethico-devotional code of conduct sprang up."[89] In the political sphere too, a feeling of identity was growing rapidly among the rulers out of internal political necessity.

But such Sanskritic culture and religion could not penetrate into the hill regions possibly due to plains people's fear of the fierce tribes of the hills or the remoteness of their villages. Of course, there could have been a process of slow penetration, but the timely arrival of Christianity stopped it. For instance, the tribes like Khasis and Garos of present Meghalaya, due to their occasional trade contacts with the plain people of Assam and Bengal, started to absorb some of the cultural traits of the Hindus. But, as Goswami rightly says, "with the arrival of the Christian missionaries, the people, for various reasons, became apathetic towards the religion of the non-tribal Hindus."[90] Over against this view, one of the native scholars in 1990 argued that it was only after the British had imposed their alien administration that the penetration of the plains Hindus into the hills was on such a large scale that the traditional ways of assimilation were ineffective.[91]

Culturally, one of the best features is community life. Though the ownership of the land, customs varied from tribe to tribe, however, general trend was a communal ownership particularly where the shifting cultivation prevailed. In

---

[87] Cf. S. Barkakati, *Assam* (1969), 7-8. As referred in Downs, *History of Christianity in India: Northeast India in the Nineteenth and Twentieth Centuries*, 217.

[88] Cf. Baruah, *A Comprehensive History of Assam* ..., 158 & 254.

[89] Ibid., 252.

[90] Goswami, "The Tribes of Assam: A Few Comments on their Societal and Cultural Ties with the Non-Tribes," 277-278.

[91] For an elaborate discussion on this, see O.L. Snaitang, "A Study of the Role of Christianity in Social Change among the Khasi and Jaintia Hill Tribes of Meghalaya from 1814 to the Present" (D. Th. Dissertation, United Theological College, Bangalore, 1990), Ch. II.

some tribes, like Khamtee, the chief was considered as the lord of the soil, but he could have only a share of the produce, the rest was divided amongst the hand who had helped the cultivation.[92] Amongst the Padams, all offerings to the Gaums (Chiefs), as well as fines, forfeiters and escheats were utilised for the benefit of the community as a whole.

One of the foundations of community life was the community centre called *Morung*.[93] This centre served as council where every evening, all men gather to discuss various issues and plan community activities. The centre in particular was used to discuss the political questions set forth by one of the chiefs; to inform one another of what has been seen or heard; and to settle what the village will do on the next day. One of the most beautiful features here was the democratic decision for community activities like hunting, fishing, filed labour as they had their own common ground for hunting, fishing ponds, river or stream, field for cultivation, drinking stream etc. Interestingly, every evening, between 10 and 11 o'clock boys are sent about the village, shouting at the top of the voice, "Tomorrow a tiger hunt; Tomorrow fishing; Tomorrow, field labour; Tomorrow, genna."[94]

Though most of the societies were stratified into three classes – the chief and his family, the chief's council members and their families, and the families of the ordinary villagers, the caste system prevailing in the rest of India is absent among them. Of course, free and slave classes were common phenomenon among some tribes. For instance, among the Padams, "The law of the master is not the law of the slaves." However, the treatment that was meted out to the slaves was very humane. Even slaves were treated as family members. It is said that "the slaves have no harder time than the other members of the family; they eat together, work together and sleep together, and to an outsider there is nothing to show their social inferiority."[95] This was claimed by Theyieu Sakhrie, a close associate of Phizo, the Naga warrior in the following words:

> ...We are all equals. Men and women have equal social status. We have no caste distinctions; no high or low class of people. We believe in that form of Government which permits the rule, not on the majority, but of the people as a whole. We govern ourselves by a Government which does not govern at all. In the life of the village the family is a permanent institution, a conscious unit polity. Every family is proud of its own and no family has ever been left by their fellowmen to the

---

[92] T. T. Cooper, *New Routes for Commerce: The Mishmee Hills* (1873), 149, in *India's North-east Frontier in the Nineteenth Century*, edited by Verrier Elwin (Bombay: OUP, 1959), 370.

[93] This was a centre of all adult males in a village as well as the recruiting ground for any emergency or for works of public service.

[94] N.M. Krick, "An Account of an Expedition amongst the Abors in 1853," *JASB* IX (1913), 119. As cited in Barpujari, *Problem of the Hill Tribes: North-East Frontier, 1822-1942*, 11.

[95] J. Erol Gray, *Diary of a Journey to the Bor Khamti Country, 1892-3* (1893), 5 f. & 9 f. in Elwin, ed., 422.

> mercy of circumstances. Possessing its own house, built on its own land, no family ever pays any tax. Forests and woodland, rivers belong to the people. We cultivate as much land as we need or desire and there is no one to question our rights. We have food to eat and drinks to drink excessively beyond our needs. Truly God has been good to us. Three square meals a day and 'zu' (rice wine) without measure. We have no beggars. Every family lives in its village. It has no landlords to harass it; and no revenue collector to knock on its doors; for the family is master of its own affairs. And wonder of wonders, we have no jail. We do not arrest nor even imprison anyone. Our civil authority is God in the matter of life and death and murder is very rare. We fear nobody, individually or collectively. We are healthy people and fear corrupts the health of man. What peace we have, no police and no CID! We use no lock. Our granaries are kept outside the village and no guard is ever needed, for there is no one to steal them. We travel as we like and it costs nothing. Wherever we go, it is our home. If, by ill fortune, a man falls sick or dies he is borne home to his family without counting the cost. We talk freely, live freely, and often fight freely too. We have no inhibitions of any kind. Wild? Yes, But free![96]

However, such communitarian life do not reflect much when it comes to the question of identity, dignity and status of women in the society. Though the treatment of women is not like in many other patriarchal societies, the epithet "weaker section" is visible in number of parables and proverbial expressions. For instance, how men valued women can be seen from the proverbs of fascination for gun such as "the youth usually prefer to have choice in the selection of guns rather than in girlfriends." Likewise, there are parables such as: "As the meat of a crab is not meat, so the word of woman is no word"; "The wisdom of a woman does not extend beyond the limit of the village water source"; and "Let a woman and a dog bark, it pleases them."[97] Women's labour was not counted as profitable work. Hannay, while writing on the Singpho women particularly the wives, writes, "Not only the whole of the household duties of cooking, cleaning the grain from the husk, spinning, weaving, dying etc. But the more laborious outdoor work of drawing water, planting out reaping the crops and even the labour of cutting and bringing the firewood."[98]

Further, the various tribes of the region in the olden days had other dark history too. The people of the region in the olden days lived in their present.

[96] As cited in Nirmal Nibedon, *North East India: The Ethnic Explosion* (New Delhi: Lancers Publishers, 1981), 19.

[97] Lal Biak Thanga, *The Mizos: A Study in Racial Personality* (Gauhati: United Publishers, 1978), 23.

[98] S.F.G. Hanny, *Sketch of the Singphos or the Hakhyens of Burmah* (Tract, 266, Calcutta, 1847), 11-12. As cited in Barpujari, *Problem of the Hill Tribes: North-East Frontier, 1822-1942*, 11.

They never took care for the future. Their life style was simple but hard. Since cultivating, hunting and fighting were their regular jobs for survival, there existed clan schisms and village feuds. Looking at such life of the tribes, the general and very persistent British perception of the people, particularly, in the hills was that they were all wild savages, and continuously at war with each other, seeking the "heads" of their enemies as trophies. In fact, various tribes were always at feud with one another. For instance, the tribes like Garos and Nagas lived in a state of constant warfare in their hills. They rendered the border areas wholly insecure by their frequent raids for the purpose of procuring human skulls which they needed for funeral ceremonies or to manifest their heroism. Among the Garos, head-hunters were glorified. It was resorted to as a means to enhance the fertility of the soil and thereby increase the harvest. It was a supreme religious obligation and that all rites would be incomplete without its fulfilment.[99] But among the Khasis, it was not religious obligation, but the enemy's head captured enhanced the prestige of a community. No Naga youth was also tattooed or distinguished as brave unless he had one or more heads to his credit whether acquired as trophies in a war or by treacherous murders.[100]

Whatever might be the arguments of the apologists,[101] doubtlessly this inhuman rite took a heavy toll of human lives.[102] In "A fairly sage estimate" Peal writes, "judging by the skulls of the Morangs would give about 12,000 murders,

[99] H. M. Bareh, *Encyclopaedia of North-East India*, vol. IV Meghalaya (New Delhi: Mittal Publication, 2001), 48-49.

[100] One of the examples of justification of head-hunting is that "Head-hunting…was not a separate entity. It was the very core of Naga [as well others] culture based upon the concept of fertility. It was the main-spring of their lives and their activities and behavior were inextricably woven round this practice. (It) gave vigour and meaning to their lives. The stone walls and palisades, village gates majestically decorated with human heads, feasts of merit, flamboyant head-dresses, elaborate textiles with patterns symbolic of head-hunting are intimately bound up with this basic activity. The aesthetic life, full of inspired dances, and songs and colourful dresses is a response to their adventurous spirit. With the disappearing of head-hunting many a good elements which was associated with it disintegrated…." R.N. Haldipur, "Policy Towards and Administration of the Tribes of North-East India," in *Tribal Situation in India*, ed. K.S. Singh (Shimla: IIAS, 1972), 307.

[101] One of the examples of justification of head-hunting is that "Head-hunting…was not a separate entity. It was the very core of Naga [as well others] culture based upon the concept of fertility. It was the main-spring of their lives and their activities and behavior were inextricably woven round this practice. (It) gave vigour and meaning to their lives. The stone walls and palisades, village gates majestically decorated with human heads, feasts of merit, flamboyant head-dresses, elaborate textiles with patterns symbolic of head-hunting are intimately bound up with this basic activity. The aesthetic life, full of inspired dances, and songs and colourful dresses is a response to their adventurous spirit. With the disappearing of head-hunting many a good elements which was associated with it disintegrated…." R.N. Haldipur, "Policy Towards and Administration of the Tribes of North-East India," in *Tribal Situation in India*, ed. K.S. Singh (Shimla: IIAS, 1972), 307.

[102] Cf. Barpujari, *Problem of the Hill Tribes: North-East Frontier, 1822-1942*, 13.

in about 40 years, in an area roughly 20 miles square."[103] Their story is narrated as follows:

> In the first of these fifteen persons were killed and the *cutchaary* of the Farmer was plundered; in the second, a second *cutchaary* was plundered and burnt and two people were killed and two wounded; in the third several huts were plundered and burnt and seven people killed and one wounded; and in the last, several huts were plundered and burnt and three persons were massacred....[104]

> ...bloodthirsty, treacherous and revengeful all Nagas, even the best are, and the Angami, though in many ways perhaps the finest and best of their tribes, is no exception. With them, as with the others, it is an article of faith that blood once shed can never be expiated except by the death of the murderer or some of this near relatives and through years may pass away vengeance will assuredly be taken some day.[105]

If an injury was done by one to another of the same clan or by one to another clan or tribe, it was incumbent on the injured to avenge wrong-doer. To satisfy the wrath of an injured at times demanded the death not merely of the murderer, but the members of whole family, and "the feud also descends as an heirloom on the children." Amongst the Garos, Hamilton writes: "Relations of the person killed, are, by custom, held bound to demand blood for blood, and ought put to death either the murderer or one of his kindred or at least one of his slaves."[106] It was not rare, therefore, to see clan against clan, family against family, as if miniature warfare was the order of the day.[107] If there is a quarrel between two Nagas of different villages, the dispute inevitably cause bloodshed and a feud is established between the villages of two disputants which nothing will assuage, and which in time as advantage offers will find issue on some dreadful massacre. The Nagas brook no insult. An insult given, it is a point of honour to have blood and bloodshed by the one party calls for a like stream on the part of the other. Bivar in his letter to Jenkins wrote that

> The Nagas are a peculiar people; they acknowledge no supremacy except that of the spear...they brook no authority, each man his (*sic*) own master...thirst for plunder and a natural desire to revenge are leading

---

[103] S.E. Peal, "Fading Histories," *JASB* LXII, Part III (1894): 13. As cited in Ibid.

[104] *Bengal Judicial Proceedings*, 25 (April, 1815), no 17. As cited in Barpujari, *Problem of the Hill Tribes: North-East Frontier, 1843-1972*, 22.

[105] V. Elwin, *The Nagas in the Ninetheenth Century* (Bombay: OUP, 1969), 55-56.

[106] Francis Buchanon Hamilton, "An Account of Assam," (1814): 91, published in *Annals of Oriental Literature* (London, 1820); also by *D.H.A.S.* (Gauhati, 1840). As cited in Barpujari, *Problem of the Hill Tribes: North-East Frontier, 1822-1942*, 8.

[107] Ibid.

> features of their character.... To induce the Naga tribes to change their habits...they may be made to feel certain that the offending individual will meet with condign punishment and this cannot be attained unless they are subjugated to such a control as would successfully be entailed by annexation.[108]

The early literatures on the cultures of NEI tribes abound with such stories of horror. Occasional space is given to describe some of the pleasing stories about them here and there. As fallout of it, the British administration followed various policies to end such a situation of turmoil among the tribes of the hills; and with this pretext, perhaps, they opened the door for Christian missionaries as civilizing agent through the power of the Gospel!

S.B.

[108] Bivar to Jenkins, 25 July, 1854, in *Bengal Judiciary Proceedings* (7 September, 1854), no 76-7. As cited in Barpujari, *Problem of the Hill Tribes: North-East Frontier, 1843-1972*, 4.

Chapter 2

Sunshine before Sunrise, Darkness before Sunset India's North-East and North-East's India

The title of this chapter is a metaphorical expression of the problem of 'distance' and the peculiarity of relationship between mainland India and the peripheral 'North-East' (NE).[1] On the surface, it is a metaphoric answer to the oft-asked mistaken or ignorant questions like – "Are you Chinese? Are you Indian? Where is North-East? How far is North-East?" or "Where is India? How far is India?" etc. In a deeper level, it is an answer to the attitudinal problem of "what the India thinks of NE" and "what the NE thinks of itself."

The dynamic of distance and tension in relation between NE and India has been there since time immemorial in terms of geophysical location, ethnic composition and cultural configuration. Despite development of modern communication of every kind and more than a half century of democratic political contact, the NE still is stranger to mainland India and vice versa. Constitutionally, NE is a part of India and Indian map has clearly demarcated its boundary, but even after more than seven decades of Indian Republic, there is a crisis of belonging that exists. It is unfortunate that many people from mainland India still do not know whether people of NE are Indians, and many people from NE too do not consider themselves as Indians.

[1] In this chapter, instead of North East India (NEI), the "North-East" (NE) is used to mean exclusively the seven states and for the sake of linguistic convenience and better expression, it is also used interchangeably to mean people of the region.

The reason for such haziness is due to lack of conceptual clarity on the perceived notion and actual tensions. Whatever the academicians talk about NE, they tend to avoid certain contentious issues. The scholars from outside the region are reluctant to do so due to fear of inviting trouble, and the scholars from within the region too hesitate to write about the interior issues of their own community. Therefore, with all limitations, a humble attempt, perhaps from a safe comfort zone, is made here to explore some of the interior conceptual haziness on 'exclusion and embrace' relation between the two entities. In order to reach this objective and as point of reference to justify the key hypothesis, seven major distances between India and NE namely, geographical, racial, politico-historical, socio-economic, cultural, religious and theological are explored in this chapter.[2]

Geographical Distance

As it is already been introduced in the first chapter, the NE is a "land-locked region" located in extreme east surrounded by four International boundaries – Bhutan, China, Myanmar and Bangladesh, which is connected with the rest of India only by a narrow corridor known as "chicken's Neck" approximately measuring just 20/22 KM. Due to such geographical location, what is NE to India or what is India to NE has always been in tension in the political history of the nation and region. Actually the reorganization of the region into autonomous political units was the initial impetus that necessitated the coinage of this neologism – North East India. In order to integrate the disintegrated region, and perhaps with a noble aim of coordinated developmental purpose, the North East Council (NEC) was formed as an apex funding and development agency in 1972 including the Sikkim. From then on, the Indian intelligentsia, the bureaucracy as well as the media began to use "North East India" or "Northeast."

However, as a matter of fact, such uncritical agenda to bunch together the various independent political units has swallowed the ethnic groups of the region into "Indian minorities" in due course of political process. Therefore, often there is resentment against the bracketing of huge population of various ethnic communities, spread over eight states altogether into what has now come to be known as NE.[3] Such homogenization of multi-ethnic setting into a unit is seen to be doing colossal damage to many tribes in social, political and economic parameters, and created a distance of belonging[4] – "The India's North East, and North East's India."

---

[2] In order make arguments through, many of the contents here is used from the previous chapter in gist. chapter.

[3] Wasbir Hussain, "India's North-East: The Problem," *Manipur Online* (May 2006), available at: http:www.manipuronline.com/North-East/May2006/NEthe problem09_1.htm (accessed January 7 2019).

[4] Cf. U. A. Shimray, "Socio-Political Unrest in the Region called North-East India," *Economic and Political Weekly* XXXIX/42 (October 16-22, 2004): 4637.

Racial Distance

NE is a minefield of tribes ethnologically belonging to various racial backgrounds mostly different from mainland India. Except some plain communities, all the tribes of the region are predominantly from the mongoloid stock. The original home of these Mongoloid people is believed to be the upper courses of the Yangtse-kiang and the Hoang-ho in the north-west China.[5] Historically speaking, the Kiratas/Bodo-Kocharis are among the earliest known inhabitants from Mongoloid stock.[6] The Bodo tribes, occupying the plains, gradually built up a distinctive culture of their own.[7] Besides, various tribes of Tibeto-Burman race as well as Negroits, the Austro-Asiatics and Dravidians also are believed to be early inhabitants of the region.

Due to such racial composition, NE is seen as a strange racial unit of India. By look, by culture and by language, there is a complete distance from mainland Indian people and their languages. Many in mainland India are still ignorant about the identity of people from NE. They are often looked and treated as strangers, and even foreigners just because of their appearance. Often they are being mistaken as people from other Asian countries and demanded of Passport in various Airports. Of course, there are good number of populations in the mainland India who are aware of the diversity of the region and the people in, but still their mind-sets and attitudes are not homely. Many of the NE people, especially the women living in different parts of Indian metropolitan cities undergo experiences of stereotyping as outsiders. Mostly they are mismatched as Chinese, Japanese, Korean, and Nepalese and so on. At times still they are called as 'chinky' or 'chinkies' with derogatory intent.[8] This shows that till today, they are not embraced as one among vast Indian population. They are still subjected to different perceptions and treatment than other communities.[9] They still encounter various kinds of

---

[5] For details See Baruah, 66-67.

[6] Edward Gait, *A History of Assam* (Guwahati: LBS Publications, 1983 [1926]), 236.; Singh.; Hussain, "Tribal Question in Assam," 1047.

[7] Kanaklal Barua, "Pre-historic Culture in Assam," in *Studies in the Early History of Assam: A Collection of Papers Published in Research Journals on Aspects of the History and Culture of Assam*, edited by M. Neog (Gauhati/Jorhat: Assam Sahitya Sabha, 1973), 207-220 (218-220). [This article appeared in two parts in *JARS*, VII/1 (April 1939), pp.6-18 & VII/2 (July 1939), 35-41].

[8] Anati K. Yeptho & Vincent Rajkumar, *The Social Reality* ..., 65. The term 'chinky' is a racist and offensive term, derived from the word "chink" which is used to describe anyone that is oriental or Eastern Asian descent, particularly ethnic slur usually referring to a person of Chinese ethnicity. Of course, it is used to describe the eyes of those of East Asian descent. Interestingly, the word usually doesn't have the same racial effect when used by two Asians. But the term is indiscriminately used against people of East Asians in racist and offensive sense such as odd look, inferior, stranger etc.

[9] Duncan Mcduie-Ra, "The North-East Map of Delhi," *Economic and Political Weekly*, 47/30 (July, 2012): 71.

discrimination just because of their racial difference and strange look. So, racially this is – "The India's North East, and North East's India."

Politico-Historical Distance

The region has traversed a long road in its political history. The plethora of distancing has its legacy in the history of their isolated political existence during pre-colonial era. The majority of the tribes have been living as an independent life isolated from each other as most of the tribes in the region lacked political or legal institutions transcending the level of their villages. The "village state" managed by Chiefs according to their culture, customs and traditions was the political organisation. Thus, though there have been some trade relations with the neighbouring people of the valley, the hill tribes were not a part of India or Assam, politically.[10] Even the then ruling Ahoms too had no control over the hills as well as the indigenous habitats in the plains.

It is only in the 19th century, the British incorporated the region into the British Indian Empire as distinct hill tracts with tag like "non-regulated", "backward", and "excluded" and administered with separate provisions unlike the administrative pattern prevailing in the rest of British India. To make the policy more effective, and Inner Line Regulation[11] was introduced in 1873 that prohibited all outsiders to enter the categorised areas without permission. Though regulation was introduced with good intentions, this on the process reinforced the barriers already separating the hills people from their plains neighbours.[12] Negatively, it has created a vast plain-hill distance in the region. Whatever the good motif might have been, it virtually cut the prospect of growing relations off.[13] It has also created "frontier within frontier" and accentuated a political and cultural schism. Internally, it has created a major cultural and communication gap and perpetuated an isolationist tendency.

The so-called preservationist or protective policy, on the long run, turned to be a pretext for the exclusion and separation from the mainland India and proliferation of conflicts throughout the region right after the independence of India. Even it was hoped that before their departure, the British might declare the region as independent political units. In the case of Nagas, for instance, when it was not likely to be so, the Naga National Council under the leadership of Zapu

---

[10] For details, see Chapter I of this book.

[11] For detail study on the background and implications of Inner Line Regulation, See Barpujari, *Problem of the Hill Tribes: North-East Frontier, 1873-1962*, 1-27.; also B.B. Kumar, *Reorganization of North East India (Facts and Documents)* (New Delhi: Omsons Publications, 1996), 83-86.

[12] F. S. Downs, *History of Christianity in India: Northeast India in the Nineteenth and Twentieth Centuries,* Vol. 5, Part 5 (Bangalore: The Church History Association of India, 1992), 22-23.

[13] M. Alemchiba, *A Brief Historical Account of Nagaland* (Kohima: Naga Institute of Culture, 1970), 150-51.

Phizo declared 14th August 1947 as day of independence and India's freedom on 15th August as day of neo-colonization of the region. This day on there has been constant contest between "self-positioned" status and "other-positioned" status of the region. Beset with denied rightful human existence, identity, dignity and self-determination, there has been growing "self-positioning" among the natives of NE. So, "There was a Sunshine in NE before the Sunrise in India!"

Socio-Economic Distance

Here is a distance between the claimed self-sufficiency and the blamed dependency. As hills were secluded and untouched by the historic civilizations, various tribes of the region persisted in the traditional forms of economy, social organisations, rituals and belief systems until recent times. In fact, the region is filled with rich natural resources. Added to this is the wealth of good-natured and indolent people with communitarian values. Therefore, NE is confident that it is self-sufficient, but because of exploitative national and state developmental policies, the region is still backward and the majority of the people particularly in the hilltops and rural plains are in utter poverty. However, on the other hand, there is a concerted idea and attitude that the region is utter headache to India since independence and treated like a "problem child of Mother India" and a "prodigal son of the Loving Father."

In fact, there has been immense effort of bridging such a socio-economic distance. Since Independence, the Indian government undertook various approached that can be categorized into four major paradigms[14] namely, *culture paradigm* (1950s and 60s), *security paradigm* (mid 60s), *politics paradigm* (early 70s), and *development paradigm* (80s). In the first paradigm, the phenomenally diverse mosaic of cultures, it was felt that those cultures must be preserved and enriched. These were seen as exotic, endangered and thus needed to be kept in museums and protected from the big bad wolf called "economic development". Secondly, after the Chinese invasion in 1962, the region was seen as a strategically significant one not only in a geographical sense but in a larger geopolitical sense of India's role in East Asia and Southeast Asia. Hence, considering the NE as a security frontier in a geostrategic sense – began to animate government thinking towards the region. Thirdly, it was felt that the diverse tribal cultures and diverse sub-nationalities required participation in 'mainstream' democratic process. This was when new states began to be formed on the idea that people here required a voice – representation in the democratic process – and that once they have voice and representation through the instrument of representative, pluralistic parliamentary democracy, many of the problems associated with this region would tend to get nullified or minimised. This led to formation of different states and granting autonomous districts. Finally, in the developmental paradigm, if government gives them development, they would forget about problems of

[14] Jairam Ramesh, "Northeast India in a New Asia," *Seminar* 550 (June 2005): 17-18.

identity associated with creating a nation out of essentially tribal communities. If institutions of development are built and money poured into the region, people will be happy and problems of politics, of society, of ethnic strife would somehow get minimised if not completely eliminated. Thus, the 1980s was the period marked by a substantial increase in public expenditure in this region assuming that people would then be *homo economicus*, not looking at aspects like what tribe they belong to, and so on.

Thus, 1980s onward there has been various developmental projects under the banner of NEC. However, many NE watchers feel that the Centre's response to its problems has always been a "knee-jerk reaction". In fact, none of these attempts appeared of much help to link the distance as it was just like an appeasement measures and the hiatus between proclaimed policy and the adopted programmes. Contrary, NE has just been given a peripheral status in the national life, which is the major cause of distancing. This has aggravated the situation as integration and peripherization went hand in hand on the part of the Centre and the increasing fear of subsumption and at the same time neglect on the part of NE.

The socio-economic problems and grievances expressed through various movements accompanied with underground wings are, however, considered as utter misplaced anger of their own innate problems generated by perplexed "stranger complex", "feeling of alienation and exploitation" and perceived "step-motherly treatment" or "second class citizens". In the nutshell, such sentiments are regarded as "deprivation drama" used as convenient lever to secure greater benefits from the Centre,[15] which Indian intelligentsia calls nothing, but *bargaining insurgencies*[16] as millions of Rupees that is being pumped into the region allocated for development purpose disappears in the hands of organised gangs – politicians, bureaucrats, middle-persons and underground outfits. Many term is as "oxygen to ethnic militants."[17] Extortion and corruption has become a cottage industry of the militant outfits and politicians. So, in such a volatile NE, perhaps "There is Darkness before Sunset!"

Cultural Distance

The contemporary political history of NE discussed above has marked a tense and contested terrain of claims and counterclaims with all its cultural overtones. The claims of belonging to the distinctive ethnic and cultural world, and a consequent claims of national identity of their own, posited against the Indian national identity has generated considerable debate and controversy among the scholars, intellectuals, social scientists, politicians and also scores of theologians.

---

[15] Cf. Udayon Misra, *The Periphery Strikes Back* (Shimla: IIAS, 2000), 55.

[16] Baruah, "Conflicts and Communities: A Northeast Indian Perspective," 29.

[17] Baruah, "Historicizing Ethnic Politics in Northeast India," 17-18.

There is an ideological play between "politics on culture" and "cultural politics."[18] The former constructs a plot for political expediency of a dominating regime, while the latter contests and reconstructs itself in an alternating mode.[19] The dominant logic of identity promulgated by the Indian state is that there is a necessity of constructing an identity that consents to an inclusion within the Indian national identity and thereby live in agreement with the territorial and constitutional authority of the Indian state. Similarly, there is a non-dominant logic of identity from NE, which assumes a space of difference for realization of its own cultural political aspiration with all other economic and social ramification. However, the Indian state with its ideological and repressive organs persuades these identities to join in Indian mainstream and coerce them into submission.

In this process, there is a domineering distinction made between the grand narratives of "nations from above" and crump narratives of "nations from bellow". In NE, the colonial ethnographic construction of tribe as a mute category of the uncivilised and powerless is used by postcolonial India to reduce the cultural self-definitions of tribes into nothingness by reducing their distinct identities into national identity. The "Politics of culture" brought forth a politics of marginalizing indigenous cultures through non-recognition of the independent specific mode of life-world. This produced a tension of difference between the "natives" and "Nation".

This is how Christianity and Christian theology too were used by the colonial "politics on culture" to reduce the native ways of life-world by replacing with a better understanding of the truth and the good. The native ways of life-world did not present a concept of God that leads to salvation. Christian theology principally aimed at explaining the native faiths over natural phenomenon and replace their faiths by way of demonstrating the order of the universe, nature and human life. Such an interpretation of native world-view forced the tribes to identify loose ends and feel ashamed of their own tradition and cultures. The Christian idea of deliverance of the sufferer by God – by way of Christ's suffering for entire humanity – provided the rationale to highlight Christ as the saviour. Such an appeal to Christ as the saviour backed by Christianity's theological capability to explain the rationale of indigenous faith clearly established the superiority of Christianity.

Over against such trend, there is a "cultural politics". It is an imaging of "an inside of thinking and imagination" over "an outside of struggle against the state and hegemonic power". It is the break with this process and the ethno-philosophy in NE, set an agenda of recovering the cultural position of ethnic

---

[18] The "politics on culture" is an attempt to subsume the cultures under the game of politics, while the "cultural politics" is an attempt to mobilize the cultural signifiers beyond a politically fixed and positioned identity of a culture.

[19] Prasenjit Biswas and Chandan Suklabaidya, *Ethnic Life-Worlds in North-East India: An Analysis* (New Delhi: Sage Publications, 2007), 108.

identities lost inside the nationalist mapping of their life-world. It resists the onslaught of nationalist-statist politics of cultural devaluation, canonization and homogenization by way of self-representation and maintenance of traditional community institutions.

As it is widely accepted, the cultural life of NE has nothing much in common with the mainstream Indian cultures. Sir Robert Reid, the governor of Assam, in the early 1940s stated that "they are not Indian in any sense of the word, neither in origin, nor in language, nor in appearance, nor in habits, nor in outlook, and it is only by historical accident that they have been tacked to an India providence."[20] While introducing the "Crown Colony Scheme", J.H. Hutton, the Deputy Commissioner of Naga Hills District showed how the hill people with racially, historically, culturally, and linguistically had any affinity with the people of the Assam plains, while their administration was wholly on different lines.[21] It was also strongly argued in the Memorandum to Simon Commission that "the backward tracts should be excluded from the province of Assam in the new Constitution. These areas have nothing in common with rest of the Province... the present artificial union should be ended."[22] Hence, there is a common cliché among the people of NE that they were neither a part of then Assam nor of the rest of India.

The aspect of "cultural politics" based on rich and distinct cultural elements goes into playing the politics of difference at the level of mainstream India. In order to resist the domination of other, they follow "cultural politics" of enclosed positioning. To this effect, even the choice of language in the multi-lingual state like Nagaland, though the Nagamese is the lingua franca of the state, English is preferred as official language instead. The logic of preference obviously is of greater influence and utility of it in contemporary India. English being a symbol of culturally dominant language it can definitely resit domination from other Indian communities. Even in the public linguistic culture, it is English not Hindi, Western dress, music and way of life than Indian. Logic here is both resistance to dominant Indian culture and greater sense of freedom, pleasure and self-satisfaction not neglecting their own cultural practices. It takes them outside the ways of Pan-Indian mainstream cultural forms. In fact, they choose the globally dominant symbols that foster a sense of being different from what is India.

---

[20] Cited in Imdad Hussain, "ASSAM: Unification and Roots of Division," in *Reorganisation of Northeast India Since 1947*, edited by B. Datta Ray and S.P. Agrawal (New Delhi: Concept Publishing Company, 1996), 16.

[21] *Memorandum of the Government of Assam to the Indian Statutory Commissioner* Vol. XIV pp. 111-122. Referred in David R. Syiemlieh, "The Future of the Hills of North-East India 1928-1947: Some British Views", in *Reorganisation of Northeast India Since 1947*, edited by B. Datta Ray and S.P. Agrawal (New Delhi: Concept Publishing Company, 1996), 25.

[22] *Memorandum to Simon Commission by Assam Government*, cited in Hussain, "ASSAM: Unification and Roots of Division," 1.

Unfortunately, it appears that the sentiment of "we don't want to be treated as museum pieces and untouchables", but getting influenced by Western cultures is apparently not a problem, rather attachment to those cultural symbols are considered to be help in bringing a sense of recuperation of what gets lost within Pan-India national identity. Hence, what is Western is less problematic than what is Indian. Forgetting about the life in their villages, many Western life-styled elite Christians of developing towns are disdainful of "Indian-ness", of its poverty and stench of rural India.[23] Even the word "India or Indian" itself is allergic to many people in certain pockets of NE. For them, there is no connection and thereby no regard at all except, the India currency. This has even led to the justification of "no harm engaging in corruption and living lavish life" as long as it is Indian money. Therefore, one can read report such as "...during elections when political parties distribute money to buy votes, acceptance of that money is seen as legitimate since it involves only 'India *Toka*' [Indian money], not 'Naga *Toka*' [Naga money].[24] This is an expression of a psycho warfare of "I don't belong". To India's eye, it is anti-national and double standard life, but to them it is distinctive life and even means of nation building.

Such repressive and regressive imaging and counter imaging of difference is widening the distance between NE and India. It has deepened the feeling of separateness in the heart of NE and the feeling of troublemaker has gone deep into the mind of India. It seems NE is in the subconscious mind of India than in the hearts, and India not in the heart of NE but just in the psyche. As sentimentalization and fantacization rules the psyche, each has failed to see the goodness in the other. Thus, NE is not getting the best of India and India is not getting the best of NE. In its obsession with the 'bad' of the people there, India has failed to harness their good and in their obsession with the feeling of 'oppressiveness' of the Indian State, NE has failed to appreciate the goodness of India. What the best of culture India gets from NE is just music, dance and handicrafts, not the indigenous wisdoms; and the best of India's culture NE gets is its Bollywood cultures and education, but not Indian wisdom. Culturally, a gap between "India's North East and North East's India!"

Religious Distance

Most of the tribes of NE, both the hills and the plains, had their own traditional religion with certain common beliefs in Supreme Being and spirits. Since all of them were inhabiting in the lofty mountains, roaring rivers, deep valleys and dense forests, they had certain beliefs in spirits. Their religion and life-world was interconnected with spiritual beings, nature and all other living beings. There is a

---

[23] Patricia Mukkim, "Whiter the Naga Struggle?" *The Telegraph*, Thursday, May 20, 2004, 16.

[24] Sanjib Baruah, *Durable Disorder: Understanding the Politics of Northeast India* (New Delhi: Oxford University Press, 2005), 74. Another justification people in general make is that since this is public's money, there is no harm in taking it; it is just coming back to the public.

belief that "If a stone rolls from the mountain, if a leaf drops from a tree, it must be a spirit of a stroll; if wind blow through the forests, the gods were indulging some healthy exercise, if winds shake the trees and howl through the valley, the *deos* or the spirits were quarrelling". They maintained their own distinct religion, tradition, taboos, social system that was quite different from the people of the valley. Animists? Yes, but not appellative animist of the dominant.

Though there are some linkages in their belief systems, Hinduism had little or no influence on the hill tribes whereas Buddhism got deep rooted among some tribes of Arunachal Pradesh. The Sanskritic religion and culture could not penetrate into the hill regions possibly due to its unappealing social practices or plains people's fear of the fierce tribes of the hills. Of course, there could have been a process of slow penetration, but the timely arrival of Christianity stopped it. As Goswami rightly observes, "with the arrival of the Christian missionaries, the people, for various reasons, became apathetic towards the religion of the nontribal Hindus."[25] A large number of people in the plains of Assam, Manipur and Arunachal Pradesh have accepted Hinduism, both Brahmaism and Vaishnavism, whereas the great majority of the hill tribes embraced Christianity. In fact, as it is stated earlier, Christianity was a choice religion of the hill tribes. This made Indian in general to perceive NE as Christian region. However, there are only about 4.5 million Christians in the region as per the 2001Census."[26]

The earliest record of Christian presence in NE dates back to the 17th and 18th centuries, but Christianity entered the region through the shadow of British Administration during 19th century. Six different streams of Christian Missions – Serampore Mission, American Baptist, Welsh Presbyterian, Roman Catholics, Anglican and Lutherans entered by the help of British Administration. It was said, "the Cross not unoften followed the British flag."[27] In Down's words, "Government found the missions useful, or so they hoped, in pacifying the hills tribes and providing education at minimal cost to itself; the missions found the government useful in underwriting, in many cases, their educational work and in providing security for both themselves and their converts."[28]

In initial stage, there has been strong resistance especially from the village chiefs. They saw Christianity as threat to their chieftainships, traditional way of

[25] B.B. Goswami, "The Tribes of Assam: A Few Comments on their Societal and Cultural Ties with the Non-Tribes," in *Tribal Situation in India*, edited by K.S. Singh (Shimla: IIAS, 1972), 277-278.

[26] Arunachal Pradesh - 89,013 (10.29%), Assam 7,44,367 (3.32%), Manipur 6, 26, 669 (34.11%), Meghalaya 11, 46, 092 (64.58%), Mizoram 5, 91, 342 (85.73%), Nagaland 10, 57, 940 (87.47%), Tripura 46, 472 (1.68%). Total Population of Seven States 3, 83, 16, 618; Christians 43, 01, 895, (11.2%). The Registrar General of India, Census of India, 2001, Series-1, Paper- 1 of 2001, Final Population Totals; *Basic Statistics of Ner 2006*.

[27] Barpujari, *Assam in the Days of the Company* (1826-1858), 300.

[28] Downs, *History of Christianity in India: Northeast India in the Nineteenth and Twentieth Centuries*, 30.

life and social order. Nevertheless, in the long run, the hill tribes accommodated themselves to British rule and began to see it, as well as Christianity, as a defence against the greater threat of dominance by and absorption into the more advanced Hindu community of the plains.[29] As it is observed, "One of the functions of Christianity, sociologically speaking, was to help the hill tribes preserve their identity in the face of the perceived new threat of assimilation into the Hindu societies of the plains."[30] By the first half of the 20th century, almost whole of the region was covered by the Christian missionary activities. At the beginning of the century, Khasi Hills and Lushai Hills (Mizoram) witnessed rapid growth[31] followed by Naga Hills and other hill tracts.[32]

In Mizoram, the natural calamities such as bamboo flowering, rat explosion, landslides and the resultant famine served as "God's strange means" to win the Mizos for Christ.[33] Among Nagas, Christianity was perceived as cement that would bring together the various tribes into a Naga nation. In general, humanitarian activities, gift of a written language and literature, modern education, the ideals of universal brother/sisterhood served as magnet to embrace Christianity.

People saw ray of hope for bright future. It served as the vehicle for the unification of isolated small communities into a larger entity.[34] It enhanced *inter-ethnic alliance*[35] or *tribal ecumenism*.[36] Indeed, the church organisations, associations, circles, councils, dioceses, conventions, assemblies and synods served as a forum for corporate identity as Naga, Mizo, Garo, Khasi and so on. In the

[29] Ibid., 15.

[30] Ibid., 4.

[31] For comprehensive history of Christianity in Mizoram (Missiological Perspective), see C.L. Hminga, *The Life and Witness of the Churches in Mizoram* (Serkawn: Literature Committee Baptist Church Mizoram, I 987).

[32] Cf. Downs, *The Mighty Works of God. A Brief History of the Council of Baptist Churches in North East India: The Mission Period, 1836-1950* (Gauhati: CLC, 1971).; Milton Sangma, History American Baptist Mission in North East India - 1836-1950 (New Delhi: Mittal Publications, 1987), 218-72.

[33] Sajal Nag, "God's Strange Means: Missionaries, Calamity and Philanthropy Among the Lushais," in *Christianity and Change in Northeast India*, edited by T.B. Subba, Joseph Puthenpurakal and Shaji Joseph Puykunnel (New Delhi: Concept, 2009), 285-304.

[34] B. K. Roy Burman, "Integrated Area Approach to the Problems of the Hill Tribes," in *Tribal Situation in India*, 80.

[35] S.M. Dubey, "lnter-Ethnic Alliance, Tribal Movements and Integration in Northeast India," in *Tribal Movement in India*, edited by K.S. Singh (New Delhi: Manohar Publications, 1982), 13ff.

[36] Downs for the first time used the term "Tribal Ecumenism" in an appendix written in C.B. Firth's book, *An Introduction to Indian Church History*. He actually used the term to refer to the development of new relationships at the intra-tribal, inter-tribal and extra-tribal levels. Cf. Appendix in C.B. Firth, *An Introduction to Indian Church History* (Madras: CLS. 1976).; Also see F.S. Downs, "Tribal Ecumenism in North East India: The Christian Role in Solidarity Movements," *Eastern Theological College Journal* 2/2 (Jan-May 1989): 48ff..; ICHR XXVIII/1 (June 1989): 23 ff.

later days, the Church, theological education and institutions served as connecting medium among the tribes, with India and wider world. F.S. Downs, argues with vivid historical evidences that

> Christianity has been one of the most powerful integrating agencies within the tribes, districts and states of the region, as well as between the peoples of the hills and those of the plains has also prayed a significant role, popular notions to the contrary notwithstanding, in the process of integrating the hills people in the North East with the rest of the country.[37]

Contrarily, the Indian intelligentsia and anti-Christian forces see Christianity as the most effective factor of distancing tribes among themselves and from mainland India. Notwithstanding the good works, it is alleged that the Christian missions at the outset fostered a negative orientation among the tribes. The missionaries and Christianity are seen behind all the separatist movements in the region. The following statements suffice the point.

> The isolation of the [tribes] was further accentuated by the advent of the western Christian missionaries in the region... these missionaries converted the [tribes] to Christianity in large numbers and reclaimed them to civilisation and, in the process, raised yet another wat, culture and religion… inculcated in them western Christian concepts of life and ethics – all of which only further served to alienate them [tribes] from populace and culture of the rest of country.[38]

> Christian missionaries in the hill areas of the region and elsewhere popularised modern education and health care. However, in so far as dissemination for the ideals of freedom and equality and a sense of belonging to the "great" Indian nation were concerned, the Christian missionaries played a negative role.[39]

> The phenomenal rise of Christianity in all North-Eastern state except in Arunachal Pradesh, during 1961-1981 became a symbol of tribal regionalism.[40]

---

[37] Downs, *History of Christianity in India: Northeast India in the Nineteenth and Twentieth Centuries*, 131.

[38] D. R. Mankekar, "Understanding the Tribals on the North-Eastern Border," in *Tribal Situation in India*, 110-111.

[39] Singh, *The Problem of Change: A Study of North-East India*, 3.

[40] B. Datta Ray, "Anatomy of Regionalism in North-East India Hills: A Preliminary Observation," in *Tribal Transformation in India: Ethnopolitics and Identity Crisis*, edited by Buddhadeb Chaudhuri (New Delhi: Inter-India, 1992), 475.

> After Independence, the role of the foreign missionaries was highly dubious, if not positively and openly anti-Indian ... they encouraged secessionist tendencies among the tribal leaders and incited them to claim free tribal states by exciting their fear that in the Indian Union their identity would be lost and their cultural heritage would be destroyed.[41]

In response, NE considers such allegations as childish, ridiculous and politically motivated. Only those secularists who are against anything Christian and have contempt for the people of the region spread such allegations. Such utter wrong picture is totally unacceptable to the local people.[42] Instead, they feel that India as a whole should be grateful to the early Christian missionaries for helping many tribes to make big forward leap, which would not have been possible otherwise.

Nevertheless, they also do not deny the fact that Christian mission left some of the dangerous legacies. In his write up - "Heathens and Baptists" Heimendorf strongly argued that "conversion to Christianity could in no way bring back the colour and joy; rather, it contributed to a loss that remained irreparable in village life of the tribes."[43] Secondly, Christianity as an identity elevator tended to be reinforcing the traditional animosity not only people of the plains but among the tribes. In fact, the Naga and Mizo movements had close association with Christianity both in the minds of their leaders and supporters. These movements had certain degree of strong Christian ideological base.[44] For instance, the first Naga Independence leader, Zapu Phizo was a convinced Baptist. In the earlier period, a substantial number of pastors joined the underground. Volunteer Gospel teams preached under armed guard which one might almost say like "gun in one hand Bible in the other". Many of the militant camps are named after Biblical places such as Carmel, Gilgal, Hebron, Jericho, Zion, etc., and conduct of those camps are ordered by Christian spiritual activities. Even the cadres did not fight on Sundays unless attacked.[45]

The slogan - "Nagaland for Christ" is a recognised rallying cry among Nagas, Even Christian elements appeared overtly in the official statements. The Constitution of the Federal Government of Nagaland, while it guaranteed free

---

[41] *Proceedings of the Northeast India History Association, Sixth Session* (Agartala, 1985), 19. As cited in Downs, *History of Christianity in India: Northeast India in the Nineteenth and Twentieth Centuries*, 117-118.

[42] L. Jeyaseelan, "Conflict Situation in North-East India: The Church's Response II," *VJTR* 63/7 (July 1999): 505.

[43] Christophe von Furer Heimendorf, *Return to the Naked Nagas: An Anthropologist's View of Nagaland, 1936-1970* (Delhi: Vikas Publications, 1974), 49.

[44] Cf. John Parratt, "Christianity ethnicity and structural violence: The North-East India Case," available at: http:/www.kanglaonline.com/index.php?template:kshow&kid=8&

[45] M. Horam, *Naga Insurgency: The Last Thirty Years* (New Delhi: Cosmos Publications, 1988), 76-77.

profession and practice of any religion, declared that Christianity would be the religion of the Naga state.[46] The *Shepoumaramth Regional Church Bulletin* 1994-95 published a column "God has chosen Nagaland for His glory" where it declared:

> The kingdom of Nagaland for Christ is very precious. Whoever commit themselves not wholeheartedly to Christ will perish and they will not see this Kingdom. The Naga nation is no longer, the smallest, it is now the largest. Nagaland's Kingdom is not only out alone but also belongs to God. Faith will rule over the whole earth, not gun and man (sic) power. Those who oppose the nation will oppose himself (sic). Nagaland is a heavy stone for the Indian and the Burmese, come together against it.... At the same time it is not only the fault of India but also Nagas. We have been suffering for many years going against God. God's children cannot be divided and time has come to become united as a bundle of five sticks.... Nagas are travelling in two boats trying to fulfil the pleasure of the world and to please God. our church becomes the centre of Politics.... God has formed to a New Jerusalem, and all nations will marvel seeing this small nation. National workers will no more be hiding in the jungles. The educated pro-Indian of the Nagas like Sanballat and Tobiah are against the sovereignty movement.... The Land of the Naga is purchased by the blood of the innocent youth. Their bones are not yet decayed, and blood not yet divided. Those who died in the jungle for the nation are still shouting for Nagaland's sovereignty, and God hears this crying.[47]

However, when such ethnic aspirations are in question, it appears "blood is thicker than the baptismal water and ethnicity stronger than the bond of faith that calls for forgiveness and reconciliation" and "Christianity is only a skin deep, faith has not sunk in it."[48] This is India's NE - "Darkness before Sunset!"

Theological Distance

Theologically too, there has been and there is still a great distance. Theologies from the region are in the periphery of so-called mainstream Indian Christian Theology. Weakness perhaps lies with the churches of NE. Though the presence of theological colleges in the region dates back to more than a century,[49] the

[46] Ibid., 61.

[47] Quote cited from Reprint, *The Shepoumaramth in the Naga National Movement* (Shepoumaramth: Government of the People's Republic of Nagaland, 1995), 225-28.

[48] L. Jeyaseelan, "Conflict Situation in North-East India: The Church's Response," 506-507.

[49] The first theological seminary specifically for the training of the clergy was founded by the Welsh Mission at Cherrapunji Meghalaya in 1887 [John Hughes Morris, The History of the Welsh Calvinistic Methodists' Foreign Mission, to the end of the Year 1904 (Liverpool, Carnarvon: CM Book Room, D.O. Brian Owen Agent, 1910), 179.] later known as Cherra Theological College.

churches in NE did not produce theology until the recent decades. Theology apart, the churches did not produce theologically trained leaders until the 1960s and even in the 70s, in the case of some Churches. The churches began to send students for theological education in great numbers only after 80s.[50]

The self-theologisation was crystallized only in 1995 with the inauguration of Tribal study centre at Eastern Theological College, Jorhat, Assam under the leadership of Renthy Keitzar. since then there has been growing interest among the theological students from NE and with the emergence of "Tribal Theology", Christianity was interpreted in terms of the best and the noblest of human virtues engraved in indigenous cultures. Native theologians moulded the indigenous meanings by taking into account available meanings within local cultures. Perhaps, Christianity was very well grounded in the people's culture and accommodated within their ethos. Here, the "Cultural politics" of Christianity was different from the colonial "politics of culture" that reduced indigenous culture to a mere object. Christian philosophy in NE sought to explain the primary form of power in the world, along with the most basic human necessity "not in dominion, but in caring presence" which has implications against the "politics of culture" in India. This also implies that while doing this, the native theologies echo the self-distinctiveness and separateness, thus distancing the distance farther ideologically. The disclaims and claims made against Indian Christian Theology in favour of native theologies, are a replica of separateness expressed in various political movements in NE. Moreover, to many outside onlookers, the "Tribal Theology" is a product of uncritical enthusiasm and romanticism about distinctiveness and uniqueness of their past cultures which appears like "mechanism of distancing". This is "India's North East!"

Conclusion

Above explorations of distances show that there is a gap between perceived notions and actual facts. There is an ardent need of right positioning of the NE on the part of the India as nation and re-positioning of self-enclosed position on the part of the NE. At an anthropological and epistemological plane, the culturally embedded practices of the indigenous life-world such as dresses, attires, languages, music and spiritual values, which are bypassed by the colonial and post-colonial Indian states in the process of political and cultural recognition are yet to be understood reciprocally. It is true that recognising many communities of

---

This college was the earliest affiliated College with Serampore at the L. Th. level following the charter revision of 1918 that started a College level theological department and latter affiliated in 1937. [Serampore College, *University Handbook for the Year 1960-62: Golden Jubilee Number 1910-19*].

[50] Cf. A. Wati Longchar, "Trends in Tribal Theology in North East India," in *Dalit and Minjung Theologies*, ed. Samson Prabhakar and Jinkwan Kwon (Bangalore: BTESSC/SATHRI, 2016), 59-60.

"scheduled tribes" with attendant cultural and political rights has certainly made them a part of the system, but not with a sense of belonging. NE has occupied only a peripheral space in India's national consciousness. Many mainland Indians do not consider people of the region as fully Indian or NE does not understand India fully.[51] Therefore, the question of indigenous, ethnic and national identity, with its attendant political, economic and cultural claims has remained unresolved paradox of "India's North East and North East's India".

Bridging the distance must emerge from the cultural resources of both. From within the culture systems one must bridge the distancing cultures. India must revisit NE, and NE must reconsider India. For, in the cultural life-world of India and NE, there is irreducible wisdom of holistic notion of human-nature, culture-nature relationship and ideal praxis. Therefore, in the sacred conceptualization of Human-Nature-Creature-Spirit relationships expressed in "Tribal Theology", people of NE must find relationship between the distancing selves; and in the philosophy of "unity in diversity", India must embrace NE. Since reciprocity emerges from something that comes from the separate and different other, both should come to the sense of with-ness belongingness through mutual respectfulness of other's otherness.

While remaining fully attached to its vision of one nation, India must recognize the distinctiveness of NE and overcome the barriers of superimpositions and while remaining fully attached to its distinctiveness, NE must recognize the reality of extreme diversity and extremity of distinct identity within, and overcome the barriers of egocentricity. The unqualified commitment to and exclusive engagement with the ideas of separateness and differences will lead nowhere. Both must be enlightened that what India thinks of NE is not what it is, and what NE thinks of India is not what it is. India must know "there is no darkness in NE before sunset!" and NE must realize "There is no Sunshine before the Sunrise!"

S.B.

---

[51] Walter Fernandes, "Globalization, Culture and Fundamentalism," in *Know Your People: Cultural Sensitivity in Formation*, edited by Peter Haokip et.al (Shillong: Orient Publications, 2005), 18-19.

Chapter 3

Hegemonic Colonial Historiography over the History NEI Tribes

The term "Colonialism" came into widespread use in academic discourses since 1920s and served as catalyst for many fields of studies. The term encompasses range of dimensions, both coercive and ideational at work in the construction and perpetuation of colonial domination and hegemony over weaker nations and peoples. It has been identified that the colonizers denied the tradition, history, identity and rights of the colonized peoples, and created among the colonial subjects, a sense of inferiority and dependency complex. And the trajectory of changes that colonizers tried to impose was set on such feeling of inferiority. In the process, there is either marginalization or a complete suppression of the weaker nations and peoples. Such control and domination occurred most in the field of education, literature, medicine, and in fact in all systems of knowledge.[1] As result of such engagement by the colonizers, produced a different kind of writings about the colonized peoples' history. In this chapter, one of such histories of NEI tribes, i.e., Ao-Nagas of Nagaland[2] is presented, particularly the Colonial Mission Hegemony and making of Colonial Historiography with brief conceptual and introductory notes on Colony, Colonialism and Colonial.

[1] K.N. Panikkar, *Colonialism, Culture and Resistance* (New Delhi: Oxford University Press, 2007), 22.

[2] The focus of this chapter in general is the colonial perspectives in writing the history of various Hills tribes of NEI. But specific examples are cited of Ao Naga History written by the outsiders.

Colony, Colonialism and Colonial in Making History

Colony, Colonialism and Colonial are words which have been used constantly by historians, social scientists and interest groups of other fields. As such these words have also had different meanings and connotations for different interest groups. For instance, European metropolis interests, which have been the major colonizers, have made the words appear to be synonymous with civilization, philanthropy, and end to ignorance, disease and tyrannical rule and the beginnings of good administration and justice. But for the Third World countries which have been at the receiving end, colonialism has neither been civilizing, nor philanthropic nor has it been an end to ignorance.[3] In fact, for the colonies the main actors of colonialism have been, to put it in the words of Aime Cesaire, "The Adventurer and the pirate, the wholesale grocer and the ship owner, the gold digger and the merchant, appetite and force, and behind them, the baleful projected show of a form of civilization which, at certain point in its history, finds itself obliged, for internal reasons to extend to a world scale the competition of its antagonistic economies."[4] The colonial situation is therefore not just an economic order but it carries with it, as Frantz Fanon shows, a socio-psychological aspect too.[5] The colonies were thus marked by polarization into two antagonistic poles: the colonizer and the colonized. "The prosperity and privilege of the former are directly based on the exploitation and pauperization of the other."[6]

In recent years, discussions of imperial experience have alerted the Third World societies to their dangers. However, another type of colonial activity now threatens the integrity of societies in developing nations is the 'colonizing the mind'. This is the form of psychological imperialism. Perhaps resistance against this force is difficult as it comes not as an active conspiracy as traditional colonialism was, but with precise way of psychological penetration that slowly and steadily influence people to embrace the Western norms and ethical imperatives as means of human achievement and national performance and thereby replace their own traditional values. Such enslavement of the mind is the most subtle of submissions – especially when it is self-imposed.[7]

The 'civilizing mission' the British undertook after the conquest marked the beginning of a new stage in colonizing process where the natives were brought

[3] Manorama Sharma, *History and History Writing in North East India* (New Delhi: Regency Publications, 1998), 61.

[4] Aime Cesaire, "From Discourse on Colonialism," in *Colonial Discourse and Post-Colonial Theory: A Reader*, edited by Patrick Williams & Laura Chrisman, 173.

[5] See Renate Zahar, *Frantz Fanon: Colonialism and Alienation* (London, 1972) and Frantz Fanon, *Wretched of the Earth* (Penguine Books, 1977) – for the ideas of Fanon, quoted in Manorama, *History* ..., 61.

[6] Renate Zahar, *Frantz Fanon: Colonialism and Alienation* (London, 1972), 18, quoted in Manorama, *History* ..., 62.

[7] Ralph Buutjens, "Colonising the Mind," *Anima*, 10/1: 15, 19.

under administrative control, presumably for improving their moral and material conditions. The opportunity for liberating the 'natives' from the 'unhappy system of oppression' of Oriental despotism was considered sufficient justification for the conquest. The setting up of administrative structures, creating ideological institutions, transforming cultural practices that followed the conquest were, therefore, approached with a reforming zeal.[8] Imbued with a sense of purpose and conviction of superiority, often tinged with racism, the British administration undertook the task of transforming the 'natives'.[9] In fact, the concept of colonialism is usually associated with territorial occupation, economic aggrandizement or cultural domination.

The new category of socio-historical location created by Colonialism and writing of history accordingly has become even more complex subject in the countries that have undergone the colonial experience. Here, the question of bias in writing and interpreting history is apparent because of the system carried with it does not allow any representation of the realities of the societies. Therefore, historians who wrote histories without critically assessing this position and aspects of colonialism fall into the pit of presenting and interpreting a subjective history and indulge in interpreting a bias historical account of the natives. Literally, the history writing was never been free from bias interpretation. Even the historians of the 19th century who thought that they were presenting ascertainable facts were not in reality in fact writing value free history. They reflected their bias.

Historiographical perspective changes and takes different shapes due to the changes in social realities or the hegemony in the society exercised by the elites. Likewise the heyday of colonial period and domination gave rise to new trends in history writing called colonial historiography whereby giving undue glorification and justification of colonialism. This perspective had produced a new kind of bias in history writing which can be termed as the colonial bias. This perspective and trend is very apparent in the historical works produced in the colonized countries of Africa, Asia and the Latin America. This trend and perspective in history writing has a far-reaching impact on the native historians.

Missionaries to the Ao-Nagas in Nagaland: Colonial Mission Hegemony

19th century ushered in witnessing the growth of new religious movements resulting in the formation of several missionary societies and agencies for missionary enterprises among different denominations in the West. Looking at the context towards the late 18th century, we find that among the educated elite of New England in the United States there began a religious awakening. The

---

[8] Harald Fischer-Tine and Michael Mann (eds), *Colonialism as Civilizing Mission* (London: 2004), 1-26 ; Michael Adad, *Machines as Measure of Men: Science, Technology and Ideologies of Western Dominance* (Delhi: 1990), 199-210. As cited in K.N. Panikkar, *Colonialism ...*, 3.

[9] K.N. Panikkar, *Colonialism...*, 3.

Puritans[10] who had escaped religious persecution in Europe during the 17th century dominated the region of New England. As they settled in this new region, they felt it was their duty and calling to begin a process of building a church and society that would based on Puritanical values.[11] It was therefore, from New England that the Puritanical and later, evangelical ideas and thoughts were developed, firmly took root and spread to other parts of the United States. By the beginning of the 19th century, the religious revival movement swept America. Moreover, after the revolutionary war and independence, the missionaries thought that it was their urgent duty to involve in the reorganization of human society in accordance with the law of God.[12] Hence, the idea of 'manifest destiny' became a watch word by the beginning of the 19th century. This means that it was the destiny of America to manifest to humankind the excellence of the divine principles.[13] Following the civil war in the latter half of the 19th century, the notion that America had a providential role to play for the progress of humankind became more prevalent.[14] With this motive – providential role, manifest destiny, reorganization of human society - and mission, the American Baptist Mission with its Puritanical and Evangelical insights and background came to work first among the Nagas in Nagaland.

The mission work among the Nagas was part and parcel of their 'manifest destiny' to Christianize the world of heathens or for that matter animist and thereby to civilize the savage or barbaric race and bring them out from darkness to light. The missionaries felt it was their manifest destiny to initiate a process of change through evangelization that would transform the socio-cultural and

---

[10] This is the name given to religious sectarians who were originally members of the Church of England but who later formed an independent group. The Puritans insisted that worship in the Church in England should be free from vestments, furnishings and ceremonies, retained from the medieval order. They opposed church government by bishops. In its most common historical usage Puritanism refers to a movement within English Protestantism in both the British Isles and Colonial America. The idea of puritans was to maintaining 'purity' of worship and doctrine so also to follow strict puritanical disciplines regarding aspects of one's social, political and economic life. The starting point for Puritan theology was an emphasis on the majesty, righteousness and sovereignty of God. Cf., Francis J. Bremer, "Puritanism," *Encyclopedia of Religion*, 2nd Edition, Vol. 11, edited by Lindsay Jones (USA: Thomsan Gale, 2005): 7518-7521.

[11] Wendy J. Deichmann Edwards, "Forging an Ideology for American Missions: Josiah Strong and Manifest Destiny," in *North American Foreign Missions - 1810-1914: Theology, Theory and Policy*, edited by Wilbert R. Shenk (Michigan: Grand Rapids, 2004), 165.

[12] Wendy, *American Mission* ..., 167.

[13] The idea is that for this blessed mission to the nations of the world, which are shut out from the life-giving light of truth, has America been chosen; and her high example shall smite unto death the tyranny of kings, hierarchy, and oligarchs, and carry the glad tidings of peace and good will where myriad now endure an existence scarcely more enviable than that of beasts of the field. See Wendy, *American Mission* ..., 168-169.

[14] Justo L. Gonzalez, *The Story of Christianity: The Early Church to Present Day, Part II* (Massachusetts: Peabody, 2004), 253.

religious worldview of the Nagas. In doing so, the Nagas were "presented with truths and technologies drawn from a post-enlightenment world in which Christianity was inseparable from specific understanding of civilization."[15] It is in this process the Nagas began to experience and embrace a history which was not of their own. Even they no longer see it as form of control or imposition from outside as it is deeply inscribed in their everyday routine.

Hegemonic Colonial Historiography over Tribes of NEI

The term colonial historiography is not just a perspective in writing history that upholds colonialism, but certain value systems, colonial discourses, assumptions, ideologies and representations that continues to affect and influence in a subtle way the minds of the people and the historians even after colonial administration as a political force and hegemony come to an end. Here, one can refer to the socio-psychological and ideological consequences of colonialism. The impact continues to be seen in the writings of many historians of the colonized countries. Thus, colonialism has to be seen not only in terms of an alien control over the land, resources and trade of the subjected countries, but as a system which had far reaching impact on the economic, social, political, cultural and intellectual development of those countries.[16] One must note that Postcolonial project is also committed to the historical and psychological recovery of the postcolonial subjects.

Colonialism have thus created and shaped various historiographical narratives in the colonies that were once colonized. Colonialism was also engaged in emptying the colonized world of meaning. Hence, a counter narrative of historical writing today (post-colonial situation) falls short in its historical analysis since certain basic ideological representation and characteristics still persists. For instance, commenting on the interpretations of Indian history, Romila Thapar has very rightly pointed out that, Indian history began with such an explanation of the past by British colonial historians. Subsequently, nationalist historians attempted to refute some of these explanations, or else to accept some… they have periodized the Indian history to support their colonial argument that the primary identity of Indian society was that of religious communities, generally antagonistic of each other. In this manner colonial administration sorted out Indian society and wrapped it up into neat packages. Unfortunately, nationalist historians did not unwrap these packages. We still have them and they have become part of how

---

[15] Jean Commaroff, 'Missionaries and Mechanical Clock: An Essay on Religion and History in South Africa,' *The Journal of Religion*, 71/1 (January 1991): 8, quoted in John Thomas, "Missionaries, Colonialism and the Writing of History Among the Nagas," *JTCA* 7&8 (2008/2009): 103.

[16] Manorama, *History …*, 64.

we see ourselves in contemporary society and politics.[17] She also raises self-critical challenge that "we have not questioned the statement of colonial writing that Indian identities are religious identities. History is what has been used by colonial scholarship to create our identities and we are continuing to use it, and even abuse it, for purpose.[18]

The Indian histories written during the 19th and early 20th centuries were written from an imperialist perspective largely to uphold the British mercantilist, and colonial and imperialist expansion of which India was an integral part. Few examples on how India is projected in the colonial historiography can be cited for our understanding. The works of early British historians of India like James Mill, Elphinstone, Macaulay and others were mainly British administrative histories intended to be read by the British public, more particularly by the officers of the government. Then first important comprehensive history of India was written by James Mill.[19] In the preface to the first volume he stated that it was "intended to serve as an introduction to the knowledge of India" for the people of Britain.[20] He even tried to establish that ancient India were barbarous in science, religion, government, law and political economy. Mountstuart Elphinstone wrote that the most prominent vice of the Hindus is want of veracity, in which they out do most nations even of the east.[21] Another historian Vincent A. Smith[22] who wrote the history at the time when Indian nationalism was beginning to emerge tried to provide the British people with better understanding to the Indians and to defend against the attacks of the nationalist. He argued that the triumphant progress of Alexander the Great demonstrated the inherent weakness of the greatest Asiatic armies when confronted with European skill and discipline.[23] In all of their writings, the Indian subjects were merely used as an object or background to claim and justify their hegemony and superiority.

In nutshell, these writings were primarily done by the British India administrators (c. 1870-1940). The British historians were concerned with the British activities and treated the vicissitudes of Indian society as outside their kin. In their opinion India society was unprogressive and decadent. What was important to them was the way in which what the British did affected Indians.

---

[17] Romila Thapar, "Reporting History: Early India," *Social Scientist*, 40/7-8 (July – August, 2012): 31-32.

[18] Romila Thapar, *Reporting History* ..., 41.

[19] James Mill, *The History of British India*, 3rd Edition (London: 1862), published in Six Volumes in 1818.

[20] James Mill, vol. I, xxix.

[21] Mounstuart Elphinstone, *The History of India: The Hindu and Mahomatan Period*, 9th Edition (London: John Murray, [1841] 1909), 213.

[22] Vincent A. Smith, *The Early History of India*, Third Edition (Oxford: Clarendon Press, 1914 [1904]).

[23] Vincent A. Smith, *The Early History of India* ..., 117.

Emphasis was placed on the successes and failure of British colonialism, the expansion of the British Empire in India, the works of the viceroys and of the British administration. Accepting the discontinuity of British India with the traditional India, Indian historiography was presented and interpreted in terms of impact of western civilization on India. These writers maintained that British could give India the best form of Government. This is the perspective from which Indian history was written during the 19th and early 20th centuries to justify British colonialism in India. In fact, this is a deliberate justification of colonizer to write the colonized subject history to showcase their achievements without considering, if the colonized subjects really needed such a history of achievement and development.

In the process, as Manorama[24] states, in these colonial countries gave birth to two identifiable trends of historiography. The first is to accept colonialism as a given phenomenon and therefore no questioning of colonialism. The only difference was that historians of the imperialist countries wrote Euro-centered histories while the historians of the colonial countries try to bring their own country back into the picture. The second trends of colonial historiography, by and large, believe in justifying colonization, and which therefore falls in line with imperialist historiography. In the case of historians writing on India are a number of Indian historians[25] who can be grouped under the first category. As in the case of historical writings in India in general, a similar trends of historiography can be identified in the North-East Indian writings. *A* case may be cited of Ao-Nagas/ Naga history.

Colonial Perspectives in Writing the History of the Ao-Nagas

The American missionaries who have worked among the Nagas as civilizing agent could be seen as a hegemonic project as they had significant control over the modes of symbolic production like – "educational and ritual processes, patterns of socialization, political and legal procedures, canons of style and self-representation, public communication, health and bodily discipline, and so on" as identified by Comaroffs.[26] For the missionaries took control over educational system, medical, hygiene, reducing the native language into written form, dress code, introduction of modernity, etc. In the process, the control over this symbolic production that took place in a very subtle way had a far reaching impact on the whole realm of the existence of the people that remained unnoticed - be it in understanding of the self, identity and history. In the process of intervention in the symbolic production, this new understanding of self and history made the Nagas feel at home. For instance, one of the landmarks in the history of Christianity in Nagaland was in 1897 where the first Ao Association meeting of the Ao-Naga

[24] Monorama, *History* ..., 66.

[25] S.P. Sen, J.N. Sarkar, S.N. Sen who wrote from Indo-centric perspectives.

[26] Comaroff..., 19-27, quoted in John Thomas, *Missionaries* ..., 103.

churches was held at Molungyimsen village from March 12-14 where some of the important topics discussed were: "... Christian benevolence, proper and decent clothing, to abandon tattooing of Christian women, to abstain from drinking and use of opium, Cleanliness and proper sanitation, compulsory education for children, burying of death bodies. [27]

This very clearly shows the efforts of missionaries to liberate the native from "darkness" into "light," from "savagery" to "civilization" in the context of evangelization and Christian benevolence. The Association at one point of time prohibited Christians from participating in war dances, pulling and making of log drums; to abstain in the celebration of feast of merit; not to pay taxes nor to impose fines to others; prohibited drinking of rice beer and taking of opium; taking oaths. Christian young man and woman must sleep in their respective dormitories under proper guidance of a warden in accordance to the Christian practices.[28]

In order to understand this, perhaps it is important to locate some of the areas where the intervention in the symbolic production took place where Nagas felt at home with a new understanding of self, identity and began to experience and embrace a history which was not of their writing.

Preaching, Music and Hymn Singing

For the missionaries to preach the Gospel was the heart of mission. For example, E.W. Clark, the pioneering missionary among Nagas, in his letter to Home Mission Board in 1871 wrote: "Tribe upon tribe of Nagas are accessible to the Gospel. It is certainly painful for us at Sibsagar to be unable to lift our eyes without seeing these hills and thinking of them who have no knowledge of Christ.[29] In another letter he wrote: "Let the main thing be preaching the gospel."[30] In his first preaching, after arrival on the Naga Soil, Clark said,

> There is only one God Jehovah, who created the heaven and earth and all that we see in them. He is the King of all these, who never dies. He created us, and so he loves us as we love our Children. In order to save us from sins and death, to stop the wars, to heal the diseases and to establish peace on the earth, He sent His only begotten Son Jesus to this world. The Bible says, "For God so loved the world that He gave His only begotten Son that those who ever believe in Him shall not perish but have everlasting life." When He lived on this earth, He did all good

[27] L. Kijung Ao, *Nokinketer Mungchen* (Gauhati: Ao Baptist Arogo Mungdang, 1972), 74; See also Mary Mead Clark, *A Corner in India*, Reprint (Philadelphia: American Baptist Publication Society, 1907; Gauhati: Christian Literature Centre, 1978), 143-144.

[28] L. Kijung Ao, *Nokinketer Mungchen* ..., 95.

[29] M. M. Clark. *A Corner of India* (Philadelphia: American Baptist Publication Society, 1907), 59

[30] *BMM, LXVIII/9* (Sept, 1888), 371.

> works, healed the sick, raised the dead, and preached salvation to the poor. In order to cover all our sins, He died on the cross, but rose on the third day and now He is in heaven with Jehovah His Father. If you believe in Him you will not die, and peace and prosperity will come to you and your children will live in peace without fear. You will not feel hungry and thirsty. So today I am calling you. If anyone of you is willing to accept this religion I would like to know.[31]

Olemkilep also recorded a similar type of preaching:

> There is one God, who is the Creator of everything. He is the Lord of Heaven and earth and all things thereof. If you believe in Him, there shall be no small-pox, cholera, famine and plague, but you shall have prosperity and good health and well-being. Therefore, stop head-hunting, do not take revenge on your enemies. God will save you from your enemies. He will take vengeance on your behalf. Do not worship the idols, but repent and believe in Jesus Christ, His Son, for the kingdom of Heaven is at hand ...[32]

Clark's content of preaching as cited above was a very simple message based on the love of God; His loving providence and in the life and work of Jesus Christ. Not only Clark but most of the missionaries followed the same pattern of preaching. Analyzing the content of preaching we find that they reminded the people of their sinful nature, eternal damnation and promised eternal life and salvation through Christ. The technologies and equipments like the violin that accompanied the missionaries in their evangelism process attracted the people - at times more than their preaching.

Hymn singing was also a contributing factor in motivating the people towards Christianity. Gospel songs were therefore, translated into the native language. Clark himself is said to have carried his violin along with him when he first landed on the soil of the Nagas. He displayed it as the evangelist Godhula sang gospel hymns which mobilized the people. It positively attracted the people. The early missionaries exploited this trait from the Ao-Nagas to their advantage in winning souls, and in consequence, made the people practice their art of community singing.[33]

---

31 *A Light to the Nagas* (Jorhat: Molungkimong Baptist Church, 1972), 27-28.

32 A. Olemkilep, *Laishir Mongchen: Nagaland Mezungbuba Arogo Otsu* (History of the First Church in Nagaland) (Mokokchung: Molungyimsen Baptist Church, 1976), 13-15. Translated by N. Toshi Ao in his book, *Mission to the Nagas: A Tryst with the Aos* (Impur: Published by the Author, 1995), 117.

33 *History of Mokokchung Town Centenary 1890-1990* (Mokokchung: ACYE Press, 1991), 78.

In short, the preaching and hymn singing gave the Nagas a sense of missionary civilization so also the idea of becoming a Christian with their superiority category.

Medical Works, Dressing and Food Habits

The missionaries moved by humanitarian consideration rendered medical help to the sick and needy. Some of the earlier missionaries even dispensed medicine without necessary medical training.[34] The 19th and 20th century missionaries who established hospitals and schools saw these institutions as aids in saving souls for Christianity.[35] There were very often epidemics in those days such as small pox, cholera, etc.[36] To the Aos all physical ailments and sickness were believed to be due to some evil forces as they did not know the physical aspects of it and the hospital facilities and modern medicines were unheard of.[37] It was Clark who first introduced modern medicines to the people though he was not a medical doctor by profession. In fact, Clark used the distribution of medicine to villagers as means of evangelization among Nagas.[38] This is the reason why most of the early missionaries distributed medicines both in the village and their own homes.[39] Through this the villagers became friends and the gospel was preached to the people.[40] After the arrival of missionaries, the people discovered the use of medicine whose action seemed faster and cheaper.[41] The missionaries introduced vaccination and inoculation as a preventive measure against small pox and cholera.

The use of modern medicine by the missionaries and the subsequent healing demonstrated white God's healing power. This was an indication of missionaries civilizing mission over the so-called uncivilized Nagas.

The school at Molungyimsen and Impur introduced the use of *dhoti* and *sari*, which created awareness among the Aos. With the advent of missionaries, clothes happened to become more popular. Along with the dress, even the hairstyle of men began to change from their traditional style to a European style. The first Ao Christian Longjanglepzuk from Merangkong village had a European

---

[34] S.K. Barpujari, "Christianity and its Impact on the Nagas," in *The Tribes of North East India*, edited by Sebastian Karotemprel (Shillong: Center for Indigenous Cultures, 1998), 119.

[35] George M. Foster, *Traditional Societies and Technological Change* (New Delhi: Allied Publishers, 1973), 247.

[36] *Merangkong Arogo Otsu (History of the Merangkong Church)* (Jorhat: Merangkong Baptist Church, 1980), 21.

[37] Mar Atsongchanger, *Christian Education and Social Change* (Guwahati: Christian Literature Centre, 1995), 72.

[38] Joseph Puthenpurakal, *Baptist Missions in Nagaland: A Study in Historical and Ecumenical Perspective* (Calcutta: Firma KLM Private Limited, 1984), 83.

[39] *BMM* LXXVI/7 (July, 1896), 298.

[40] M.M. Clark, *A Corner in India* ..., 76-77.

[41] M.M. Clark, *A Corner in India* ..., 73, 76-78.

haircut and wore *dhoti.*[42] Thus, there was remarkable change in their style of living standard. The western idea of clothing was introduced to the people. A new convert was therefore required to meet the white missionaries' requirement in terms of their physical outlook, cleanliness, etc. Sanitation and hygiene brought new understanding of cleanliness and healthy living. The converts as well as students in schools were taught basic knowledge of cleanliness and sanitation. Because of this practice of cleanliness others could judge 'who is a Christian.'[43] Note that when the Ao Baptist Church Association was formed in 1897, they resolved that every Christian should keep their body, dress and houses neat and clean.[44] This idea demonstrates the white civilization process.

Educational System

Introduction of educational system was another aspect of civilization and modernity. The missionaries often exalted the Bible as the ultimate source of authority and made it as a condition that if an individual had to worship God aright, he/she must be able to read.[45] This is the reason why Christianity and education were inseparable. The first thing that attracted the Ao-Nagas towards the missionaries was to learn how to read and write. The first school was established in 1878. The primary object of the missionaries was to spread Christianity to the people, but along with it, they had a strong desire for bringing the people to the enlightenment of knowledge through education.[46] In fact, the missionaries used schools as platform for evangelism. It is perhaps clear from the statement made by Clark that "the main object of establishing schools is the proclamation of the gospel to the people."[47] Clark was fully convinced that without the help of educational system it would be virtually difficult to convert the people. The school would therefore serve as an agency to propagate the Gospel and to indoctrinate the Christian faith. To furtherance of his vision he established a Training School at Impur in 1895 to impart Bible teaching and general education. Perrine in his report remarked that, "With hill men no mode of missions can compare with education. Through schools the Gospel is made to reach the mountaineers more rapidly and permanently than by any other means."[48] In all counts, introduction of

---

[42] *Merankong Arogo Otsu* ..., 17-18, 33-34.

[43] M. Horam, *Nagas Old Ways and Trends* (New Delhi: Cosmo Publication, 1988), 90; W.C. Smith, *The Ao Naga Tribe of Assam: A Study of Enthology and Sociology* (London: Macmillan and Co., 1925), 198 ff.

[44] L. Kijung Ao, *Nokinketer Mungchen* ..., 74.

[45] M.A. Laird, *Missionaries and Education in Bengal, 1793-1837* (London: Clarendon Press, 1972), 3-4.

[46] Mar Atsongchanger, *Christian Education and Social Change* (Guwahati: Christian Literature Centre, 1995), 32.

[47] *BMM* LXXVI/7 (July, 1884), 259.

[48] Perrine, *Annual Report of ABMC* (December, 1904), 58.

education in their evangelizing process was a project of modernity and civilization of the savage.

Note that Christianity demanded certain moral standards from the people. The missionaries without proper articulating the deep philosophy beneath the cultural and religious practices termed all the practices of traditional religion and culture as 'heathen practices'. Hence, they tried to prohibit forcefully most of the practices. These prohibitions were very much antithetical to the Ao-Naga way of life. The 19th century protestant missionaries understanding of Christianity was the idea that becoming a Christian means a new mode of life.[49] They saw conversion as a conscious moral turnabout.[50] Hence began to oppose the local socio-cultural and religious practices by terming it as hidden practices having no moral code. Their whole idea therefore, was to convert as much as they can and report to their mission Boards the success story of their labour among the lowly-cultured people. The missionary attitude and its presupposition towards the people are clearly evident in the writing of M.M. Clark. She wrote, when we entered "A Corner of India" the darkness seemed impenetrable.... Mine album is the savage breast, where darkness broads and tempest rest without one ray of light...."[51] W.C. Smith in his book criticized such attitude of missionaries that Christianity was presented to the Nagas as little more than the adoption of another set of taboos, and taboo is no new element in the life of any group on a preliterate cultural level.[52] J.P. Mills[53] was also critical about the attitude of missionaries towards the culture. He was critical towards the errors of method employed by the mission.

Through preaching, medical work, dressing, hygiene, education, etc., the missionaries introduced new institutions and practices to replace the traditional ones being termed as savage, uncivilized and sinful. The missionaries who were furthering these changes felt that they are being benevolent in making this transition possible. Had they been not benevolent and sacrifices not been made, they thought that the people would still be living in darkness and in savagery. Even lot of gratitude was extended to the 'benevolent' missionary for making the

---

[49] Frederick S. Downs, "Faith and Life-Style: How Christianity was Understood by Nineteenth Century Converts in North East India," *BTF* 14/1 (January-June, 1982): 22.

[50] Richard M. Eaton, "Religious Conversion in Nagaland," in *Encounter Between Gospel and Tribal Culture*, edited by A. Wati Longchar (Jorhat: Tribal Study Centre Eastern Theological College, 1999), 12.

[51] M.M. Clark, *A Corner in India* ..., vii, 162.

[52] W.C. Smith, *The Ao Naga Tribes of Assam: A Study in Ethnology and Sociology* (London: Macmillan and Co., Ltd., 1925), 224.

[53] He opined that "Of all the mistakes made by the Mission, the gravest, in my opinion, and the most fraught with danger for the future is their policy of strenuously imposing an alien Western culture on their converts. I think I am right in saying that no member of the Mission has ever studied Ao Customs deeply, but nearly all have been eager to uproot what they neither understand nor sympathize with, and to substitute for it a superficial civilization." J.P. Mills, *The Ao Nagas*, 1926, 2nd Edition (London: Oxford University Press, 1973), 420-421.

'savage' being 'born again' into a 'civilized' and 'christianized' being. In fact, this transition did not take place in a sudden and ostentatious manner but, in a silent and inconspicuous manner, over a period of seven to eight decades.[54] Among other things, the adoption of this history as one's own also became a pre-requisite for becoming a Christian.[55]

Select Historiography on the Nagas: Analysis

Due to political instability in Nagaland after India's Independence, the missionaries were slowly forced to leave Nagaland by 1950s. However, even after the exodus of the missionaries, the understanding of the self, identity and history immersed on the native people and it had been taken as normative of reading and writing of their history. For instance, a book was published in 1997 by Nagaland Baptist Church Council with a title – *From Darkness to Light* as commemoration of the 125 years of Christianity in Nagaland. One of the statements reads: "The absence and ignorance of the unique revelation of God among any people, groups or individuals could be said as living in darkness. The Nagas in this sense would be termed as living in darkness. It was in Jesus Christ that the Nagas found the Light of life, hope, peace and love."[56]

Writing of histories of missionary works from an ecclesiastical, theological or secular perspective continued within the colonial missionary paradigm which failed to locate the missionary work within the larger picture of colonization process. The history writers continued to retell and rewrite their history romanticizing that they were once barbaric, bondage in darkness, uncivilized, sinful, etc. But due to the benevolent and sacrificial works of the missionaries, they have been transformed and have seen the light from darkness. For instance, to name a few like F.S. Downs,[57] whose writings from early 1960's to mid-1970 were done within institutional framework with chronological and narrative structures dealing with missions and churches and their leaders. However, since late 1970s, he attempted to write from the sociological perspective taking into serious consideration the perspective of indigenous socio-cultural factors. In most of his writings he argued that Christianity among the tribals is rooted in their own culture and tradition, and that they have created a Christian community distinctively their own. In other words, Christianity is in many ways indigenized

[54] John Thomas, *Missionaries …*, 113.

[55] John Thomas, *Missionaries …*, 115.

[56] O. Alem, "From Darkness to Light," in *From Darkness to Light*, edited by Alongla P. Aier (Kohima: Nagaland Baptist Church Council, 1997), 30.

[57] *The Mighty Works of God: A Brief History of the CBCNEI, The Mission Period: 1836-1950* (Guwahati: Christian Literature Centre, 1983); *Christianity in North East India: Historical Perspective* (Delhi: ISPCK, 1983); *History of Christianity in India: North East India in the Nineteenth and Twentieth Centuries*, vol. V, Part 5 (Bangalore: CHAI, 1994). Apart from these books there are several others articles and periodicals.

among the tribals. In summary, Downs did not give priority to the role of native people and their religion in the process of conversion. He advocated the theory of acculturation in relation to the whole process of change.

In his book A. Bendangyabang,[58] a native historian has dealt extensively on the role of Christianity in the field of social change among the Aos and the Nagas. The book covers various aspects of political ecclesiastical, economic, social and cultural issues of the people. It further looks on the socio-political changes and examined how effectively Christianity has contributed to the development of the people. Like most of the writers, he also asserted that once the missionaries started their work among the people their intention was not only to convert the people but also social transformations were aimed at. For this venture the missionaries introduced various civilizing programmes like education, hygiene, literary composition, medical aid and so on. Missionaries helped the people to change their value system through the spread of Christian message. As the title of the book suggest, the author's aim was to explore that the agency of social change was through the work of the mission apart from conversion to Christianity. The book highlights that it is the missionaries who started the process.

Puthuvail Thomas Philip[59] wrote about the growth of Baptist Church in Nagaland from a missiological perspective. He has so ably brought out the process of the continuous expansion of the mission throughout Nagaland among different Naga tribes. He looked at the growth of Baptist Churches in Nagaland from a missiological perspective where he highlighted the factors like the environmental, sociological, psychological, Christian and religious, that was being involved in the expansion and growth of the church. He concluded the book with an analysis on the effect and opportunity of the churches that the impact of Christianity on the Naga culture is tremendous on individual, social and religious levels. The tribal people accepted Christianity as a basis of their progress. The writer further states that Christianity brought an over-all change in the religious life of the Naga people.

Joseph Puthenpurakal[60] in his book tried to look from an ecumenical perspective of the Baptist Churches in Nagaland. The main objective of the book was to understand better the Baptists of Nagaland. To understand this, the author explores with the origin, growth and content of Baptist Christianity in Nagaland and the history of their evangelization work with special attention to its content and method, and by assessing them in an ecumenical perspective. In light of this perspective, he seeks to answer the questions such as "Who are the Baptist? What is

---

[58] *History of Christianity in Nagaland, Social Change: 1872-1972* (Bangalore: Shalom Ministry Publications, 2004).

[59] *The Growth of Baptist Churches in Nagaland*, Second Edition (Guwahati: Christian Literature Centre, 1983).

[60] *Baptist Missions in Nagaland: A Study in Historical and Ecumenical Perspective* (Calcutta: Firma KLM Private Limited, 1984).

their origin? What is their understanding of the New Testament Church? What is the circumstances which led the Baptist of America to launch into foreign mission work? How did they reach the Naga Hills? How did the Baptist mission start among the Aos, then among the Angamis, the Lothas and the Semas? Why was their attitude to the Naga cultural expressions unsympathetic?" The author has added a chapter on the survey of the growth and spread of the Baptist Movement upto 1955 after its beginnings in the Ao Area. Here too, the emphasis was made to the contribution of the Christian mission among the native people.

Conclusion

It is clearly evident that the colonial hegemonic perspective of the understanding and writing of history is still visible and have become the normative of writing history of indigenous people. The missionary history constructed upon the understanding of people's past history as barbaric, savage, and uncivilized and how they were civilized and liberated by the benevolent missionaries are still the tone of history writings even today. The consciousness of their own history is still under the hegemonic control of missionaries in the past. This has in fact, created a bias historical interpretation. Therefore, it is very imperative at this point to be aware and locate the colonial historiography and its influence on the local historians. Positively historians of the colonized countries have deconstructed the colonial historiography by identifying the characteristic feature like civilizing mission. The time has come to look forward for new narratives of our own histories which have for long been given undue consideration.

W.T.

Chapter 4

Oral History: A North East Indian Tribal Reading

Though Oral History is steadily moving from the periphery to the mainstream of academic studies and is employed as a research tool by historians, anthropologists, sociologists, medical therapists, documentary film makers, and educators at all levels,[1] the written documents are still considered as the original/primary and authentic source for academic research and discourses. The validity of Oral History within the established tradition of historiography is still under question. The written text which has become the dominant hermeneutical premise still overshadows the Oral History of the communities at the margins. Generally speaking, the Oral History in India[2] has not found its rightful place in historical writing. And it is more so in the historiography of North East India (NEI). This in fact is a big challenge to the indigenous communities in writing their own history using their own oral resources. Their experiences, civilization and history which are deeply embedded and evolved in oral traditions transmitted from generation to generation in non-literary forms in and through cultural expressions are not yet taken into consideration in writing their history. It is with these question and

---

[1] Donald A. Ritchie, ed, *The Oxford Handbook of Oral History* (Oxford: Oxford University Press, 2011), cover page.

[2] Unlike the US, Britain, Australia and Malaysia, where rigorous oral history is integral to critical popular history, India has no oral history association. There is only one oral history archive in India tucked away in the Nehru Memorial Museum and Library in New Delhi, and that too is not popular in orientation. Today we see the existence of Oral History Associations. See Anirudh Deshpande, "Remaking the Indian Historian's Craft: The Part, Present and Future of History as an Academic Discipline," *Economic & Political Weekly*, XLVIII/7 (February 16, 2013): 66.

challenge in mind, this chapter intends to highlight and explore the possibility of placing the Oral History as one of the prerequisites of writing historiography of North East India Tribal community.

What is Oral History?

Oral History is the history of the ordinary people. The term – "Oral History" perhaps means many things. In simple words, it is a record of oral tradition, compiled of stories handed down from one generation to the next, as well as the recording of personal history or experiences. It may take the form of eye-witness evidence about the past, but can include folklore, myths, songs and stories passed down over the years by word of mouth.

As an emerging discipline, it also means "the recording, preservation and interpretation of historical information" that involves a formal interview examining a particular topic or issue. The discipline has now democratized the study of the past by recording the experience of people. In so far, the most distinctive contribution of Oral History has been to include within the historical record the experiences and perspectives of groups of people who might otherwise have been marginalized or 'hidden from history.'[3] It can provide new information, alternative explanations and different insights which are potentially of enormous value. Oral History therefore, has offered space to groups, communities, gender or races, cultural and ethnic minorities to interpret their history.

Development of Oral History and Methodological Consideration

In the 18th century, Samuel Johnson commented that "all history was at first oral," but the term 'Oral History' was first used in reference to troubadours and oral tradition only in mid-20th century.[4] At first Oral History did not attach itself to interviewing until an article appeared in the *New Yorker* in 1942 about Joe Gould.[5] This led to the process of development of Oral History. Oral History was established in 1948 as a modern technique for historical documentation when Columbia University historian Allan Nevins began recording the memoirs of persons significant in American Life. But it was Paul Thompson who made the

---

[3] Robert Perks and Alistair Thomson, eds, *The Oral History Reader* (London & New York: Routledge, 1998), i, ix.

[4] Donald A. Ritchie, "Introduction: The Evolution of Oral History," in *The Oxford Handbook of Oral History*, edited by Donald A. Richie (Oxford: Oxford University Press, 2011), 3.

[5] Joe Gould, a Greenwich Village bohemian who claimed to be compiling "An Oral History of Our Time." Gould told of interviewing the "shirt-sleeved multitude" in saloons and on park benches, because "what people say is history." Gould's quest earned him many free meals, but was later revealed to be figment of his imagination. He left no manuscript. The label stuck, however, and in 1948, when the Columbia University history professor Allan Nevin established the first archives to conduct and preserve interviews, he called it the Oral Research Office. "Joe Gould Dead; 'Last Bohemian,' New York Times, Aug, 20, 1957; Joseph Mitchell, Joe Gould's Secret (New York: Viking, 1965), quoted in Donald A. Ritchie, *Introduction* ..., 3.

first large scale Oral History programme in Britain in which 459 Edwardians born between 1872 and 1906 were interviewed about their family and work.[6] Paul Thompson, among others, charts the prehistory of the modern Oral History movement, explaining that historians from ancient times relied upon eye-witnesses accounts of significant events. It was in the 19th century that ushered in the development of an academic history discipline which led to the primacy of archival research and documentary sources, and a marginalization of oral evidence until the mid-20th century.[7]

However, after the post-World War II,[8] led to the gradual acceptance of the usefulness and validity of oral evidence in the use of memory as a source for historical research so also the increasing availability of portable tape recorders, underpinned a revival of Oral History.[9] The timing and pattern of this revival and emergence differed markedly around the world.[10] But there are sets of ideas and debates which proved to be critical in shaping contemporary approaches to Oral History. We find an increasing interest in "people's history" in the 1960s and the parallel creation of regional and national Oral History associations inspired

---

6 One of the best sources on the history of oral history is Paul Thompson's *The Voice of the Past: Oral History* (Oxford U.P. 2nd edition, 1988 orig. 1978).

7 Paul Thompson, *The Voice of the Past: Oral History* (Oxford University Press, 2000), 25-81, quoted in Alistair Thomson, "Memory and Remembering in Oral History," in *The Oxford Handbook of Oral History*, edited by Donald A. Richie (Oxford: Oxford University Press, 2011), 78-79.

8 After WW II the expansion of higher education meant that thousands of lower-class people entered tertiary education for the first time and began to notice the absence of their own ancestors from the history books. The hegemonic controls of the literary elite were also being challenged by the insistent demands of the new mass communications markets. Historians such as G.D.H. Cole and H.L. Beales, radicals from the Thirties, founded the Society for the Study of Labour History and for the first time the history of the common people began to be studied in earnest and without condescension by historians such as Edward and Dorothy Thompson. By the mid-Sixties a new lower-class intelligentsia had started to ask radical questions about the lack of primary sources from which a more democratic history could be constructed. The wealthy and educated insiders had left many records. Not only in the mass of material concerned with government and high politics, but in the literature, in the records of legal cases, property transactions, in personal journals and correspondence, and in every kind of document from wills to laundry lists. The poor had no rooms and seldom entered any records on their own terms. They appear as servants, criminals, recipients of charity or as turbulent or obedient subjects. It was in the heady atmosphere of Sixties cultural revolt that Oral History arose to fill this void.

9 Cf., Robert Perks and Alistair Thomson, *The Oral History Reader* ..., 1, and Alistair Thomson, *Memory and Remembering* ..., 78-79.

10 For example, the first organized oral history project was initiated by Allan Nevins at Columbia University in New York in 1948, and in the interest in archival recording with white male elites was representative of early oral history activity in the United States. In Britain in the 1950s and 1960s oral history pioneers were more interested in recording the experiences of so-called 'ordinary' working people – George Ewart Evans, for example, determined to 'ask the fellow who cut the hay' – and this interest fused with political commitment to a 'history' amongst many social historians in Britain and around the world from the 1960s. See Robert Perks and Alistair Thomson, *The Oral History Reader* ..., 1.

a burgeoning Oral History movement. The lived experience of working-class women or black history was undocumented or ill-recorded for which the Oral History was an essential source for the "history from below" fostered by politically committed social historians in both community and academic contexts.[11] We must note that the European oral historians were more rooted in social and cultural history, and allied with political movements that were left out. They examined history from the 'bottom up,' intending to include the voices of those previously excluded from national narratives. A sense of social responsibility motivated this approach, which challenged the social and intellectual status quo by interviewing those who had been overlooked or oppressed. In the United States, the 'bottom up' approach also emerged in the 1970s with American oral historians increasingly turning their attention to race, class, gender and local communities.[12] Slowly, the Oral History movement spread worldwide. It went beyond the United States and Western Europe and expanded into Eastern Europe, Africa, Asia, and Latin America. People found Oral History useful for confronting and understanding the injustices in their societies. Australians have reexamined their relations with Aboriginals, just as America and Canadian interviews with Native American and First People helped explain their diverse cultures.[13]

Most significantly, Oral History is predicated on an active human relationship between historians and their sources, which can transform the practice of history in several ways. The narrator not only recalls the past but also asserts his or her interpretation of that past, and in participatory Oral History projects, the interviewee can be a historian as well as the source.[14] Oral History has challenged the historical enterprise in many ways. The historian has to learn the skills and techniques required for recorded interviews and have to draw insights and adopt the methods from different intellectual disciplines like sociology, anthropology, psychology and linguistics so as to better understand the narratives of memory. In nutshell, the interview is a historical document created by the agency of both the interviewer and the interviewee.

Michael Frisch[15] argued against the attitude that Oral History provided "a pure sense of how it 'really' was," and asserted that memory – "personal and historical, individual and generational" – should be moved to center stage "as the object, not merely the method, of Oral History." Used in this way, Oral History could be a powerful tool for discovering, exploring and evaluating the nature of the process of historical memory – how people make sense of their past, how they connect individual experience and its social context, how the past becomes

[11] Alistair Thomson, *Memory and Remembering*..., 78-79.

[12] Donald A. Ritchie, *Introduction* ..., 4-5.

[13] Donald A. Ritchie, *Introduction* ..., 6.

[14] Robert Perks and Alistair Thomson, *The Oral History Reader* ..., ix.

[15] Michael Frisch, *A Shared Authority: Essays on the Craft and Meaning of Oral and Public History* (Albany: State University of New York Press, 1999), 188.

part of the present, and how people use it to interpret their lives and the world around them. Thus, memory becomes the subject as well as the source of Oral History, and the oral historians began to use an exhilarating array of approaches – linguistic, narrative, cultural, and psychoanalytic and ethnographic – in this analysis and use of Oral History.[16] Much of the initial scholarly resistance to Oral History had to do with its "subjective nature." Memory can change overtime, and is dependable on perception. Documents were unchangeable and therefore seen to be objective. Although oral historians recognize the fallibility of memory, they do not put more weight on a source just because it has been written down.[17] Luisa Passerini[18] while divulging on the role of subjectivity in history asserted that – the consciousness and unconscious meanings of experience as lived and remembered – and showed how the influences of public culture and ideology upon individual memory might be revealed in the silences, discrepancies and idiosyncrasies of personal testimony. Passerini's pioneering work on subjectivity and silence is one of the most widely referenced contributions to the literature of Oral History. She stated that we should not ignore that the raw material of Oral History consists not just in factual statements, but is pre-eminently an expression and representation of culture, and therefore includes not only literal narrations but also the dimension of memory, ideology and subconscious desire.

Considering the credibility and validity of memory we can say that we all work with memory everyday of our lives. Most people offer profound insight about their own memories and remembering and about their past experience and its meaning and significance in the present. The most accepted definition of memory comes from psychology that the individual brain's ability to store, retain, and subsequently retrieve information, which encompasses both experiential and learned memory.[19] However, Allessandro Portelli argues that

> But what is really important is that memory is not a passive depository of facts, but an active process of creation of meanings. Thus, the specific utility of oral sources for the historian lies, not much in their ability to preserve the past, as in the very changes wrought by memory. These changes reveal the narrators' effort to make sense of the past and to give a form to their lives, and set the interview and the narrative in their historical context.[20]

---

[16] Alistair Thomson, *Memory and Remembering* …, 80.

[17] Donald A. Ritchie, *Introduction* …, 12.

[18] See Luisa Passerini, "Work Ideology and Consensus under Italian Fascism," in Robert Perks and Alistair Thomson, eds., *The Oral History Reader* (London & New York: Routledge, 1998), 53-62.

[19] Anna Green, "Can Memory be Collective," in *The Oxford Handbook of Oral History*, edited by Donald A. Ritchie (Oxford: Oxford University Press, 2011), 104.

[20] Alessandro Portelli, "What Makes Oral History Different," in Robert Perks and Alistair Thomson, eds, *The Oral History Reader* (London & New York: Routledge, 1998), 69.

Recent memory research by neuroscientists and psychologist has confirmed Portelli's claim that memory is not a passive depository of facts, but an active process of creation of meanings.

While challenging orthodoxies about historical sources, methods and aims, Oral History has generated fierce debates; for e.g., about the reliability of memory and the nature of the interview relationship, or more generally about the relationship between memory and history, past and present.[21] In his article '*Movement without Aim*', published in 1975, Ronald J. Grele[22] lamented the rather limited critical discussion among oral historians about the theoretical and methodological issues underpinning their work. That charge could not be leveled at oral historians in the late 1990s. This article outlined some of the North American debates concerning the reliability of memory and the representativeness of individual testimony, about research standards in interviewing, comparison between written and oral source or was interpretative history in its own right. He argued that oral historians should explore three significant relationships: the linguistic and 'performative' aspects of an interview, and the connection between individual and social historical consciousness. He in detail explains that

> … we need a larger and more general concept of historical cognition, because without some larger context within which to place the information we gather, and the various aspects of the interview – linguistic, performatory, and cognitive – which will synthesize these structures, we risk not only the possibility of misunderstanding what is happening in the interview, but also of misunderstanding what is being said and why. It is only then larger context which makes the information conveyed in an interview unambiguous. Also, if we fail to see our interviewees as bearers of a culture and thus people with their own view of the past, be it formed as part of a hegemonic ideology, or in opposition to that ideology, or as some combination of myth and ideology, or even a secret history, we will, because the information must be structured, infuse our own vision of the past into the interview. Such a situation is exactly what we do not want to do. Our aim is to bring to conscious articulation the ideological problematic of the interviewee, to reveal the cultural context in which information is being conveyed, and to thus transform an individual story into a cultural narrative, and thereby, to more fully understand what happened in the past.[23]

---

[21] Robert Perks and Alistair Thomson, *The Oral History Reader* …, ix, x.

[22] This article is reproduced in Robert Perks and Alistair Thomson, eds, *The Oral History Reader* (London & New York: Routledge, 1998), under the title "Movement Without Aim: Methodological and Theoretical Problems," pp. 38-52.

[23] Ronald J. Grele, *Movement without Aim* …, 48.

Alessandro Portelli,[24] challenged the critics of Oral History and so-called 'unreliable memories' head-on in 1979 by arguing that 'What makes Oral History different' – orality of oral sources,[25] narrative form,[26] subjectivity,[27] the 'different credibility' of memory,[28] and the relationship between interviewer and interviewee[29] – should be considered as strengths rather than as weaknesses, a

---

[24] See Alessandro Portelli, *What Makes Oral History Different*..., 63-74.

[25] Oral sources are oral sources. Scholars are willing to admit that the actual document is the recorded tape; but almost all go on to work on the transcript, and it is only transcripts that are published. Occasionally, tapes are actually destroyed: a symbolic case of the destruction of the spoken words. The most literal translation is hardly ever the best, and a truly faithful translation always implies a certain amount of invention. The same may be true for transcription of oral sources. The disregard of the orality of oral sources has a direct bearing on interpretative history. At this juncture, one distinguishing factor is the place of form – language. But language which is composed of another set of traits, also cannot be contained within a single segment. The same statement may have quite contradictory meanings, according to the speaker's intonation, which cannot be represented objectively in the transcript, but only approximately describe in the transcriber's own words. Traits which cannot be contained within segments are the sites (not exclusive, but very important) of essential narrative functions: they reveal the narrators' emotions, their anticipation in the story, and the way the story affected them. See Alessandro Portelli, *What Makes Oral History Different* ..., 64-66.

[26] Oral history sources are narrative sources. Therefore, the analysis of oral history materials must avail itself some of the general categories developed by narrative theory in literature and folklore. Oral sources from nonhegemonic classes are linked to the tradition of the folk narrative. In this tradition distinctions between narrative genres are perceived differently than in the writing tradition of the educated classes. See Alessandro Portelli, *What Makes Oral History Different* ..., 66-67.

[27] The unique and precious element which oral sources force upon the historian and which no other sources possess in equal measure is the speaker's subjectivity. Oral history tell us not just what people did, but what they wanted to do, what they believed they were doing, and what they now think they did. Subjectivity is as much the business of history as are the more visible 'facts'. What informants believe is indeed a historical fact, as much as what really happened. See Alessandro Portelli, *What Makes Oral History Different*..., 67-68.

[28] Oral sources are credible with a different credibility. The importance of oral testimony may lie not in its adherence to fact, but rather in its departure from it, as imagination, symbolism, and the desire to emerge. Therefore, there are no 'false' oral sources. The diversity of oral history consists in the fact that 'wrong' statements are still psychologically 'true' and this truth may be equally as important as factually reliable account. Of course, this does not meant that we accept the dominant prejudice which sees factual credibility as a monopoly of written documents. The prejudice is that the oral sources are distant from events, and therefore undergo the distortion of faulty memory. Indeed, this problem exists for many written documents, which are usually written some time after the event to which they refer, and often by nonparticipants. Oral sources might compensate chronological distance with a much closer personal involvement. See Alessandro Portelli, *What Makes Oral History Different* ..., 68-70.

[29] The control of historical discourse remains firmly in the hands of the historians. It is the historian who selects the people who will be interviewed. But at times things may also be the other way round. The historian may validate his/her discourse by 'ventriloquizing' it through the narrator's testimony. The first person narrative of the interviewee stands the first person of the

resource rather than a problem. He concluded that the Oral History can never be told without taking sides, since the 'sides' exist inside the telling. And, no matter what their personal histories and beliefs may be, historians and 'sources' are hardly ever on the same 'side'. The confrontation of their different partialities – confrontation as 'conflict', and confrontation as 'search for unity' – is one of the things which make Oral History interesting.[30]

With this brief general introduction to historical development of Oral History and methodological consideration, we shall now look at the North East tribal communities on how to draw from the methodological insights of Oral History to construct their history within their own social and cultural locations.

Oral History and Tribals: North East Indian Case

Looking at the North East India (NEI) tribal context, Manorama stated that, one of the main problems in development of historical writings in the North East has been a serious shortcoming in the methodological and theoretical orientation.[31] It is high time that the historians of this region must give paramount importance to the development of Oral History. In fact, there are many societies and communities in NEI that are still facing with lack and scarcity of recorded history of their evolution and civilization. Therefore, the Oral History becomes the indispensable sources for tracing, analyzing and construction of their historical development. In this, the one of the foremost tasks is to develop a methodology to understand the Oral History tradition. In this regard, the emergence of Oral History in the intellectual academic discourse and its popularity among many historians has provided space on how to develop Oral History methodology. But ironically, Oral History is being looked today from the prism of suspicion by several historians of the older school of historical interpretation and intellectual elite. The importance of documented history and text has so overtaken us that any deviation from it is being considered dangerous.

At this point, the question is, what is text? We need a new emphasis and a larger view in regard to text/s. Written and sacred texts are not the only kind of texts in a culture like the Indians. It is the oral traditions of every kind that produce texts.[32] Cultural performances of every sort, whether written or oral acts of composition, plays, rituals, games, etc., contain texts. Every cultural performance

---

historians, without whom there would be no interview. Therefore, informants are historians; and the historians, a part of the source. The narrator pulled into the narrative and becomes a party of the story. See Alessandro Portelli, *What Makes Oral History Different …*, 72-73.

[30] Alessandro Portelli, *What Makes Oral History Different …*, 73.

[31] Manorama Sharma, *History and History Writing in North-East India* (New Delhi: Regency Publication, 1998), 22.

[32] A.K. Ramanuja, "Who Needs Folklore? The Relevance of Oral Tradition to South Asian Studies," *Manushi*, No. 69 (March-April, 1992): 4.

not only creates and carries texts, it is a text.[33] Texts then are also contexts and pretexts for other texts. Language, like other communication systems, depends on both fixed or invariant forms and free or variant ones. Our ordinary language is full of fixed forms. In fact, some things are not subject to variation and not open to innovation. Orally transmitted texts have fixed components, formulae, refrain, obligatory descriptive passages, and traditionally defined motifs and narrative structures.[34] The different genres in varied categories and proportions convey and express meanings.

It is important to note that the cherished possession of two of our most oppressed groups in India – the Dalits and the Tribals, whose cultures are oral and non-literary – is their oral traditions[35] and their rich fund of folk stories, proverbs, narratives, etc. Their folklore[36] is endowed with remarkable performative character. Therefore, oral tradition is not simply a question of mode of communication. It has a deep, human, cultural and social significance, as it symbolizes the dignity and selfhood of the lowly and the marginalized.[37] It is also very contextual in their form and meaning. It is interesting to note that the anthropologist and folklorist have discovered that culture has a mix of both the oral (non- literate) and literate. Research on the question of whether a culture is purely literate or oral, have discovered that neither a society is entirely oral (non-literate) nor entirely literate, but a mixture of both.

Oral traditions/literatures such as ballads, legends, fables, anecdotes, songs, tales and proverbs serve as an important category and ideas of primary sources that deserves serious consideration. For such traditions/literatures, particularly the ballads, which comes from the hearts and lips of whole people projects a bright prismatic light upon their manners, customs, beliefs and inner emotions. Similarly, if pressed into service, the legends too yield data of great historical value. As a branch of folklore, the legends relate to a sacred person, place or an event.[38] Myths also contains values, laws, explanation and philosophy of a people. These are symbolic features of social and religious reality of human existence. Folk

---

[33] A.K. Ramanuja, *Who Needs Folklore* ..., 4.

[34] See A.K. Ramanuja, *Who Needs Folklore* ..., 7.

[35] Some researchers find it helpful to distinguish between "oral tradition" and "oral history," the former being the umbrella category in which the oral history method can be placed. "Oral tradition" among many Native American people refers to stories handed down for multiple generations that can also involve nonhuman subjects. This differs from the more recent academic use of the term "oral history," in which personal stories are collected from an individual.

[36] The 'lore' in folklore refers basically to the expressive forms of the people – verbal (folk stories, folksongs, ballads, proverbs, riddles, aphorism, etc) and non-verbal (Folk art, folk festivals, folk dances, etc). See Felix Wilfred, *The Challenge of Folklore* ..., 6.

[37] Felix Wilfred, "The Challenge of Folklore to Indian Theologizing," *Jeevadhara*, XXIV/139 (January, 1994): 71.

[38] Cf. Saraswathi Venugopal, "Oral History and Folklore," *Journal of Tamil Studies*, no. 53 & 54 (June & December, 1998): 203.

songs record history and tells how historical events affect the lives of the people.[39] These, perhaps often neglected sources, are extremely valuable in developing and evolving history of a community.

When we look at the history of the advent of Christianity in India, we find oral traditions serving as great resource in writing the written history. For example, till the advent of the foreign missionaries, the history of the Syrian Christians was wrapped in oral traditions like folk songs and myths. Though it is very difficult for historians to dissect the myths and find the kernel of truth in them in relation to the origin of the Syrian Christians,[40] the history is written based on those sources. For Kerala, undoubtedly, possessed a rich oral traditions which was reflected fully or partially in their folk sọngs[41] and oral traditions are the sole source of writing history in absence of written materials or documents.

Oral tradition poses a serious question with regard to the differences and relations between written and spoken media. For the relations between oral and written traditions in any culture are not simple opposites. They interpenetrate each other and combine in various ways.[42] There is a certain inter-relationship and communication between the two spheres and it is here that we have to identify the specificity of the oral tradition and the experience it embodies. There are two processes that are at work. On the one hand, there is the process by which elements from the classical (written) and the folk (oral) are adopted by the folk, and on the other, there is the process by which what was once an element of folk experience, history or worship is taken over and made part of the classical realm.[43]

Perhaps, in both cases it is the people who are the subjects. In the former case, people play the role of the interpreting and transforming the classical in keeping with their experience-base, and in the latter, they remain the original creators of the elements and the forms, which in the course of time, the classical realm. Though oral tradition like folklore may have both these dimensions, it is the experience and interpretation of the people which remains as its foundation and base. Folklore provides a certain perspective of wholeness and realism. It enables to see the aspect of human passion, rage, anger and release of energy, which all make up the world of concrete life-experience.[44] In all cultures, especially the Indian,

---

[39] Suganthy Krishnamachari, "Songs of the Soil," *The Hindu (Friday Review)*, 4 January 2013, 1.

[40] Joseph Pulikunnal, "Religion and Culture of the St. Thomas Christians During the Pre and Post Portuguese Period," *A Paper Presented during the Silver Jubilee Celebration of the Federated Faculty for Research in Religion & Culture, Kottayam on 4 July, 2005* (Kottayam: Mar Thoma Seminary, 2005), 1.

[41] A.M. Mundadan, *Indian Christians Search for Identity and Struggle for Autonomy* (Bangalore: Dharmaram Publications, 2003), 4.

[42] A.K. Ramanujan, *Who Needs Folklore* ..., 6.

[43] Felix Wilfred, *The Challenge of Folklore* ..., 61.

[44] Felix Wilfred, *The Challenge of Folklore* ..., 62.

the oral and the written are deeply intermeshed in various ways. If we distinguish composition and transmission, we find that a work may be composed orally but transmitted in writing or vice versa.[45] Thus, everyone concerned with written texts has to reckon with the oral materials around. Therefore, it is necessary that we rediscover the oral traditions' worth and significance.

Most of the studies today are based on the context of written texts and documents. One of the interesting aspects of oral tradition or in other words folklore is that most of its contents or items are context-sensitive. This contextuality is basically related to an oral tradition which is based on daily experiences of people. Unfortunately, the general and dominant genres of study, in India had been and still are from the prism of cognitive categories and frames of interpretation from the West. Felix Wilfred strongly challenges this in following words:

> ... experience, like language, is not simply a question of meaning and interpretation. It is truism to say that an experience cannot be conveyed and recorded in its full depth and intensity. For any language, so to in experience there is a texture (as for example rhyme and alliteration in a local proverb) which cannot be rendered in another language even though its sense and meaning can be translated. The texture can be perceived only in the language of the people concerned and in their life-context, which is also the performance context. All this indicates the serious limitations of interpreting Indian experiences through alien cognitive tools, and the imperative need to enter into cultural categories, divisions and classifications which people have developed in interpreting their own experience and which are intelligible only in the particular experience-context.[46]

The above statement critiques the language and politics of identity. Edward Sapir defined language as a "purely human and non-instinctive method of communicating ideas, emotions, and desires by means of voluntarily produced symbols."[47] According to Sapir, it is an illusion to imagine that one can adapt to reality without the use of language or to assume that language is merely a means of solving specific problems of communication or thought. Language is in fact, a determining factor in the way in which its users perceive the world. As such it is the interface between individual thought and the real world.[48] Language is a dialect and dialects carry oral literature. Oral literature or text that composed of folklore, folktales, ballads, etc., can be termed as literature of the dialects.

---

[45] A.K. Ramanujan, *Who Needs Folklore ...,* 8.

[46] Felix Wilfred, *The Challenge of Folklore ...*, 77.

[47] Edward Sapir, *Language* (New York: Harcourt, Brace & World, 1921), 8.

[48] David J. Hesselgrave & Edward Rommen, *Contextualization: Meanings, Methods and Models*, Second Printing (Michigan: Baker Book House, [1989] 1992), 159, 161.

Since the mid–1980s, oral historians have increasingly examined language as the invisible force that shapes oral texts and gives meaning to historical events. The tribal communities should seriously take this aspect of language/linguistic theories along with the other aspects like narrative, memory construction, narrative form, subjectivity, performative aspects of an interview, etc., in developing their own history. It is important to note that, linguistic theories are far from new in the interdisciplinary field of Oral History; the more recent turn to post-structuralism suggests a more intensive concern with both linguistic structure and cultural discourses determining oral narratives as well as skepticism about any direct relationship between experiences and representation. This theorizing perhaps enriches our understanding of Oral History.[49]

In the history of the tribals, the vulnerable experiences and their traditional stories, myths, symbols, dances, songs, and their connectedness to land and environment become the vital resources[50] for developing their own history. Oral tradition like folklore contains obvious traces of people's lives so also describe the reality. It is important to acknowledge how their culture, class position and political worldview shaped the oral histories. Tribal Oral History must therefore, be developed by the tribals utilizing the vital resources to project their experience and history which is embedded in their oral traditions. The tribal festivals, myths, rites, rituals, customs, cultures, and spirituality should be taken into account while developing their Oral History. For these elements represent and reflect their whole aspiration and lived-reality. As stated, the raw material of Oral History consists not just in factual statements, but is pre-eminently an expression and representation of culture, and therefore includes not only literal narrations but also the dimension of memory, ideology and subconscious desire. In the tribal context, these dimensions and elements are unconsciously and silently embedded in oral tradition.

In the ancient pre-literate tribal societies, oral tradition played a fundamental role as the source and document of knowledge and wisdom, chronicle of history which directed them in all space of their existence. For instance, among the Nagas, there was no written script or text of their own. And yet their culture and Oral History flourished. They had an effective medium of communication and records that have been preserved for many centuries through the oral tradition based on deep-rooted and time-tested foundations. Any oral narrative of traditional history, origin and migration of the people, formation of the village, events of war, peace, and festivals and so on are transmitted orally from one generation

[49] Joan Sangster, "Telling Our Stories: Feminist Debates and the Use of Oral History," in Robert Perks and Alistair Thomson, eds, *The Oral History Reader* (London & New York: Routledge, 1998), 94.

[50] A. Wati Longchar, "An Assessment of the Tribal Theology: Trends and Challenges for Future," *Paper Presented at D.Th Research Methodology Seminar, 2007* (Bangalore: United Theological College, 2007), 4-5.

to another through folk songs, poetry, ballads, prayers, sayings, stories and tales. Indeed, the very history of the Naga people, their religion and the entire socio-cultural and political life is being shaped by their oral tradition.[51] As in the past, even today in the Naga society oral narration is a powerful tool for administrating a concrete solution in any conflict situations and matters. A rich Oral History is one of the many treasures of Naga history.

Conclusion

Of late, precisely from the second half of the 20th century, the Oral History has become an agreed and consensus methodology among historians in writing history of the pre-literate oral culture. Oral History has now become an important means in which ordinary common people can actively engage in making their history. Importantly, it is used as an alternative to elitist form of historical writings by which the marginalized folks are slowly finding space in the construction of history. Oral History certainly have given voice to those who were 'hidden from history.' Many scholars are turning to Oral History as a methodology with the radical and democratic potential to reclaim the history of the ordinary people. For it is realized that the oral tradition like the folklore, folktales, folksongs, ballads, etc., serves as an important category of primary sources for historians. This development challenges the tribals in NEI to write their own history as there are enough folklore, ballads, legends, fables, myth, dances, songs, tales and proverbs with every community. The time has come for each tribal community of NEI to construct their own history using Oral History and methods available within and around.

W.T.

---

[51] Cf., Lanusashi Longkumer, "Oral Tradition in Contemporary Conflict Resolution: A Naga Perspective," (*indianfolklore.org/journal/index.php/IFL/article/view File/105/116/conflict resolution and oral tradition*).

Chapter 5

Reconstructing Tribal Historiography: A Subaltern Perspective

The history of the tribals in India is a history of conquest, subjugation, domination, alienation, discrimination, oppression and dehumanization. In all spheres of life, the tribals are placed at the margins and disposed as subaltern groups[1] with no due space and dignified identity in society as people. However, with the emergence of tribal movements and awakening of tribal history in 1930s and 1940s, and the subsequent efforts of systematic academic study since 1960s, the Tribal history has indeed undergone significant shifts. After Independence significant changes were made in the historiography in India both in quality and quantity.[2] Since the 1970s the focus of history of Christianity in India has been shifted to the people and their experiences. The Tribal history has now become a subject of intensive research in the disciplines of sociology and social history with the development of subaltern studies in the early 1980s which seriously critiqued the elitist historiography.[3] Today, the Tribal history in general and the history of Christianity in particular written from the perspective of the dominant that made very scanty references and represented fragmented and distorted images with pejorative and derogatory terms are greatly challenged.

---

[1] Saurabh Dube, "Entangled Endeavours," in *Postcolonial Passages: Contemporary History – Writing on India*, edited by Saurabh Dube (New Delhi: Oxford University Press, 2004), 198.

[2] V.V. Thomas, "Research Methodology: History of Christianity," *Paper Presented at D.Th Research Methodology Seminar*, 2008 (Bangalore: United Theological College, 2008), 5.

[3] Martin Fuchs & Antje Linkenbach, "Social Movements," *Sociology and Social Anthropology*, Vol. 2, edited by Veena Das (New Delhi: Oxford University Press, 2003), 1537.

"Rewriting history", as rightly remarked by K.N. Panikkar, "is a continuous process into which historians brings to bear new methodological or ideological insights or employ a new analytical frame drawn upon hitherto unknown facts,"[4] there is a positive development that the subaltern historians write history of their own people. Perhaps, the critical theoretical tools offered by the Subaltern School are great contribution in writing the history of Christianity in India. Therefore, keeping in mind such theoretical tools, an attempt is made in this chapter to reconstruct tribal historiography and its implications for writing the history of Christianity in India from a tribal perspective.

Subaltern Historiography

The Term Subaltern

The term subaltern is derived from the writings of the Italian Marxist Antonio Gramsci which means of 'inferior rank', whether of class, caste, age, gender, or office.[5] In line with this, Ranajit Guha also termed the word Subaltern as people of inferior rank, and it was used as a name for the general attitude of subordination in South Asian Society whether this is expressed in terms of class, caste, age, gender, and office or in any other way.[6] Subordination is one constitutive term in a binary relationship of which the other is dominance.[7] The value implication creates some difficulty in using the term subaltern, yet it has come to stay. Specific groups belonging to the subaltern classes may vary from place to place due to the regional disparity in social and economic development in the country. However, Subaltern classes usually refer to those social classes and groups not included under elite.

Subaltern historiography touches the areas of race, class, gender and other hegemonic practices. It is to be noted that the Subaltern studies began with Indian, European and American scholars in the late 1970s and early 1980s that focused towards understanding peasant consciousness in India, in so far as any and all consciousness was a product of material conditions. Consciousness here, is broadly viewed by subaltern writers in the traditional Marxian sense as a manner of thought determined by one's place in the production system; yet at the same time, these writers also view consciousness as a form of subjectivity which can and does

[4] K.N. Panikkar, "Outsider as Enemy Politics of Rewriting history in India," *ICHR* 36/2 (December, 2002): 73.

[5] E. Sreedharan, *A Textbook of Historiography: 500 BC to AD 2000*, Reprinted (Delhi: Orient BlackSwan, 2009), 493.

[6] Ranajit Guha, "Preface," in *Subaltern Studies I: Writings on South Asian History and Society*, edited by Ranajit Guha (New Delhi: Oxford University Press, 1982), vii.

[7] P.T. Mathew, "Religious Experience of the Christian Mukkuva Community," in *Religion and Politics from Subaltern Perspective*, edited by Thomas Kadankavil (Bangalore: Dharmaram Publications, 1999), 88.

develop modes of resistance to that system.[8] Since then, the concerns of subaltern studies have blossomed into global phenomenon with strong institutional support from mainstream academia in Africa, South America, Ireland and China, as well as India, Europe and America.

Emergence of Subaltern Studies in India

Subaltern studies as stated began in India in the 1980s with an explicit but not exclusively Marxist and Gramscian focus. It emerged in an atmosphere of widespread negative response to Marxian orthodoxy in the academic research in analyzing and understanding the Indian society and the nation.[9] Therefore, Subaltern school may be characterized as post-Marxian search to come to terms with the indigenous self of Indian society and look at its unique experiences on its own terms.[10] In applying the term subalterns as a methodological tool in analyzing the hegemonic systems and structures of any society, Gayathri Chakravorthy Spivak writes: "Subaltern historiography raises questions of method that would prevent it from using a ruse. For the 'figure' of women, the relationship between woman and silence can be plotted by woman themselves; race and class differences are subsumed under the charge. Subaltern historiography must confront the impossibility of such gestures. The narrow epistemic violence of imperialism gives us an imperfect allegory of the general violence that is the possibility of an episteme."[11] Subaltern historiography is thus to locate the subjectivity of the subalterns in developing their history.

In fact, Subaltern School started with a criticism of the historiography of Indian nationalism, which has for a long time been dominated by elitism – colonialist elitism and bourgeois-nationalist elitism.[12] The publication of *Subaltern Studies I: Writings on South Asian History and Society* (1982) and *Elementary Aspects of Peasant Insurgency in Colonial India* (1983) by Ranajit Guha was a significant development in subaltern history.[13] Nationalistic approach to history was the dominant features in the post-independent writings of history wherein the contributions of subaltern or the marginalized people were not acknowledged adequately. Ranajit Guha asserts that in this nationalist thought the making of

[8] Laurie Louise Patton, "Subaltern Studies," *Encyclopedia of Religion*, 2nd Edition, Vol. 13, edited by Lindsay Jones (USA: Thomsan Gale, 2005): 8800.

[9] George Oommen, "Historiography of Indian Christianity and Challenges of Subaltern Methodology," *Journal of Dharma* 28/2 (April – June, 2003): 221.

[10] George Oommen, *Historiography* ..., 221.

[11] Gayatri Chakravorthy, "Can the Subaltern Speak?," in *The Post Colonial Studies*, edited by Bill Ashcroft, Gareth Griffiths and Helen Tiffin (London: Routledge, 2004), 28.

[12] Ranajit Guha, "On Some Aspects of the Historiography of Colonial India," in *Subaltern Studies 1: Writings on South Asian History and Society*, edited by Ranajit Guha (New Delhi: Oxford University Press, 1982), 1.

[13] Since then eleven volumes and several other books have appeared representing this school of history.

the Indian nation and the development of the consciousness – nationalism – were exclusively or predominantly elite achievements.[14] He further states that in the colonialist and neo-colonialist historiographies these achievements are credited to British colonial rulers, administrators, policies, institutions and culture; in the nationalist and neo-nationalist writings – to Indian elite personalities, institutions, activities and ideas.[15] This statement conveys that the struggle of subaltern from their subjectivity is totally neglected. Therefore, the historical writing of this kind cannot explain Indian nationalism for us. For it fails to acknowledge, far less interpret, the contribution made by the people *on their own, that is independently of the elite* to the making and development of this nationalism.[16] K.N. Panikkar rightly aptly remarked that one of the weaknesses of the national movement was that it did not have an effective programme to ensure the inclusion of the depressed and socially excluded classes into the nation.[17] Guha asserts that parallel to elite politics, there was domain of people's politics in which the principal actors were the subaltern classes and groups constituting the mass of the population.[18]

Subaltern history is the history of a suffering, oppressed and the marginalized people who were forced silence by dominant elite group. In India these people are the dalits, tribals, women, etc. Too much history of Christianity has been from the standpoint of the 'shepherds' and too little from that of the 'flock'. However, it is in studying the activities of ordinary people that we can see most clearly the history of a past age.[19] Interestingly historians have now come to realize that unless the common people are included in the framework of history it would be an incomplete history. The methodology of subaltern people is from below, the grass root. Today the Subaltern historiography has emerged as an alternative to all the existing historiographies. It has now become a new genre in writing history in India. One of the central concerns of the Subaltern school of history is to give due recognition to the subaltern as a subject of history. This involved a mode of analysis and writing that would bring out the voice emphasizing the 'rebel consciousness' – its sovereignty, consistency and logic.[20]

---

[14] Ranajit Guha, *Historiography* ..., 1.

[15] Ranajit Guha, *Historiography* ..., 1.

[16] Ranajit Guha, *Historiography* ..., 3.

[17] K.N. Panikar, "Was Indian Nationalism Inclusive?," *The Hindu*, 23 February 2010, 8.

[18] E. Sreedharan, *A Textbook of Historiography* ..., 492.

[19] S. Immanuel David, "History of Christianity in India: Changing Perspectives," *ICHR* 30/1 (June, 1986): 8.

[20] Martin Fuchs, *Social Movements*..., 1539.

Methodological Issues in Subaltern Historiography

Some important features of methodological issues in subaltern historiography are:[21]

1. The subaltern school stands in counteract the historiography of Indian nationalism for their elitist nationalist approach. Their starting point of a new historiography is nation and nationalism as against representation of the elitist discourse;
2. Autonomy of subaltern consciousness and action. For the subalterns, collective consciousness plays a pivotal role thereby giving impetus to the method of analyzing society and people, which were ignored and silenced by elite discourses;
3. The restoration of subject to people that were either silenced or taken away by elitist discourses and to make the subaltern classes the subject of their history. This means Recategorization and Deconstruction of historical texts;
4. Subaltern studies take the texts seriously and therefore advocating a different theory of reading, i.e., Rereading the Historical Texts and reconstruct history from their own perspective;
5. To redefine the understanding of the text. This means to incorporate the written and oral traditions, myths and popular religiosity, rituals, etc.

The contribution of the subaltern methodology is the restoration of the silenced space created by elite domination. Their focal perspective is that the agency of change is located in the subaltern. Although Subaltern Studies started twenty years ago, only recently has subaltern historiography emerged as a methodological challenge to be reckoned with by theological researcher.[22] Subaltern perspective can be a critical tool in writing the history of Christianity in India from a new perspective. Within this framework let us examine to reconstructing the tribal historiography in Indian context. However, it is not the intention here to deal extensively on the theoretical tools or aspects of the subaltern methodology.

---

[21] See George Oommen, *Historiography* ..., 216-217, 219-231; Felix Wilfred, "Subaltern Religious Experiences," *Journal of Dharma* 23/1 (Jan-Mar, 1998): 57ff; David Hardiman, "Subaltern Studies at Crossroads," *EPW,* No.21 (1986): 289; V.V. Thomas, "Re-Reading the History of Christianity in India with Special reference to the ST. Thomas Tradition," *UBS Journal* 3/2 (September, 2005): 11-15.

[22] Subaltern Studies and their methodology have received international academic attention and it is recognized as one of the most unique Asian or Indian contribution to the academia. Cf. George Oommen, *Historiography* ... 220.

Reconstructing Tribal Historiography

Understanding the Term Tribal

In the Indian context the term 'tribal'[23] or 'tribe' has a sense of pejorative, negative and derogatory connotations. It suggests primitive people living in hills and forests, backward and uncivilized people who are the original but not developed inhabitants. Tribes are characterized as autochthonous, isolated, without history, economically and culturally primitive and politically subjugated.[24] Historically, the tribals have been accepted as the first settlers of India. They are known as *adivasis* or the indigenous people. However, it is strange that on the international forums like the U.N the Government of India denies the presence of the indigenous people in India.[25] Their history can be traced beyond the pre-historic times of Mohenjodaro and Harappa.[26] The Tribal population of the country, as per 2011 census, is 10.43 crore, constituting 8.6% of the total population. In all, 705 Scheduled Tribes exists at present in India.[27] The largest concentration of the tribal people, excluding Africa, is in India. There are three major groups of tribals

---

[23] The English word 'tribe' is derived from the Latin word *Tribus* (*Tri* = three, *bhuour* or *bu* = to be) which means 'to be three'. It was used to identify the three basic divisions of the Romans – the Tintienses, Ramnenses and Lucreres. All Roman citizens were enrolled in one or other of the tribe. This division was made for the purpose of taxation, military conscription and census taking. In the process the anthropologist used this term to denote a 'group of people speaking a common language, observing uniform rules of social organization, and working together for some common purposes such as trade, agriculture, or warfare. See K. Thanzauva, *Theology of Community: Tribal Theology in the Making* (Aizawl: Research & Development of AICS, 2004), 10-20; A. Wati Longchar, *An Emerging Asian Theology: Tribal Theology, Issues, Method and Perspective* (Jorhat: Eastern Theological College, 2000), 2-7; Nirmal Minz, "Identity of Tribals in India," in *The Indigenous Question: Search for an Identity*, edited by Walter Fernandes (New Delhi: Indian Social Institute, 1993): 23-25; C. Lakra, "Christianity and Tribal Identity," *Religion & Society* 36/2 (June, 1989): 30-32; Jaganath Pathy, "What is Tribe? What is Indigenous? Turn Towards the Metaphor for Social Justice," *Religion & Society* 38/3&4 (Sept – Dec, 1991): 18-26; B.K. Roy Burman, "Who are the Indigenous and Tribal People of India?" *Religion & Society* 38/3&4 (Sept – Dec, 1991): 3-10; T.S. Wilkinson, "Isolation, Assimilation and Integration in their Historical Perspective," *Religion & Society* 8/3 (October, 1961): 13-25; Joseph Bara, "Alien Construct and Tribal Contestation in Colonial Chhotanagpur: The Medium of Christianity," *Economic & Political Weekly* 44/52 (Dec 26, 2009 – Jan 1, 2010):90-91.

[24] Martin Fuchs, *Social Movements* ..., 1537.

[25] Jhakmak Neeraj Ekka, "Cultural Deterioration, A Threat to Indigenous/Adivasi Identity: Defining the Church's Theological Response for Cultural Restoration," *Dharma Deepika* 12/1 (January – June, 2008): 10. He has validated this statement from a research done by Martinez found in Bengt Karlsson, "Anthropology and the "Indigenous Slot": Claims to and Debates about Indigenous Peoples' Status in India," *Ordeal and Voices of the Indigenous Tribal People of India*, edited by Joseph Bara (Guwahati: ICICTP, 2006): 23-47.

[26] Nirmal Minz, *Identity*..., 23.

[27] *Statistical Profile of Scheduled Tribes in India 2013* (Ministry of Tribal Affairs Statistical Division Government of India), 25.

in India.[28] The tribal population in India is spread over the length and breadth of the country.[29] The more commonly used classifications are: the Himalayan region, middle India, western India, south India and Islands or north-eastern India, middle India, Southern India, north-western Himalayas and Andaman and Nicobar Islands.[30]

History of Tribal Quandary and Methodological Issue

History points that majority of the Christians in India comes from the tribals and the dalits who are the oppressed sections of the society. The community of tribals in fact is significant and important in India. The history would never be complete unless taking into account the experiences and aspirations of this people. The tribals in India are so diverse in culture, language and origin, their only commonality being the poverty, exploitation and alienation they suffered from time immemorial.[31] They are culturally alienated, socially stigmatized, economically exploited, poor and politically powerless[32] and theologically unheard and voiceless and finally historically did not find much space of their contributions. Tribal historiography therefore, should be situated within the context of cultural space, political consciousness and religious belief systems.

Today the tribals exist under the forced mercy of the dominant society of India. Nirmal Minz argued that the tribals social and cultural values reflecting deep human values of equality are ignored and pushed aside by the dominant society.[33] It is at this juncture that a search for a common historiography for the tribals should come to the forefront to do away the wrong notion and concept of tribal history and the people. It is pertinent therefore, that the tribal history needs to be reexamined and reconstructed. The tribal historiography in the context of

---

[28] 1) Those who are of the Munda language family, like the Santhals, the Mundas, the Saoras, etc. 2) Those who belong to the Monkhamer lanuage family, like the Bodos, the Nagas, the Garos and others and 3) those who belong to the Dravidian language family, like the Gonds, the Kui, the Oraons, etc. Cf. A. Wati Longchar, "The Need for Studying Tribal Theology," in *An Exploration of Tribal Theology*, edited by A. Wati Longchar (Jorhat: Eastern Theological College, 1997), 1-2; Nirmal Minz, *Identity*..., 23.

[29] It is found in almost all the states and the union territories of India with exception of Punjab, Haryana, Jammu and Kashmir, and the Union Territories of Chandigarh, Delhi and Pondicherry. However, given the migration of tribal population into states or regions outside their traditional habitats, one can assume that a scattering of tribal population may be found in all parts of India. Cf., Virginius Xaxa, "Tribes in India," *Sociology and Social Anthropology*, Vol. 1, edited by Veena Das (New Delhi: Oxford University Press, 2003), 380.

[30] Virginius Xaxa, *Tribes in India* ... 380.

[31] They have suffered from the hands of Aryan invaders, the Muslim rulers, the British administrators and the privileged people of India today.

[32] K. Thanzauva, *Theology of Community* ..., 22-13.

[33] Nirmal Minz, "Mission in the Context of Diversity – Mission in Tribal Context," *Religion & Society* 36/1 (March, 1989): 10.

depressed class movement is in the process of recovery through writers such as Nirmal Minz, F.S. Downs[34] and a host of other young writers.[35] The emergence of tribal history in the recent past in the limelight of historical writings is attributed to experiences of various forms of injustice and exploitation in the context of their assertion for right and identity of the people from the subjects of people, land, power and divines. It is a resistance history to affirm justice, identity, and dignity. Tribal people lived by a set of cultural values which can be accepted more or less as human values universally. This values comprises equality, community life, co-operation, honesty and truthfulness, democratic decision making, facing life with dance and songs, mutual respect, etc.[36] But this identity, tenets and values are eroding today because of modernization and by the elite discrimination and domination.

In the history of the tribals, the experiences of oppressions and hardships, and their traditional stories, myths, symbols, dances, songs, and their connectedness to land and environment become the vital resources[37] for developing their own history and methodology. Their history is from 'below' and 'bottom layer of history' to restore their identity which had been under the bondage at the hands of the elite society. Considering the fact that a significant number of tribals are Christians in India, the tribal context in general and the Christian tribal context in particular need to be taken seriously in writing the history of Christianity in India. For instance, looking at the development of Indian Christian Theology (ICT) in the wake of nationalism we find that it failed to incorporate tribal experiences and aspiration in developing theology.[38] According to Santhianathan

---

[34] Downs books are all confined to the North East Christianity. Some of his books are: *History of Christianity in India: North East India in the Nineteenth and Twentieth Centuries*, Vol. V, Part 5 (Bangalore: CHAI, 1992); *The Mighty Works of God: A Brief History of the Council of Baptist Churches in North East India: The Mission Period 1836-1950* (Guwahati: Christian Literature Centre, 1969); *Christianity in North East India* (Delhi: ISPCK, 1983). Apart from these books he has also written several articles on North East Christianity.

[35] Lalsangkima Pachuau, "Christian Mission from Below: Methodological Developments toward a Subaltern Affirmation," *Re-routing Mission: Towards a People's Concept of Mission (Indian Perspective)*, edited by George Mathew Nalunnakkal (Thiruvalla: Christava Sahitya Samiti, 2004), 35.

[36] Cf., Nirmal Minz, "Religion, Culture and Education in the Context of Tribal Aspiration in India," *Journal of Dharma* 12/2 (April – June, 1987): 152; C. Lakra, *Tribal Identity* ..., 39; Barnes L. Mawrie, "Experience of the Tribal Socio-Political, Historical and Cultural Context: Quest for a Tribal Theology," *Mission Today* 10/ 1 (January – March, 2008): 53.

[37] A. Wati Longchar, "An Assessment of the Tribal Theology: Trends and Challenges for Future," *Paper Presented at D.Th Research Methodology Seminar, 2007* (Bangalore: United Theological College, 2007), 4-5.

[38] Cf., R.H.S. Boyd, *An Introduction to Indian Christian Theology* (Madras: CLS, 1975); Sunand Sumithra, *Christian Theologies from an Indian Perspective* (Bangalore: Theological Book Trust, 1995). However, credit must be given to R.S. Sugirtharajah and Cecil Hargreaves, editors of *Readings in Indian Christian Theology*, Vol. 1 (Delhi: ISPCK, 1993) for including at least one essay of a tribal theologian among the 25 essays produced in the book.

Clarke, there are three different phases in the development of ICT: 1) the neo-orthodox missionary theology when it had a western influence; 2) during the 19th century when it embraced Brahmanic traditions and Hindu philosophy to establish Christian truth against Brahmanism; and 3) the 20th century national independence leading to a theology of Indian renaissance.[39] Wati Longchar is of the view that most of the theological educators at that time were mostly from high caste converts to Christianity. They use freely the concepts, doctrines and symbols of other religions, particularly Hinduism to interpret the Christian faith. This sort of perspective and approach to theological education in India indirectly sanskritized the tribals who are alien to Hindu culture.[40] Arvind Nirmal and Nirmal Minz called this as Brahmanic tradition.[41] Yesudas Choondassery also argued that Brahminino-centered ideology must be denounced by ICT.[42] Insofar ignored the voices of the tribals and deeply failed to interpret and integrate the experiences of the tribal community.

The ignorance to hear the voices and experiences of the tribals was largely due to the general popular understanding of the term 'tribals' as designating somebody backward, illiterate, scantily-clothed, unmannered, wild, violent, feared as a head-hunter, and living in interior forests and high hills far away from modern civilized societies.[43] It is indeed a time to explore the new dimensions to providing space for a tribal perspective in the making of history. The tribals should not be an object but must become the subject of history. Critical look at the writings of Christian history we find that it is more of denominational history[44] rather than an ecumenical history. This perspective would only legitimate in producing history of exclusion and dehistoricization. In this line Abraham Ayrookuzhiel blamed to certain extent the church historians for the distortion of truth in history.[45] The

[39] Santhianathan Clarke, *Dalits and Christianity: Subaltern Religion and Liberation Theology in India* (New Delhi: Oxford University Press, 1999), 36-42.

[40] A. Wati Longchar, "Tribal Theology and Theological Education in India," *Journal of Tribal Studies* 5/2 (July – December, 2001): 24.

[41] Arvind P. Nirmal, "Towards a Christian Dalit Theology," in *Indigenous People: Dalits – Dalit Issues in Todays's Theological Debate*, edited by James Massey (Delhi: ISPCK, 1994), 215; Nirmal Minz is of the view that this tradition (Brahmanic) has further pperpetuated institution interiority oriented approach to the theological task in India. One wonders whether this kind of Indian Christian Theology will ever have a mass appeal. See his article, "Theological Interpretation of the Tribal Reality in India," in *Readings in Indian Christian Theology*, Vol. 1, edited by Sugirtharajah and Cecil Hargreaves, (Delhi: ISPCK, 1993), 45.

[42] Yesudas Choondassery, "Indian Christianity and the History of Exclusion," *Voices from the Third World* 30/2 (December, 2007): 11.

[43] Nirmal Minz, *Theological Interpretation* ..., 46.

[44] Cf., A.M. Abraham Ayrookuzhiel, "Dalits' Challenges to Religious Systems: A People Ignored by Church History," *ICHR* 23/2 (December, 1989): 127-128.

[45] He is referring to the plight of the Dalits in the church and in the making of dalit Christian history by historians which is a distorted one. This similar situation is also being faced by the tribal

dimension and perspective of the neglected sections of the common people need to be taken into consideration if the history of Christianity in India looks for an objective and ecumenical history.

Sources for Reconstructing Tribal Historiography

Tribal historiography must be developed by the tribals utilizing the vital resources to counter their experiences from enormous and manifold forms. The elitist mindset and of the perception in the writings of the tribal history has to be erased in order to find space for the tribal communities in the making of a common history of Christianity in India. It is to re-read and re-write the history from a tribal perspective by including and incorporating their contribution in the making of history. Roger Gaikwad writes, should the Indian Christianity fail to relate to the tribal context and neglect to provide space for tribal Christianity, then it would be guilty of not giving a holistic expression to the gospel of Jesus Christ in India.[46] Of course his statement contains a sort of missiological implication and expression but the idea to incorporate the perspective of tribals in the making of the history of Christianity in India is evident. Therefore, reconstructing of tribal historiography becomes an important task today. All history, right or left, is constructed, and indeed must be reconstructed anew in the light of the changing exigencies of present needs and future hope of the people.[47] The extreme plight of the tribals comes from deep existential life situation not from the world of conceptualization. The subaltern tools and methodology must be a medium in interpreting the plight of the tribals to foster a holistic and objective history.

The formation of Church History Association of India (CHAI) was a mile stone that paved the way for writing the history of Christianity in India from the people's perspective. The CHAI, whose membership is wide and inclusive, has felt the need to write the History of Christianity in India with a new perspective.[48] Thus the Editorial Board declared that perspective in which the history of

---

Christians. Cf., A.M. Abraham, *Dalits ...*, 127.

[46] Roger Gaikwad, "Rethinking Indian Christianity from a Tribal Perspective," *Religion & Society* 44/4 (December, 1997): 108.

[47] Rudolf Heredia, "Subaltern Interrogation of Hindu Nationalism: II: Need for a New Hermeneutic," *Vidyajyoti* 66/11 (November, 2002): 916.

[48] This means it has to be people oriented, to be bottom up; it should be about Christianity and not the church (so a change from 'Church History' to 'History of Christianity'; it should emphasis the subaltern; History of Christianity to be seen in the light of local history; the source of writing need to be wide – not only Church Records and missionaries' reports and the like, but also government records, local/native written and unwritten sources, etc. Another issue is the Indianness of the History of Christianity. See D. Arthur Jeyakumar, "Methodological Issues in the History of Christianity," *Paper Presented at D.Th Research Methodology Seminar*, 2007 (Bangalore: United Theological College, 2007), 3.

Christianity had been written in the past is in serious need of revision.[49] There was a time when various groups or communities of men and women had a kind of private history of their own, when histories were studied and written in isolation of one another. But this is not possible now.[50] The CHAI felt that the cultural, social and related aspects of the Indian Christians need to be given due place. As a result the CHAI[51] launched to write six-volume comprehensive History of Christianity in India from an Indian contextual and ecumenical perspective. Guidelines were indicated as to how the historiographical perspective has to be used in writing the History.[52]

Keeping in mind the perspective of CHAI historiography, several historians and reputed scholars such as J.W. Gladstone, George Oommen, Dick Kooiman, Geoffrey A. Oddie, Duncan Forrester, John C.B. Webster, etc., have done some commendable work from the subaltern perspective specifically on the Dalit Christian movements and Fidelis De Sa on the tribal communities of Mundas and Oraons. [53] Analyzing the theories and motives on conversion movements among the Dalits and Tribals in India we find that it is very much integral to their struggle for social improvement. Most of the historian who have dealt with this issue agreed to it. In fact while investigating the conversion movement history their outcome were divergent within a specific social structure and people but

---

[49] A. Mathias Mundadan, "Rewriting History: Orientations," *Journal of Dharma* 28/2 (April – June, 2003): 164.

[50] Joseph Cardinal Parecattil, "Objective History: The Best Teacher," *ICHR* 19/2 (December, 1985): 96.

[51] So far the CHAI has published Volumes I, II, III, IV part 2 and V part 2 & 5. What ever has been published so far maintains a wider and contextual perspective.

[52] For detailed explanation see, "A Scheme for a Comprehensive History of Christianity in India," *ICHR* 8/2 (December, 1974): 89-90.

[53] J.W. Gladstone, *Protestant Christianity and People's Movements in Kerala: 1850-1936* (Trivandrum: Kerala United Theological Seminary, 1984). Few articles were also written and published in Journals from this perspective; George Oommen, "Dalit Conversion and Social Protest in Travancore, 1854-1890," *BTF* 28/3&4 (September-December, 1996): 69-84; "Christianization or Dalitization: The Twentieth Century Experience of Dalit Christians in Kerala," *ICHR* 37/1 (June, 2003): 1-22. See also his book with John C.B. Webster, *Local Dalit Christian History* (Delhi: ISPCK, 2002); Dick Kooiman, *Conversion and Social Equality in India: The London Missionary Society in South Travancore in the 19th Century* (New Delhi: Manohar Publications, 1989); Geoffrey A. Oddie, *Social Protest in India: British Protestant Missionaries and Social Reforms* (Columbia: South Asia Books, 1978); See also his edited book, *Religion in South Asia: Religious Conversion and Revival Movements in South Asia in Medieval and Modern times* (New Delhi: Manohar Book Service, 1977); Duncan Forrester, *Caste and Christianity: Attitudes and Policies of Anglo-Saxon Protestant Missions in India* (London: Curzon Press, 1980); John C.B. Webster, *The Christian Community and Change in Nineteenth Century North India* (Delhi: The Macmillan Company of India Ltd., 1976). See also the book by the same author *A Social History of Christianity: North-West India Since 1800* (New Delhi: Oxford University Press, 2007); Fidelis De Sa, *Crisis in Chota Nagpur: With Special Reference to the Judicial Conflict Between Jesuits Missionaries and British Government Officials, November 1889 - March 1890* (Bangalore: Redemptorist Publications, 1975).

without ignoring the spiritual and psychological forces their consensus is that they all advocated upward mobility, justice and identity as important factors in conversion movements among the Dalits and Tribals in India. However, one important lacuna in their findings is that they did not give serious attention to the religious dimension and its role in the conversion movements. For instance when looking at the North-East tribals the aforementioned factors are not the main contributing factors to their Christian conversion movement. The religious aspects played a pivotal role in their conversion to Christianity. But this is not highlighted in any of the historical writings.

In the present writings of history we find that the tribals were and are uncivilized, illiterate, savage, backward, etc., and therefore, all the socio-cultural changes and modernization are highly attributed perhaps without contention to the works of Christian missions. In fact it is certainly true. But the raw fact is, the immense contributions of the tribal people are ignored in their writings. Therefore, while dealing with the Christian movements they did not give adequate space to the religious factors, i.e., their religious belief system and practices. It is important to note that Subaltern studies takes into account not only the issues of race, class, gender or ethnic but also all the aspects of the subaltern condition and experiences, for instance their belief system, spirituality, rituals, mortality, etc. Therefore, Felix Wilfred asserted that subaltern religion emerges from the experience of being subjugated, dominated. They have always sought in their religious experiences and symbols an important means to counter the domination they suffer.[54] George Oommen in one of the case studies of tribal conversion movements among the Malayarayan of Kerala stated that the "pre-existing religious ideas played a role in their conversion to Christianity.[55] C. Lakra also opined that there is a symmetrical relation between tribal religion and Christianity. There are elements of God the Father as creator, protector and redeemer from whom all blessings flow over the tribe, family, children, cattle, crops, fields and jungles.[56] Their assertion needs serious attention in reconstructing tribal historiography.

The tribal festivals, myths, rites, rituals, customs, cultures, and spirituality should be taken into account while reconstructing the tribal historiography from an Indian Christian perspective. These elements represent and reflect their whole aspiration. The subaltern school advocates the small voice or silenced voice to speak which had been silenced by the dominant discourse in the making of history. The tribals who were silenced by the dominant in regard to their socio-cultural and religious realm must find space and be represented adequately. As stated for quite long even in the theological discourse, the religion of the tribals was termed as 'animist' or 'primitive' hence not philosophically deep for

---

[54] Felix Wilfred, *Subaltern* ..., 58, 64.

[55] George Oommen, "Re-reading Tribal Conversion Movements: The Case of the Malayarayans of Kerala, 1848-1900," *Religion & Society* 44/2 (June, 1997): 82.

[56] C. Lakra, *Tribal Identity* ..., 36-37.

articulation.[57] This is incorrect and unjustified perception towards the tribal Christians in India. If this is the general notion then it will certainly fail to see the cultural values and spirituality of the tribal people which is imbedded in their history. No doubt for long the tribal had no written texts unlike the elite classes. However, written literature/document/text cannot be taken as a measuring rod of a people or religion. At this point, the subaltern tools of recategorization[58] and deconstruction[59] of history should be taken into account in reconstructing the tribal historiography. The silenced voice need to be restored to provide an objective tribal history which was ignored by elitist discourses. Indian Christian tribals are going through a period of transition and struggle between the past and the present. The pertinent task is to erase the prejudices against cultures which was the trademark in the past and look forward to find solution in the present. This is the point in which the question of reconstructing tribal historiography becomes indispensable.

One of the components of subaltern methodology is rereading and redefining the historical texts. The assumption here is that historical texts are the product of an agenda and there is nothing like a neutral or objective text, narrative or evidence. Every text therefore, is a product of a given time, and as an agenda, it evolves in the context of politics and affiliation to circumstances.[60] The subaltern school has thus produced tools for critical reading of the text in favour of the subaltern even if the sources of the information are almost entirely the creation of the elite.[61] So in reading the text one should unearth the power structure dominating the discourse and must find out the consciousness of the subaltern reflected in the discourse. In this sense, to redefine the text from a tribal perspective is to use the elements like the myths, rites, rituals, customs, cultures, and spirituality. This would help unravel the rebellious consciousness of the subject. In this process the oral text also has to be considered. The tribals

---

[57] Cf., A. Wati Longchar, "People's Theology," *CCA News* (September, 2007): 5.

[58] Subaltern Schools' search for new categories, which transcends several domains of human experiences and masses. Subaltern Studies considers all aspects of subaltern condition, material as well as spiritual, past as well as present as important. Hence clearly rejects the exclusive materialistic view of human condition and existence. Therefore, historians and others who are engaged in research should free themselves of the dominant narratives and materialistic categorization. This recategorization has a direct challenge to theological researchers whose task is to understand human experience in a holistic manner. See George Oommen, A Commentary on Subaltern Studies Collective: Methodological Implications for Theological Research," in *Interweaving Methodology and Praxis – Exploring Disciplinary Options in Today' World*, edited by John Mohan Razu (Bangalore: BTESSC/SATHRI, 2007), 133-134.

[59] For elaborate theoretical explanation on deconstruction of history See George Oommen, *Subaltern Studies Collective* ..., 134-137.

[60] V.V. Thomas, *Understanding Subaltern History: Theoretical Tools* (Bangalore: BTESSC/SATHRI, 2006), xvi. See also George Oommen, Subaltern Studies Collective ..., 137.

[61] V.V. Thomas, *Theoretical Tools* ..., xvi; George Oommen, *Subaltern Studies Collective* ..., 137.

take pride in having enough of the above mentioned elements at their disposal to rereading and redefining the texts to create their own history and to determine their future. These tools of rereading and redefining the historical text should be incorporated in reconstructing the tribal historiography.

Conclusion

The emergence of Subaltern historiography has opened a viable perspective to discover the silenced spaces in history. The Subaltern historiography has emerged as an alternative to all the existing historiographies. This is a very positive shift in the writing of history from a new perspective wherein silenced or ignored people would find autonomous space in the making of history. Looking at the present context the tribal Christianity needs to be given a respectful place in Indian Christianity. The emergence of CHAI historiography in the present context needs to be appreciated. Nevertheless, more has to be done to incorporate and include the contributions of the common people in the making of a vibrant history. In fact, writing history from Tribal perspective has found a remarkable but too little a space in the making of people's history. It still remains a challenge that the tribal historiography written from the dominant perspective is re-read and re-written from their own resources and perspectives. For "History is not one but many stories; only a few have been written. The challenges to build on the advances so far are many."[62] Demand of such a time as this, is writing history of the stories of alienated and feeble voice of tribals so far ignored and silenced.

W.T.

[62] Upinder Singh, "Changing Interpretations of Early Indian History," *The Hindu*, 30 June 2008, 10.

Chapter 6

Recovery and Reconstruction of Her-Story: Feminist Historiography

"Feminist" is a common term used to describe those who seek to eliminate women's subordination and marginalization.[1] To put in other way, a feminist is one who reflects on the struggle of women created by exclusion, untold experience and alienation in male dominated structures and committed for gender equality and liberation of women. In cognate, the "Feminist Historiography" is a field of study which challenges the uncritical History, traditionally written by man as "His-Stories", ignoring the Her-Stories.[2] It is indeed a fact that all historiographies are selective view of the past undeniably written in gender bias that ignored and undermined the contributions of women in history making. The challenge of feminist historiography against such history is rediscovering and reconstructing "Her-Story" in the domain of "His-Story."

Christian Feminist Contention and Perspective: A Historical Background

With regard to the contribution of women in history of Christianity, Daniel D. Chetti, few decades back, made the following profound statement:

---

[1] Elisabeth Schussler Fiorenza, "Feminist Hermeneutics," *Anchor Bible Dictionary*, Vol. 2, edited by David Noel Freedman (New York: Doubleday, 1992), 783.

[2] I have borrowed the terms "His Stories and Her Stories" from Barbara. See Barbara J. MacHaffie, *Her Story: Women in Christian Tradition*, Fifth Printing (Philadelphia: Fortress Press [1986] 1989), 1.

> … a profound lacuna exists in our understanding and appreciation of the contribution of women to our church's history. It is said that "memory" is a powerful 'geist' which animates our historical sense and imprints our present self-perception of who we are. Conversely, "loss of memory", therefore, is a debilitating condition which can destroy the psyche of an individual. Without a 'past' which they can recall to their "memory" women in the history of Christianity can be seen as victims of collective amnesia. Their lives, works and contribution are largely ignored and left out from the memory of our history.[3]

It is indeed a fact that there is always a 'Past' in the history of human civilization and this past is recreated through 'Memory.' The memory recalls the past and it creates a heuristic category to create one's identity and empowerment. Perhaps, memory plays role as both subject as well as source. In fact, the memory research by neuroscientists and psychologists has confirmed that memory is not a passive depository of facts, but an active process of creating meanings. Analyzing history from this perspective, on the one hand certainly brings to light how women were ignored, silenced, subordinated and marginalized, but on the other hand, it is also forward looking towards creating a space of their identity, liberation and empowerment.

The basis of feminist discourses and arguments are primarily from the prism to critique on 'Patriarchy'. The critique of patriarchy is basically the critique of power and relation.[4] Historically the male dominant patterns in Christianity originated from a time when the church and patriarchal society were integrally related. The church borrowed patterns of organization from patriarchal society and buttressed those patterns with theological symbolism and argumentation.[5] The contemporary feminism, according to Barbara, has in fact brought a new approach to the study of the past. This approach recognized that the Christian tradition is intertwined with patriarchy and on many occasions and in many places, functioned to oppressed and degrade women.[6] Thus, though both men and women have been agents in the making of the history, all history traditionally has been His-Stories.[7] Indeed, women are and have been central, not marginal, to the making of society and to the building of civilization. But they are completely neglected and ignored. According to Gerda Lerner,

---

[3] Daniel D. Chetti, "Making Visible: The Role of Women in the Nineteenth Century Protestant Christianity in India," *ICHR* 32/1 (June, 1988): 6.

[4] Ofelia Ortega, "Women in Dialogue: Approximations and Challenges of Feminist Theology," in *A Reader in Feminist Theology*, edited by Prasanna Kumari (Madras: Gurukul Lutheran Theological College & Research Institute, 1993), 7.

[5] Rosemary Radford Ruether, "Women's Difference and Equal Rights in the Church," *Concilium* 6 (1991): 12.

[6] Barbara, *Her Story* …, 2.

[7] Narola Imchen, *Issues in Modern Historiography* (Delhi: ISPCK, 2012), 16.

> Women have also shared with men in preserving collective memory, which shapes the past into cultural tradition. This oral tradition was kept alive in poem and myth, which both men and women created and preserved in folklore, art, and ritual. Historians have selected the events to be recorded and have interpreted them so as to give them meaning and significance but the irony is that these historians have been men, and what they have recorded is what men have done and experienced and found significant. They have called this History and claimed universality for it. What women have done and experienced has been left unrecorded, neglected, and ignored in interpretation. Historical scholarship, up to the most recent past, has seen women as marginal to the making of civilization and as unessential to those pursuits defined as having historic significance.[8]

Though women were equally participated in the dimension of evolvement of human civilization and history, they were consciously ignored in the documented records of history. Their significances in history were thus left unrecorded, neglected and misrepresented. This recorded history recorded by men became 'the absolute' and 'the universal' in the interpretation and annul of history.

While looking at the Bible, the Feminists see that all the narratives are products of an androcentric patriarchal culture and history[9] and strongly question the androcentric valuation of "historical significance." They also challenge that many historical sources on women are prescriptive rather than descriptive. Despite their lives and actions being reality in history, women are neglected in the writing of history. Hence, feminist historians seek to comb the androcentric records in order to bring feminist meaning by re-appropriating the patriarchal past for those who have suffered not only the pain of oppression but also participated in its social transformation and development.[10] For, the story about women has been thoroughly obscured by the ways in which women have been excluded from the processes by which cultures find meaning, interpret and explain their past and present and orientate themselves to the future, as all this is expressed in texts, which may simply represent the views of the most privileged and atypical members of a given community of language users.[11] In Gerda's words, by making the term "man" subsume "woman" and arrogate to itself the representation of all humanity,

[8] Gerda Lerner, *The Creation of Patriarchy* (New York/Oxford: Oxford University Press, 1986), 4.

[9] Elisabeth Schussler Fiorenza, *In Memory of Her: A Feminist Theological Reconstruction of Christian Origin* (New York: Crossroad, [1983] 1988), xv.

[10] Fiorenza, *In Memory of Her* ..., 85.

[11] M.R. Miles, Image as Insight: Visual Understanding in Western Culture and Secular Culture (Boston: Beacon Press, 1985), 152, quoted in *Feminist Theology: A Reader*, edited by Ann Loades (London/Kentuchy: SPCK/W/JKP, 1990), 2.

men have built a conceptual error of vast proportion into all of their thought.[12] Thus, in the process of documenting historical text, women became the victims and victimized. They have made history but are denied of their space and rights in interpreting it and systematically excluded in the process of creating their identity and empowerment. The significance of feminist historiography in the Christian tradition, therefore, is to represent "Her Story" not in isolation of the whole history, but focusing on the status of women in the Christian tradition.[13]

In the Christian tradition, the construction of gender difference is associated with the reception of the philosophical school of Platonism,[14] Neo-Platonism and Aristotalism,[15] which were blended into the Bible. Despite their emphasis and influence on particular contexts, the Bible and Greek philosophy were in agreement over the claim that the man was the principal and that the humanity of woman was derived. To claim that the man was the principal meant that he was the beginning and had the vocation to rule. According to Elisabeth,

> This presupposition was not questioned either by the church fathers or by most of the medieval scholasticism. The construct 'woman' was essentially explained as a negation or a reduction of the construct 'man'. Although there are counter-traditions which deviate from this andronormative picture of human beings, right down to modern times the main tradition of official theology has proved to be the dominant influence in history because time and again it has been endorsed by the church. The counter tradition, whether grounded in plurality of theological schools or conveyed by female mystics or poets, have been out to one side. Because, the same biblical text has continually been interpreted down the centuries, the andronormativeness of the picture of human beings has transcends the bounds of particular periods.[16]

Christianity inherited from its historical past, a fundamental contradiction in its views and treatment of one half of humanity, the women. On the one

---

[12] Gerda Lerner, *The Creation of Patriarchy* ..., 220.

[13] Barbara, *Her Story* ..., 1.

[14] In the *Laws* Plato concludes that a woman has less potentiality for virtue than a man; he says further that it is women's weakness and timidity that makes them sly and devious (781 b 2-4). Again Plato shows his contempt for women: 'Human nature being twofold, the better sort was that which should therefore be called man' (*Timaeus* 42 e). And twice he says: 'Evil and cowardly men are reborn as women that being the first step downward to rebirth as animals '(42 b3-c4; 90 e 6-91 a 4. See Mary Ann Rossi, "The Legitimization of the Abuse of Women in Christianity," *Feminist Theology*, No.4 (September, 1993): 61.

[15] Aristotle sees woman as a misbegotten male (*De Generationel* IV 6; *Metaphysics* X 9). This Aristotelian conception is adopted with approbation by Augustine and Aquinas. See Mary Ann Rossi, *The Legitimization of the Abuse* ..., 61.

[16] Elisabeth Gossmann, "The Construction of Women's Difference in the Christian Theological Tradition," *Concilium*, Vol. 6 (1991): 50.

hand, Christianity proclaims the Universalist Soteriological egalitarianism – salvation knows no distinction between human beings; whereas, on the other hand, the Christian understanding of the nature of being, both of God and Christ and of normative humanity, has been cast in male generic terms. This male generic understanding of being has been used to subordinate women.[17] The legitimization of gender construct derived from the Misogynistic assumptions of the Christian teachings derived from Augustine,[18] Thomas Aquinas,[19] Gratian, and other founders of the Christian precepts are grounded in the Aristotelian conviction that females are defective males.[20] Furthermore, for instance, John Chrysostom[21] and Martin Luther[22] also have demeaned the personhood and dignity and integrity of a woman. In fact, the attitudes towards women up until now were being determined in no small way by several theological teachers and writers whose teachings were prevalent during the first six centuries. The category called the Church Fathers indeed made strong statements that degrade women and the feminism. Their theological commentaries tried to dismiss women's spirit and diminish their humanity. This is hurtful and hateful of patriarch. Women therefore, were kept subordinate in church and society so also strongly opposed the idea of women exercising ecclesiastical functions. The exclusion of women from ordained ministry, and indeed from all public leadership in past Christian societies, has been rooted in this male generic understanding of human and

---

[17] Rosemary Radford Ruether, "Women's Difference and Equal Rights in the Church," *Concilium*, 6 (1991): 11.

[18] Augustine locates the source of original sin in the male erection and women are the cause of it. The depersonalization of women into whore, wife or mother may be traced to his writings. Most damaging is his reiteration of the precept that the wife must submit completely to her husband, even to the point of physical abuse and death. He formulated the idea that women were good only for reproduction and unqualified for anything connected with mind and intelligence. Thus Augustine was the inventor of what the Germans call the three K's, Kinder, Kuche, Kirche: that is children, kitchen and church. Cf., Mary Ann Rossi, *The Legitimization of the Abuse* ..., 59. Augustine also states that any women who act in such a way that she cannot give birth to as many children as she is capable of makes herself guilty of that many murders. For further readings refer the book by Kari Borreson, *Subordination and Equivalence in Nature: The Nature and Role of Women Augustine and Thomas Aquinas* (Washington D.C: University Press of America, 1981).

[19] Thomas Aquinas claimed that woman was created as subordinate and inferior to man. Not only was she second in the order of creation, but she was endowed with less intellectual capability and, consequently, less ability to make right moral decisions. He added that women were 'defective' human being/males.

[20] See Mary Ann Rossi, *The Legitimization of the Abuse* ..., 56.

[21] He stated, 'Among the savage beasts, none is held so harmful as a woman.'

[22] Martin Luther says, women are created for no other purpose than to serve men and be their helpers. If women grow weary or even die while bearing children, that doesn't harm anything. Let them bear children to death; they are created for that. Cf. D. Martin Luthers Sammtiliche Werke. Erlangen and Frankfurt, 1826-57, 20, 84 quoted in Merry Wiesner, "Luther and Women: The Death of Two Marys," in *Feminist Theology: A Reader*, edited by Ann Loades (London/Kentuchy: SPCK/W/JKP, 1990), 123.

divine.[23] This encrypted concept was furthered to disabling gender construct. Of late it has come to recognize the omission and erasing of women from the androcentric texts of early Christian history.[24]

Over against such history, number of outstanding women historians, theologians and biblical scholars in recent times have come up to look the history from feminist perspective by uncovering new sources regarding women in history, scripture and the early church community. Rosemary Ruether, in her book *Sexism and God-Talk* categorically states that "Whatever denies, diminishes, or distorts the full humanity of women is, therefore, appraised as not redemptive, not reflecting the divine or an authentic relation to the divine; what does promote the full humanity of women is of the Holy." She also points out that "it is not claiming the critical principle, full humanity, but the fact that women claim this principle for themselves. Women name themselves as subjects of authentic and full humanity."[25]

Hence, Elizabeth Schussler Fiorenza's in *Memory of Her*[26] calls for rediscovering the women heritage in the early Christian community, and make women's stories an integral part of the proclamation of the gospel.[27] She argues that all the institutions of our culture tell us through words, deeds, and even worse silence that we are insignificant. But women's heritage is the source for women's power. Attempt to reconstruct early Christian history as women's history in order not only to restore women's histories to early Christian history but also to reclaim this history as the history of women and men.[28] In this way, the Feminists seek to reconstruct heuristic models and concepts that allow to perceive the human reality articulated insufficiently in androcentric texts and research. Fiorenza further challenges that the patriarchal religion have erased women from history

---

[23] Rosemary, *Women's Difference* ..., 11.

[24] For instance in Romans 16:7 probably reveal a female leader of the early church. Here, Andronicus and Junia are commended for their outstanding work in spreading the gospel. However, the translator in the past has found it inconceivable that a woman would be called apostle and so they use the male name Junias. Junia, however, was a common female name in the first century. Cf., Barbara, *Her Story* ..., 26. Another one is, many interpreters of the New Testament in the past have translated the name in Co 4:14 as the male name "Nymphas", it is generally agreed that the verse correctly reads, "Nympha who had a church in her house." Cf., Barbara, *Her Story* ..., 24. Archeological clues, such as catacomb painting of women celebrating the Eucharist (with a modern reproduction transforming the women into men), and locating a Bishop Theodora in the church of St. Prassede in Rome (with the last part of her name scratch out). Mary Ann Rossi, *The Legitimization of the Abuse* ..., 61.

[25] Rosemary Radford Ruether, *Sexism and God-Talk: Towards a Feminist Theology* (Boston: Beacon Press, 1983), 18-19.

[26] Elisabeth Schussler Fiorenza, *In Memory of Her: A Feminist Theological Reconstruction of Christian Origin* (New York: Crossroad, [1983] 1988).

[27] Mary Luke Tobin, "Women in the Church: Vatican II and After," *The Ecumenical Review* 37/3 (July, 1985): 300.

[28] Fiorenza, *In Memory of Her* ..., xiv.

and made them 'non-being' and in her book, *Bread Not Stone*, she underlines the following:

> "The critical rereading of the Bible in a feminist key and from women's perspective is in the process of uncovering lost traditions and correcting mistranslations, of peeling away layers of androcentric scholarship and rediscovering new dimensions of biblical symbols and theological meanings. In Bible study groups, sermons, and seminary, women rediscover our biblical heritage and realize that this heritage is part of our power today. The rediscovery on a popular and academic level is made possible by two basic shifts, in our perception of the world and reality, and in our perception of the function of biblical texts and interpretations."[29]

The critique of patriarchal ideology and the construct about women and the narration of history from such prism clearly shows that women are completely excluded and erased from both the ecclesiastical administration and the very history of Christianity. This calls for a rediscovery, redefinition and reconstruction of the image and portrayal of women in historical writings by which women find their rightful space in history, and dignity in Church and society at large.

Methodological Consideration: Indian Perspective

While looking at the methodological issues in feminist historiography from Indian perspective, first and foremost, one must consider the experiences and the roles assigned to women in society. It must begin by recognizing that women have been excluded from the mainstream of history and literature. For even though women are indeed participants in the processes of culture and society, they have been silenced, marginalized, and perceived as being unessential to the making of civilization. Their works and contributions have been left almost entirely unrecorded, leading to historical and literary invisibility.[30] Perhaps, it is the traditional male scholarship that perpetuated the exclusion of women by making men the normative and dominant representation of humanity and placing women as subordinate and secondary to men.[31] Secondly, it must critic and deconstruct the male cultural paradigm of mis-representing women, and the traditional androcentric approach to historical writings. Also, an area of methodological consideration we need to take note is the search for an alternative history and tradition that support the inclusion of women as full historical being. In Indian

---

[29] Elisabeth Schussler Fiorenza, *Bread Not Stone: The Challenge of Feminist Biblical Interpretation* (Boston: Beacon Press, 1984), 1.

[30] Wanda Deifelt, *Feminist Methodology* ..., 203.

[31] Wanda Deifelt, "Feminist Methodology as a Critique and Renewal of Theology," in *Feminist Theology: Perspectives and Praxis*, edited by Prasanna Kumari (Madras: Gurukul Lutheran Theological College & Research Institute, 1999), 201.

contexts, this means, recovery and reconstruction of lost or forgotten traditions and history of women, their role, leadership and writings.

Speaking about the character and abilities of Indian woman it is written in *Manusmriti* that "She lacks the ability of true appreciation and balance of mind and does not possess much depth of reason .... It may be admitted that women have but little sense of justice and this is no doubt connected with preponderance of envy in their mental life."[32] Manu, for this very reason, perhaps assigned to women perpetual legal minority, making them subject to fathers in Childhood, husbands in youth and sons in old age. In family and society a woman was part of a relationship, not a person in her own right. Social obligations overwhelmed the individual who was only the means to an end. Her responsibility was to marry and bear a son and remain faithful even after the death of her husband.[33] The cruder depictions and portrayals of *Manusmriti* are indisputably a picture of Indian women. Literature spoke of the infirmity and imperfection of women and protected them for the sake of family honour. This is the reason why during the hey-days of Protestant missions in India, they were reluctant to introduce any social reforms by interfering in personal laws so also that had anything to do with religion.[34]

However, despite their limited values, status and role, we see women joined the national movement; boycotted foreign goods; courted arrest and went to jail. We also see women in general, and Christian women in particular, contributing to the women educational system and for emancipation and empowerment by which women even excelling far better than men in some areas. Unfortunately, the socio-cultural and religious construct of women as weaker and polluted being in several ways still depict and deprive their significant participation.

One must understand that the very root of the disproportionate relationship that exists between men and women is sexism. Sexism simply means the unjust treatment meted out to women because of their sex. In fact, it is the direct violation and denial of women's rights to access to power, curtailing the right to control their destiny and the denial of equal opportunity. It is within this socio-cultural and religious context we need to locate the place and significance of women in the writing of the history of Christianity in India. Perhaps, we need to investigate objectively whether women been given enough space or their role and contribution acknowledged in the historical text and narrative discourses.

---

[32] R.M. Women in Manu and His Seven Commentator (Varanasi: Kanchana Publication, 1962), p. 40, quoted in Daniel, *Making Visible* ..., 20.

[33] Vera Augustus, "Women in Indian Society," in *Feminist Theology: Perspectives and Praxis*, edited by Prasanna Kumari (Madras: Gurukul Lutheran Theological College & Research Institute, 1999), 41.

[34] However, Sati was abolished in 1829; Widow Remarriage was legalized in 1856; Female Infanticide was banned in 1870; and there was legislation against Child Marriages in 1929.

As already stated, most of the histories were written being dominated by men from their perspective making it invisible the contributions, status and place of women in history. Of late, secular Indian historians like Kumkum Sangari, Janaki Nair, Gayatri Spivak, Kamala Visweswaran, Susie Tharu, Tejaswini, Niranjana, Lata Mani are few examples who have been considering the question of writing history from the feminist perspective and the issues arising out of it. [35] They have initiated and developed Feminist historiography in the light of distorted, omission, and incomplete history in India, which has impacted the historical research during the last ten to fifteen years in India. However, the feminist historiography in India is yet to find considerable space in the history of Christianity in India. Perhaps, one of the pioneering Christian feminist historiography, which deserves appreciation, is not written by Christian historians, but by the secular historians – Uma Chakravarthi[36] and Gauri Visvanathan[37] on Pandita Ramabai and Conversion respectively.[38]

Even hardly we see mention of the role and contribution of women in the writings of well-known modern Church Historians like William R. Cannon,[39] Kenneth Scott Latourette,[40] Williston Walker[41] and Justo L. Gonzalez.[42] For instance, except Gonzalez, we do not see any of the historians mentioning about the role and contribution of the great 14th century women, Saint Catherine of Sienna.[43] Beside Catherine, there are several other women whose role and

---

[35] V.S. Elizabeth, "Inevitability of Rewriting Indian History from a Feminist Perspective," *Journal of Dharma* 28/2 (April – June, 2003): 237.

[36] *Pandita Ramabai: Rewriting History through the Life and Times of Pandita Ramabai*, Delhi, 1998.

[37] *Outside the Fold: Conversion, Modernity, and Belief*, Delhi, 1998.

[38] Uma Chakravarthi analyses how the colonial state had changed gender relations in a fundamental manner. She holds that the case history of Pandita Ramabai was not about silencing or invisibility but was one of suppression by the Brahminic patriarchal structures and how she threatened the then Hindu nationalist. Whereas Gauri Visvanathan examines through the life and experiences of 'converts', the vexing issue of the role of belief in modern society, and shows how it is arguably one of the "most unsettling political events in the life of a society," basically it is a cultural study focusing on the role of religions in modernity, and demonstrates how religious ideologies can alter patterns of modern society. Cf., George Oommen, "Historiography of Indian Christianity and Challenges of Subaltern Methodology," *Journal of Dharma* 28/2 (April-June, 2003): 217.

[39] William R. Cannon, *History of Christianity in the Middle Ages: From the Fall of Constantinople* (Michigan: Baker Book House, 1960).

[40] Kenneth Scott Latourette, *A History of the Expansion of Christianity: The Thousand Year of Uncertainty*, Vol. 2 (New York & London: Harpers & Brothers, 1938), 359, 375.

[41] Williston Walker, *A History of the Christian Church* (New York: Charles Scribner's Sons, 1959).

[42] Justo L. Gonzalez, *The Story of Christianity*, Vol. 1 (New York: HarperSanFrancisco, 1984).

[43] Catherine of Siena was more orthodox in her influence. She began to have visions while still quite young, and was soon making prophesies. After an injury disfigured her and made her marriage prospect nil, her parents consented to her desire to enter the Dominican Second Order of

contribution in the making of the history of the church was being ignored and silenced.[44] The obvious reason for the omission could be the gender bias because of the perspective of Institutional history during this period.[45]

Coming to the Indian context, from James Hough to C.B. Firth, the same bias attitude is visible in the writings of history of Christianity in India. Firth, however, devoted some valuable sections to the contribution of women, but the damage had already been done since the women's contribution was not fairly treated in the early writings in India. Even during the formation of the CHAI all the Editorial Board members were men, which did not give much importance to the study of the role of women in the History of Christianity in India.

To make the point clear, we can cite the case of a noted woman, Lilavati Singh. Though despite of rigid social and cultural barriers, made immense contribution to Indian church and ecumenism, she did not find adequate space and recognition in the writings of the history of Christianity in India.[46] In order to justify her contribution, it is appropriate that we make a brief note on her life and ministry.

> Lilavati Singh was born in 1868 and grew up as a child in the dusty village of Gorakhpur. Her family originally came from Nepal Hindu background but became Christian and moved to North India. Lilavati

nuns. There she became persuaded that she wore a marriage ring given to her by Christ, and that she bore the *stigmata* (i.e., the wounds of Christ) as well. Only she could see the ring. The stigmata too were given to her invisible, at her request, lest she take too much pride in bearing publicly the signs of Christ's passion. The remarkable thing is that her contemporaries believed her claims to be true and saw her as an exemplary model of a saint. Her long *Dialogue with God*, dictated while in a mystic trance, were widely circulated. And we have over 350 of her letters addressed to the great and near great of her time. In 1375 she urged Queen Joan of Naples to go on crusade. In 1376 she was ambassadress to reconcile Pope Gregory XI with the Florentine. Between 1376-78 she appeared before Gregory in Avignon and, in the name of God, commanded him to return both himself and the papal office to Rome and thus end the long papal Avignon residence. She felt free, indeed compelled, to communicate to the Pope these marching orders, mediated to her through the direct inspiration of God. Her letters are full of criticism of priests, cardinals and even Popes. She was a practical leader of the church whom princes, both secular and clerical, took most seriously. She died in 1380 and was named a saint in 1461. In 1970 Pope Paul VI, hardly a feminist, named her a 'doctor' of the Roman Catholic Church. Cf., Earl Kent Brown, "Women in Church History: Stereotypes, Archetypes and Operational Modalities," *BTF*, X/2 (July-December, 1978): 85-86.

[44] For instance, Empress Pulcheria Augusta, a defendress of faith, who was the first empress regnant in Roman imperial history; St. Hildegard, Jeanne d' Arc, Teresa of Alva, Ann Lee, Jeanne d' Albert, a good friend of John Calvin, Clare in the 13th Century, Julien of Norwich, St. Bridgett of Sweden, etc.

[45] See F.S. Downs, "Women's Issues in Theological Education: A Historical Perspective," *Transforming Theology for Empowering Women: A Theological and Hermeneutical Reflection in the Context of North East India*, edited by R.L. Hnuni (Jorhat: Eastern Theological College, 1999), 79-82.

[46] Lilavati Singh's story is an extract from an article written by Daniel, *Making Visible* ..., 14-18.

lost her mother when she was still a child and her father, unable to take of her, put her in a girl's boarding school in nearby Lucknow, run by Isbella Thoburn. Her story is a fascinating one of rise from total obscurity to the glare of International forum and fame. Her progress as an inmate in the boarding school is describe as "bright", "eager", and "promising", but also "willful", "undisciplined" and "trying". Yet there was something in the life and personality of Lilavati which made Isbella Thoburn recognize in her qualities of leadership. After graduating from Calcutta University in M.A. she went to Dhaka to work as Professor of English. She returned to Lucknow to become the first Indian woman on the faculty of I.T. College, on a salary of 75 Rupees per month. She remained there for the next nineteenth years, distinguishing herself as an educator, administrator and organizer. Above all, she was an important role model for the educated woman of India. She was also an active member of YWCA and World Student Christian Federation.

Her talents as student organizer and as public speaker made her popular both in India and outside. On her capacity as the Chairperson of the prestigious Women's Committee of W.S.C.F. Lilavati travelled and spoke in conferences in Continental Europe, England, U.S.A. and Japan. She was also the first Indian to address the World Missionary Committee of Christian Women (an international Ecumenical Missionary Organization representing all the Women's Missionary agencies from North America and Europe) in April 21, 1900, in New York. Lilavati captivated her audience with the eloquence and force of her call on behalf of her Indian Sisters. Sitting among the audience was the President of the United States, Benjamin Harrison, who purported to have said, "If I had contributed one million dollars to missions, and had seen only one such convert I would consider it a profitable investment." Perhaps a less sweeping, and a more realistic assessment of Lilavati Singh was made by Ruth Rouse, Secretary of Women's Coommittee of W.S.C.F. scribbled in her hand writing on the back of her letter she received from Lilavati: the death of this great Indian Christian woman leader was a blow to the women's work of the Federation, as well as her other interests and above all to the Isabella Thoburn College, Lucknow. She was the Chairperson of the Women's Sub-Committee of the Federation; made a great impression at Tokyo Conference, 1901 and W.S.C.F was counting on her presence at Oxford 1909." Lilavati of course could attend the Oxford Conference of W.S.C.F in April 1909 because she died in February 1909, after prolonged illness and surgery.

A closer examination of Lilavati's speeches and correspondence would indicate to us that women had played a far greater role in leading

> Churches towards "Ecumenism" than hitherto acknowledged. She was also addressing issues of women's concerns and national concerns in public gatherings long before Bishop V.S. Azariah of Dornakal gave his passionate plea on behalf of the Indian Church at the famous International Missionary Council in Edinburgh in 1910.

In India, Subaltern Studies have indeed ushered a new dimension and perspective in the writing of Indian history by critiquing the dominant discourse in the writing and interpretation of history. It has uncovered and discovered the agency that the subaltern has always exercised and contributed but ironically denied, ignored, omitted and erased and to extent to term as insignificant in the narratives of the imperialist, nationalist and even in the Marxist histories. Today the subalterns are finding space in the historical narrative. Subaltern studies however, have its limitation in understanding the subordination of women and their suffering because of gender discrimination. They therefore, Spivak remarked: "...is scrupulous in its consideration towards women. They record moments when men and women are joined in struggle, when their conditions of work or education suffer from gender or class discrimination. But I think they overlook how important the concept-metaphor woman is to the functioning of their discourse."[47] She cited an example from the subaltern led revolt during the 19th century because men were unwilling to accept female leadership:

> With the deposition in 1836 of Ananta Bhupati, the 17th Zamindar of Golgonda, the Collector of Vishakapatnam istalled Jamma Devamma, widow of the 15th Zamindar, in his place. This was an affront to the *muttadar* and *mokhasadars* of Gudem who were not consulted ... and who protested that they had never before been ruled by a woman ... In Rampa, the death of the Mansabdar Ram Bhupati Dev in March 1835 was followed by a revolt of *muttadar* against the daughter who had been appointed as the successor (1.102).[48]

The above statement is one of the examples where the subaltern studies overlooked the gender dimension and agency of women in their writing from a new perspective. Just discussing these events and the nationalist, Marxist or subaltern historians' neglect of the female subject should give us an idea of the difficulty of writing an Indian history from a feminist perspective. At the same time it reveals the need for analyzing and understanding the silence and the omissions of women in all histories. It also reveals the possibilities that are

---

[47] Gayatri Chakravorty Spivak, "Subaltern Studies: Deconstructing Historiography," in *Subaltern Studies IV*, edited by Ranajit Guha (Delhi: Oxford University Press, 1985), 356.

[48] Spivak, *Deconstructing Historiography* ..., 357.

inherently present in these very omissions of rewriting a history of women[49] or for that matter Her-Story.

In this process of historical discourse we need to critically look for the methodology/ies that would help unearth the distorted text/s from feminist perspective. The tools of 'Recovery' and 'Reconstruction' need further deliberation in this process of articulation. The term recovery generally implies the action or process of getting back something that has been lost, stolen or forgotten. In the context of intellectual historical and theological discourse it means to recovers for us the dimension of text/s or documents that has been distorted or forgotten because of socio-cultural and theological imposition and limitation. Thus recovery designates the dimension of the activity that uses the text to change the horizon of its recipients. Reconstruction simply means the process of changing or improving the condition of something or the way it works. Thus, reconstruction describes the historical work done in order to understand the original context in and for which the text was produced.[50] We need to recover the texts or documents which are distorted and reconstruct relevantly by interpreting the text or documents from the original context in which it was produced from the feminist perspective.

To imply the tools of recovery and to reconstruct, we need to look for the relevant methodology. In the light of recovery and reconstruction, the methodological issues in the feminist historiography lies within the structure of deconstruction, re- defining, re-reading, re-writing, etc., that has to be articulated in the context of their specific experiences and questions.

In a deconstructive reading the text in question is shown to harbour contradictory logics which are standardly ignored. Very often it is a matter of locating certain marked binary opposition and showing that their order of priority is by no means a stable as the text seeks to maintain. That is to say, there is counter-logic at work whereby those distinctions can be shown to breakdown, or to generate a reading markedly at odds with author's overt intent. This leaves open the possibility that texts may mean something other and more than is allowed for by any straightforward appeal to the authorial intention. It looks for what is not present rather than what is present. It looks for the points of crisis and breakdown in a system or a rationalization rather than its more obvious positivities.[51] Deconstruction questions not only the definitive meanings of texts, but the

---

[49] V.S. Elizabeth, *Inevitability of Rewriting ...*, 240.

[50] Francis Martin, *The Feminist Question: Feminist Theology in the Light of Christian Tradition* (Michigan: William B. Eerdmans Publishing Company, 1994), 85-86.

[51] George Oanthanmackel, "Deconstruction of Derrida's Differance: A Possible Way to Metaphysics," in *The Post Modern: A Siege of the Citadel of Reason*, edited by Johnson J. Puthenpurackal (Delhi: Media House, 202), 82-82.

societies and institutions which validate their use.[52] It involves the questioning of many hierarchical oppositions and writing in order to expose the bias.

Deconstruction as a methodology looks for deconstruction of binary, resist the polarization and advocate for interdependence which focuses on the reality of hybridity. This methodology seeks for the restoration of the people who are ignored in the historical discourse. Deconstructing certain myth about 'Sati', Arshia Sattar stated that the myth of Sati has nothing to do with widows or funeral pyres but a symbol of empowered woman. It is about a married woman's anger and frustration.[53] The greatest gift of deconstruction is to question the authority of the investigating subject without paralyzing him, persistently transforming conditions of impossibility into possibility.[54] This method will help to recover and reconstruct the history of women whose subjectivity, experiences and contribution were being ignored or represented inconsequentially in the historical texts.

Another issue is the source of historical construction. Here the methodology of rereading of the historical texts and sources becomes pertinent. The position and assumption here is that all texts are the product of an agenda and there is nothing like a neutral or objective text, narrative or evidence. Every text, knowledge, information is a product of an affiliation, politics, and agenda.[55] Rereading the text critically from feminist perspective even if the sources or the text are almost entirely the creation of men would unearth the power structure dominating the discourse. This will validate the consciousness and experiences of women that is reflected in the discourse. While considering the text in historical research it is important for any historians to investigate the discursive practices within which statements/documents are produced. This is required not in order to discern bias, rectify it and thereby arrive at untainted, proper narrative of things past, unsullied by the context within which narrative was produced. It is necessitate by the fact that most of the statements about the dominated are produced within well-defined fields of power.[56] This means to analyze the text critically and not necessarily the bias of the writer. In this process, criticism must therefore start not by naming a bias but by examining the components of the discourse, vehicle of ideology, for the manner in which these might have combined to describe any particular figure

---

[52] Margaret Davies, "Poststructural Analysis," in *Anchor Bible Dictionary*, Vol. 5, edited by David Noel Freedman (New York: Doubleday, 1992), 425.

[53] Arshia Sattar, "Sati, Symbol of Empowered Woman," *The Hindu* (Friday Review), 3 March, 2017, 4.

[54] Spivak, *Deconstructing Historiography …*, 336.

[55] George Oommen, *Historiography …*, 227.

[56] Shahid Amin, "Approver's testimony, Judicial Discourse: The case of Chauri Chaura," in *Subaltern Studies V*, 2nd Impression, edited by Ranajit Guha (Delhi: Oxford University Press [1987] 1992), 167.

of past.[57] This articulation will strengthen to come to closer approximation in the examination of the text or sources. In this sense it is the question of objectivity in history. Rereading will unravel the unequal power structure on the basis of gender behind the text or sources. This will eventually deconstruct the unequal power equation and find space of the subjectivity.

To redefine the text requires a perspective to the understanding of the text or sources. The elements like the myths, rites, rituals, customs, cultures, etc., are to be incorporated to redefine the very understanding of the text. Recovery of oral text is an important component in this process of historical reconstruction. Oral history has now become an important means in which ordinary common people can actively engage in making their history. Importantly serves as an alternative to elitist form of historical writings. In this, the marginalized folks find space in the historical construction. Oral history thus gave a voice to those who were 'hidden from history.' In fact, narrativisations of different kinds like novels, songs, paints, embroidered works, testimonials, and autobiographies can be redefined and read differently to give rise to a different kind of representation of women. This representation will not understand itself as the true picture of the woman but as one effort in documenting a woman's experience.[58] Susie Tharu and K. Lalita writes that what they have tried to do "is to create a context in which women's writings can be read, not as new monuments to existing institutions or cultures but as documents that display what is at stake in the embattled practices of self and agency.[59]

In the recent past, an Art Historian, William Varvel[60] from Texas solved the mystery of the Mona Lisa's enigmatic smile in his book "*The Lady Speaks: Uncovering the Secrets of the Mona Lisa*." He states that in Mona Lisa's smile, he sees a feminist. He argued that the history remembers the Mona Lisa as Lisa del Giocondo, who was a 16th century feminist who favoured a greater role for women in the Catholic Church. As stated redefining the text includes the arts and paintings too that would serve as a context to portray the representation of women. Incorporating the elements that would constitute in redefining the text will help in the recovery and reconstruction of history from feminist perspective.

---

[57] Ranajit Guha, "The Pros of Counter-Insurgency," in *Subaltern Studies II*, 2nd Impression (Delhi: Oxford University Press, [1983] 1995), 9.

[58] Mrinalini Sebastian, "Implications of Postcolonial Thinking for *Feminist Praxis in India,"* in Feminist Theology: Perspectives and Praxis, edited by Prasanna Kumari (Madras: Gurukul Lutheran Theological College & Research Institute, 1999), 99.

[59] Susie Tharu and K. Lalita, in their "Introduction," to Women Writing in India: 600 B.C to the Present Vol. 1: 600 B.C. to the Early Twentieth Century (1991; London: Pandora Press, 1993), p. 36, quoted in Mrinalini Sebastian, *Implications of Postcolonial Thinking ...*, 99.

[60] "In Mona Lisa's Smile, U.S. Historian Sees a Feminist," *The Hindu* (Chennai), 14 March 2014, 17.

Conclusion

Indian history or the history of Christianity in India will remain incomplete without the narration of Her-Story. The effort to write Indian history or that of history of Christianity from a feminist perspective is hard, but not impossible. History of Christianity in India has come a long way wherein historians have discovered several paradigm shifts in the historiography and methodology thereby making concerted efforts to making a people's history. Writing history from Women's perspective has found a remarkable but too little space in the making of people's history. More space and efforts should be made to include women in the subject for the discourses which has so far did not get due attention. The consequential alienation by His-Stories should be the starting point of the feminist recovery and reconstruction of Her-Stories.

W.T.

Chapter 7

History of Dalits and Tribals Conversion in India: Theories and Motives

The key objective of this chapter is to examine the theories and motives of conversion movements in India during 19th and 20th centuries with special reference to the Protestant missions. As there is certain force behind every action, there was forces at work behind the expansion of Protestant Christianity in India. Though it was beginning to be felt only from the beginning of the 18th century, it was the 16th century Protestantism of Europe which had greatly impacted on the modern missions, particularly in India. By the turn of the middle of 19th century we see Protestant Christianity assuming a significant turn and a tremendous growth and wide expansion in the history of Christianity in India 20th century. Perhaps, owing to the favourable political situation in India during these periods several Protestant missions came from Europe and America and established their respective missions resulting into great expansion of Protestant Christianity through their vigorous mission activities. Considering this fact, and attempt is made in this section to examine the theories and motives behind the conversion movements in India especially among the Dalits and Tribals.

Context

As already noted, the conversion movement of the depressed strata of people and the aboriginal tribes has to be credited for the rapid growth and expansion of Protestant Christianity in India during 20th century. Perhaps, it was from the beginning of the 19th century, the Christian missions began to pay attention to many aboriginal depressed class peoples of India. The main reason for the growth of the church in India was not the conversion of a few people here and there as 'solitary unit' but 'mass conversion' where "whole villages or sections of the community, or groups of families" embraced Christian faith. It was not only the experience of Protestant missions of 19th and 20th centuries, but such mass movements were visible in India during the time of Roman Catholic missions of the 16th and the 17th centuries.[1]

Historically, the mass movements in India took place more commonly in the regions of Kerala. According to Gladstone, the main reason for this conversion movement was that by the middle of the 19th century a kind of self-awareness and consciousness strongly developed among the people and their society. The impact of this consciousness expressed itself in various ways and led to movements of various types. It was in such a context Christianity was introduced.[2] The Christian missionaries involved in the life of the society in various ways. The active role of the missions in the field of education, religion and society were some of the factors which created a new awareness among the people to struggle for their betterment and stability. The Christian missions' involvement in the various social and economic issues on the one hand created much disruption in the society, especially among the dominant society, but on the other hand, a large number of suppressed people found a possibility to break the chains which had bound them for centuries. The conversion movement according to Dick Kooiman therefore "is not to be narrowed down to an individual movement, because it is closely linked with social aspiration of groups that suffer from discrimination and oppression."[3] Therefore, it is necessary that the nature of the conversion movement among the Dalits and the Tribals and the theories and motives behind this movement are critically analyzed.

Theories of Christian Conversion Movement in India: Selected Areas

Several scholars and historians have already given attention on this subject and came out with several reasons and factors behind conversion movements.[4] However, still there is need of close analysis on the theories and motives of conversion movements in India focusing select communities.

---

[1] J.W. Gladstone, *Protestant Christianity and People's Movements in Kerala: 1850-1936* (Trivandrum: Kerala United Theological Seminary, 1984), 1.

[2] Gladstone, *Protestant Christianity* ..., 75.

[3] Dick Kooiman, *Conversion and Social Equality in India: The London Missionary Society in South Travancore in the 19th Century* (New Delhi: Manohar Publication, 1989), 1.

[4] For a comprehensive analysis on the motivating factors for conversion to Christianity, see Geoffrey A. Oddie, "Christianity and Social Mobility in South India 1840-1920: A Continuing Debate," *South Asia* 19 (Special Issue, 1996): 143-159. For a sociological perspective on Conversion, see S.M. Michael, "Sociological Perspectives of Conversion in India," *Indian Missiological Review* 5 (January, 1983): 40-52.

Conversion Movements in South India

Looking at the conversion movements in south India, one of the major features in the history of conversion movements is attributed to the grievous famine which occurred during the periods of 1876-1878. Missionaries extended their help to the depressed classes during these periods of crisis which simultaneously led the people to embrace Christianity. However, this reason should not be the only criterion to assess the Christian conversion movements in South India. To give a clear perspective to the history it is imperative to see the other dimensions to determine the Christian conversion movements. This could be possibly done by looking at their social history that prevailed during these periods of transition. As stated, the conversion movements took place more commonly in the regions of Kerala. Several missionary societies from the west penetrated Kerala during these periods (i.e., the 19th and 20th centuries). Prominent among them were the London Missionary Society (LMS), Church Missionary Society (CMS) and the Basel Mission. Large conversion occurred only in Travancore. The work of Basel missionary was confine to British Malabar. The work of the LMS and CMS resulted in massive conversion movements whose missionary works were confined in Travancore.

Several historians and scholars have studied on the conversion movements among the low castes community in South India. There is undisputed consensus among them on the theories and motives of conversion of these depressed classes (viz., Nadars,[5] Hill Arrians,[6] Pulayas[7] and

---

[5] Nadar (also referred as *Nadan, Shanar*) is a caste of Tamil Nadu & Kerala, South India. The term, *Nadar,* in Tamil literally means one who rules the land/lord of the land/who is the owner of the land, or the 'Authority' of the land. Nadar caste was regarded as one of the agricultural castes. This caste is found in the state of Tamilnadu and in the Southern part of Kerala and was one of the most socially and economically depressed class. They were conditioned by the social structure which did not give any freedom to them.

[6] Malayarayan Tribal people were known by several names such as Mulla Vellens, Mulla Nairs, Hill Arrians and Malayarayans. While Hill Arrian was used by all Anglican sources, the Government of Travancore and ethnographers like Thurston used the name Malayarayan which means the Arayan of the hills to distinguish them from the fishing community on the Kerala coasts, the Arayans. The Hill Arrians were severely oppressed by the government officials in the form of forcing them to carry hill products to the plains. The government and the Rajah's were in the habit of extracting extortions and unjust taxes from this oppressed people. They were socially and economically exploited. They were victims of extreme external exploitation and oppression. George Oommen, "Re-reading Tribal Conversion Movements: The Case of the Malayarayans of Kerala, 1848-1900," *Religion & Society* 44/2 (June, 1997): 68-70.

[7] It is believed that the word Pulayan is derived from pula, meaning pollution. They are also known as Cheramar and Cheruman and are concentrated in the Trivandrum (Thiruvananthapuram), Quilon, Pattanamthitta, Alleppey, Kottayam and Ernakulum districts of Kerala. They have been defined as a Malayalam caste of agricultural serfs, and as members of an inferior caste in Malabar, who are, as a rule, toiler attached to the soil. In the Madras Census Report, 1891, it is stated that "this caste is called Cheruman in South Malabar and Pulayan in North malabar. Even in South Malabar

Parayas[8]). According to Gladstone, the acceptance of the new religion was part of their struggle for their advancement and emancipation. As they accepted Christianity many of them gained impetus to improve their economic condition and their efforts at social liberation that attracted people of the lower classes to Christianity.[9] George Oommen also viewed on the same thought on the Pulayas conversion. For him the act of conversion was a "language of protest" of down-trodden Pulayas against the "the landlords' ill-treatment and inhumanity." They saw their situation as "unjust and dehumanizing" and so they were seeking a new image for their community through altered practices.[10] It was a form of protest against the oppression of high castes, and a means of achieving social improvement.[11] Thurston remarked that many Parayas became converts to Christianity, and thereby receive a rise in the social scale, and a freedom from the disabilities under which their lowly position in the social scale places them.[12] Dick Kooiman also maintains that the Dalits of South Travancore, Kerala[13] converted in large numbers to Christianity during the second half of the 19th century for material benefits and "also social reform and a rise in social rank."[14]

Another historian Duncan B. Forrester also maintains the same view. After analyzing the pre-conversion situation of the Dalits, he concluded that they were seeking to escape from an intolerable status and condition within the Hindu social

---

where they are called Cheruman, a large sub-division is called Pula Cheruman. The Pulayas were the agricultural labour outcastes. See K.S. Singh, *The Scheduled Castes*, Revised Edition (Calcutta/Chennai/Delhi/Mumbai: Oxford University Press, 1999), 1098-1102, and Edgar Thurston, *Castes and Tribes of Southern India*, Vol. II (Delhi: Cosmo Publications, 1975), 45-46.

[8] Bishop Caldwell is of the opinion that the name Paraiyan/Parayan is from the Tamil word parai, a drum, as certain Paraiyan act as drummer at marriages, funerals, village festivals and on occasions when government or commercial announcements are proclaimed. They are distributed in Tamil Nadu, Kerala and Pondicherry. In Kerala Paraiyans belong to a very low caste of the agrestic serfs of Cochin, next to Pulayas in order of social precedence. Their traditional economic resource is forestry and their occupation is basketry. Besides, the Parayan are also engaged in agricultural labour, sweeping, drum-beating and skin and hide work. See K.S. Singh, *Castes* ..., 1057-1060.

[9] Gladstone, *Protestant Christianity* ..., 118. See also J.W. Gladstone, "Christian Missionary Work and Socio-Religious movements in Kerala: 1850-1910," *ICHR* 30/1(June, 1986): 33; J.W. Gladstone, "19th Century Mass Movement in South Travancore – A Result of Social Liberation," *ICHR* X/1 (June, 1976): 52-66.

[10] George Oommen, "The Struggle of Anglican Pulaya Christians for Social Improvement in Travancore, 1854-1966," (Ph.D Thesis, University of Sydney, 1993), 122.

[11] George Oommen, *Struggle of Anglican Pulaya* ..., 434. See also George Oommen, "Dalit Conversion and Social Protest in Travancore, 1854-1890," *BTF* 28/3&4 (September-December, 1996): 75-77; S. Albone Raj, "Mass Religious Conversion as Protest Movement: A Framework," *Religion and Society* 28/4 (December, 1981): 58-66.

[12] Edgar Thurston, *Castes and Tribes of Southern India*, Vol. VI (Delhi: Cosmo Publications, 1975), 130.

[13] The Pariahs, Shanars, Pulayas, Kuravars, etc.

[14] Dick Kooiman, *Conversion* ..., 82.

structure. In that situation Christianity to them was a better alternative in their quest for equality, dignity, self-respect and a new sense of identity.[15] Sundarajan Manickam is also of the view that the conversion to Christianity was a great blessing at least to a sizeable number of the Dalit converts, if not to the entire lot. It created in them a new awareness and gave then a new identity, re-discovery of themselves and developed an intense feeling of self-respect and self-reliance that they never had before.[16] According to K.L. Sharma these socially deprived sections often converted to Christianity in the desperate hope of a better life, access to modern education and dignified social status.[17] For a radical social empowerment, religious conversion is envisaged as one of the important solutions by many great leaders of Dalits in the past, including Ambedkar in the later years.[18] In short we may conclude that the prevailing social structure alienated the Dalits from all their deserved privileges. They were reduced to a status where their existence as a human was at the mercy of the high caste people. There was no space for them for improvement and emancipation. In Christianity these people found an alternative for social emancipation and identity.

The beginning of contacts between the Telugus and the Christianity dates back to the 16th century.[19] Enormous efforts were being made both by the Roman Catholics and Protestants[20] to introduce Christianity to the Telugu community. However, it was only in the 19th century that concerted efforts were made to convert the Telugus to Christianity. The protestant and the Roman Catholic missionaries during the 18th and the first half of the 19th centuries concentrated their evangelization among the dominant castes in the community. It was however, only from the second half of the 19th century that the missionaries concentrated to the Dalit communities resulting to large conversion movement. The state of Andhra Pradesh probably by contrast experienced the largest Christian conversion

---

[15] Duncan B. Forrester, *Caste and Christianity: Attitude and Policies on Caste of Anglo-Saxon Protestant Missions in India* (London: Curzon Press, 1980), 69-92.

[16] Sundarajan Manickam, "Origin and History of the Christian Dalits in Kerala and Tamilnadu," *Religion and Society* 34/3 (September, 1987): 7-25. See also his book, *Social Setting of Christian Conversion in South India* (Wiesbaden: Franz Steiner, 1977).

[17] K.L. Sharma, *Social Stratification and Mobility* (New Delhi: Rawat Publication, 2002), 171.

[18] For more details see John C.B. Webster, *Religion and Dalit Liberation* (New Delhi: Mahohar Publication, 2002).

[19] See Joe S. Sebastian, *The Jesuit Carnatic Mission: A Foundation of Andhra Church* (Secunderabad: Jesuit Province Society, 2004). In this book the author highlights at least four attempts by Catholic missionaries to introduce Christianity to the Telugus during the century. The Catholic missionary activities during the 16th century were mostly the Franciscans, The Theatines and the Jesuits. Later in the early 18th century intensive missionary work was done in the regions of Chittor, Krishna, Godavari, Visakhapatnam and Hyderabad.

[20] Benjamin Schultz, a German missionary, was the earliest Protestant missionary to have shown missionary interest towards the Telugu communities. However, this was limited to the Telugu community in Madras (Chennai). When the Protestant missionaries began their work in the early 19th century, they found both European and local, already active in Christian expansion.

movements in India whereby all the missions involved actively. The LMS mission gave a bolster in the conversion movement in the 1840s, the CMS in the 1860s, and the Lutherans in the 1880s and it was the Malas who converted in large numbers through the missions. Among the Madigas, the American Baptists played an active role during the 1870s and 1880s. The Methodists in the Medak area experienced mass movements first among the Malas in the 1880s and 1890s and then among the Madigas after 1906, while those in Hyderabad-Vikarabad area experienced both between 1905 and 1913. In the 1920s and 1930s there were huge mass movements of Malas and Madigas in the Anglican Diocese of Dornakal. In some parts of Andhra the Dalit Christian conversion movements led to mass movements among Sudras.[21]

Initially, Protestant missions in Andhra Pradesh met with favourable response from among the untouchable segments of the population.[22] Family, kinship and wider group movements among the outcaste Malas and Madigas in favour of Christianity gained increasing momentum and continued well into the early decades of the 20th century. In 1931 it was estimated that nearly 20 per cent of the depressed classes in West Godavari, 32 per cent in the Krishna and 57 per cent in the Guntur districts had been converted to Christianity.[23]

In analyzing the conversion of the Madigas and the Malas in Andhra Pradesh, Duncan B. Forrester remarked that the search for material improvement or enhancement of status is seldom if ever the sole or even the dominant motive in a mass movement. Dignity, self-respect, patrons who will treat one as an equal, and the ability to choose one's destiny – all these are powerful incentives to conversion."[24] It was the famine which first gave the decisive impetus sometimes spectacular to this conversion movement because of the relief works. But relief work of itself did not create Christian conversion movements. He therefore, further suggest that the various aspirations – spiritual, psychological, social and material – which expressed themselves in mass movement were best able to surface and become effective in times of social and economic dislocation, and that such conditions, of which famines represented an extreme case, were generally present throughout the second half of the 19th century.[25]

---

[21] For the conversion of Sudras see G.A. Oddie, "Christian Conversion among Non-Brahmans in Andhra Pradesh with Special Reference to the Dornakal Diocese: 1900-1936," in *Religion in South Asia: Religious Conversion and Revival Movements in South Asia in Medieval and Modern Times*, edited by G.A. Oddie (New Delhi: Manohar Book Service, 1977): 67-99. (Hereafter referred to as G.A. Oddie, *Christian Conversion*). See also J.W. Pickett, *Christian Mass Movements in India* (New York: The Abingdon Press, 1933), 294-312.

[22] See, G.A. Oddie, "Christian Conversion in Telugu Country, 1860-1900: A Case Study of One Protestant Movement in the Godavaery – Krishna Delta," *Indian Economic and Social History Review* 12/1 (January-March, 1975): 61-79.

[23] G.A. Oddie, *Christian Conversion* ..., 69.

[24] Duncan B. Forrester, *Caste and Christianity* ..., 75.

[25] Duncan B. Forrester, *Caste and Christianity* ..., 75.

In the conversion movements, be it in great or small scale, is the perennial problem of groups which demands greater recognition, status and better treatment from other dominant groups within the existing society. Often the Dalit converts were in a position where their morale bolstered due to the missionary attention which gave them the hope or realization of economic, social and educational advancement. Telugu society in this period – among the established classes as well as the downtrodden – there exist dissatisfaction with the established social categories and practices. The Dalit communities of Malas and Madigas attained a new outlook and meaning through their conversion to Christianity during the second half of the 19th century. They found fulfillment in their religious and social aspiration. It gave them a new social and religious identity. Christianity was both catalyst and beneficiary in this situation. M.E. Prabhakar opined, the social history of the Andhra Church reveals that the mass movement of 'outcaste' or 'depressed class' groups into the fold of Christianity happened because of their search for self-identity, human dignity, equality and fellowship, more than for economic gain or social mobility; the latter were incidental rather than intentional.[26] The elements of upward social mobility, dignity and identity were evidently present in the conversion movement history.

Conversion Movement in North India

The North Indian society during the 19th century was made of a large number of groups which the Census Commissioner called castes, tribes or races. In the Punjab the communities of the Jats and the Rajputs, who were land-owning agriculturalist, were numerically the largest. In Uttar Pradesh (U.P), the Chamars, outcastes whose traditional occupation were leather-working and (generally landless) agricultural labour, were the most numerous; second to them were the Brahmins at the very top of the caste hierarch.[27] The British annexed the Punjab in 1849 resulted in the inauguration of a new era of change in both these North Indian provinces. By the 19th century Protestant Churches in Britain and the United States sent missionaries first to the United Provinces and then to the Punjab. The missionary activities in both the provinces were effective. Educational mission played a vital role in shaping the lives of the people. This was subsequently followed by the conversion movement comprising mainly from the Chamars (leather workers), Chuhras (a sweeping community in the Punjab), and Lal Begis (a sweeper community in the U.P) classes. Members of these three sub-castes were considered outcastes, or outside the Varna system. They were considered literally untouchable, they were denied access to temples, and they had to use separate wells. One of the reasons for this treatment was that their

[26] M.E. Prabhakar, Caste in Andhra Churches: A Case Study of Guntur District, *Religion and Society* 34/3 (September, 1987): 46.

[27] John C.B. Webster, *The Christian Community and Change in the Nineteenth Century North India* (Delhi: The Macmillan Company of India Ltd., 1976), 1-2.

occupations were considered unclean and defiling.[28] It is difficult to come to any definite conclusions about the theory and motives for conversion to Christianity in North India. Clearly these were many and varied and mixed.

Pandit Harikishna Kaul, the superintendent of the 1911 Census in the Punjab, suggested that the motives to conversion to Christianity of the Chamars and the sweeper caste were primarily social and to some extend economic as well. It states, the number of cases in which conversions are based on an intelligent recognition of the psychological superiority of a religion is never large, and converts to Christianity are not always free from the weaknesses of human nature. The depressed classes are in condition of peculiar social and religious disadvantage and gain most by the equality of treatment preached and secured by the Missions. Their status is raised. An untouchable becomes touchable by adopting Christianity, and has the satisfaction and advantage of receiving spiritual instructions from highly educated and sympathetic clergymen exactly in the same familiar way as his fellow-beings of the highest position. He can receive education and follow better pursuits than his degraded hereditary calling.[29]

Missionaries seemed to agree with Kaul's conclusion in the motives of conversion to Christianity. Most of the missionaries agreed that the most dominant motive was for their betterment. The people could now see in Christianity the possibility of human betterment, of education, of concern and help in the crisis of famine, of "friends in courts"; they could also begin to see, as time went on, the differences becoming a Christian did, and did not, make the lives of those who had converted. These perception in turn affected the motivation of subsequent inquires and converts.[30] Though the motives of the conversion movements were different but their dominant motive was a quest for dignity, not only for one's self but for the whole community of which they were inseparable part.[31] There now appears to be scholarly consensus that the underlying motivation was the search for improved social status, for a greater sense of personal dignity and self-respect, for freedom from bondage to oppressive land owners. On this line, Webster in his study on these communities, i.e., the Chamars, Chuhras and Lal Begis, concluded that these Dalits become Christians "in order to improve their social status and in particular to remove the stigma of untouchability." They could do this by changing their old group name (Chamar, Chuhra or Lal Begi) to a new

---

[28] J.H. Hutton, *Castes in India: Its Nature, Function and Origin*, 4th Edition (London: Oxford University Press, 1963), 192-193.

[29] Harikishna Kaul, Punjab, Part I. Report, Census of India 1911, Vol. XIV, Lahore, 1912, 192, quoted in Webster, *Christian Community* ..., 61-62.

[30] John C.B. Webster, *The Dalit Christians: A History*, Reprint (Delhi: ISPCK, 2000), 57-58.

[31] Webster, *Christian Community* ..., 64.

one (Christian) which had no particular caste status connected with it.[32] Duncan B. Forrester also maintained the same view.[33]

Conversion Movement in Tribal Belt

To analyze the Christian Conversion Movement among the Tribals, the tribes of Mundas and the Oraons of Chota Nagpur have been selected. Though there are several other tribes in Chota Nagpur, these are the two important Tribal groups in terms of their population as well as by reason of their influence. The Mundas and Oraons closely encountered the forces of colonial education, British idea of rule by law and Christianity.[34] By the middle of the 19th century Christian missions began to arrive in Chota Nagpur. In 1845 the first Christian missionaries (Lutheran), four of them from Gossner's Evangelical Lutheran Mission began to start their mission work.[35] This was followed by the Anglican Mission (Society for the Propagation of the Gospel) in 1869.[36] The third mission to arrive in Chota Nagpur was the Roman Catholic Mission on 24 November 1868. The Christian missions entered Chota Nagpur at a time when the inhabitant Tribals were passing through severe economic and social exploitation from the hands of the landlords and moneylenders. The society was in acute agrarian crisis. They were forced to sell their lands and became landless in their own land and subsequently reduced them to forced and bonded agricultural labourers. There was no limit of their exploitation. The people were finding it difficult to adjust to the new and changing conditions imposed on them by the outsiders. The people had found no suitable means to adapting to the new prevailing conditions. It was in this deplorable condition the Christian missions worked among these economically exploited and socially oppressed Mundas and the Oraons.

Their socio-political, economic and religious system began to disintegrate beginning from the 17th century. In 1585, the Raja of Chota Nagpur was made a tributary of the Moghul Emperor under Akbar. Due to non-payment of annual tribute to the Emperor[37] the Raja was imprisoned in 1616 till 1628. It was in prison that he developed to imprint new ideas which had a lasting effect on

[32] Webster, *Christian Community* ..., 62. See also Webster, *Dalit Christians* ..., 8-19; 46-52.

[33] Cf., Duncan B. Forrester, *Caste and Christianity* ..., 69-92.

[34] Joseph Bara, "Alien Construct and Tribal Contestation in Colonial Chhotanagpur: The Medium of Christianity," *Economic & Political Weekly* 44/52 (December 26, 2009 – January 1, 2010): 91.

[35] Cf., C.B. Firth, *An Introduction to Indian Church History* (Delhi: ISPCK, 2000), 197 (Hereafter referred to as C.B. Firth, *Church History*; J.W. Pickett, *Mass Movements* ..., 45-46. For further treatment on the Lutheran Mission, see Fidelis De Sa, *Crisis in Chota Nagpur: With Special Reference to the Judicial Conflict Between Jesuits Missionaries and British Government Officials, November 1889 - March 1890* (Bangalore: Redemptorist Publications, 1975), 72-110.

[36] Cf., C.B. Firth, *Church History* ..., 198; Stephen Neill, *A History of Christian Missions* (Baltimore: Penguin Books, 1964), 362; J. W. Pickett, *Mass Movements* ..., 46.

[37] The Moghul during this period was Jehangir and the Raja was Durga Sal.

the people.[38] Upon his return to Chota Nagpur in 1628, he assumed the title *Maharaja* and act as a King. He brought in Hindu castes people from outside Chota Nagpur to be at his service and eventually had intermarriages with them. The people had to pay to the outsiders for their services and when they could not pay in cash, the *Maharaja* handed over to the outsiders his right to supply from the villagers. This was a kind of service grants to be paid for the services rendered. At a later stage this practices led to the establishment of landlordism in Chota Nagpur. In no time the outsiders became their landlords. This gave rise to disputes between the landlords and the people. These changes impacted on the traditional way of life of the Mundas and the Oraons leading to agrarian troubles. The outsiders even introduced the new idea of rent reducing the people to the rank of rent-paying tenants. This suppressive measures and exploitations of the people resulted to migration of the Tribals to other parts of India.[39]

In 1765, the British[40] consolidated their power in Chota Nagpur by defeating Moghul Emperor. However, they first entered into the region only in 1772 when the *Maharaja* requested them to help him in a revenue matter. In the face of escalating Tribal resistance to the colonial rule, the colonial state was bent upon showing the tribes as barbarous.[41] The advent of the British colonialism resulted in the influx of Indian traders which added to the problems of the Tribals. The outsiders migrating into the region in large numbers and having greater economic stake, came to monopolize the expanded British bureaucracy at the crucial subordinate level.[42] The British people regarded the revenue collector (Zamindars) who were the outsiders as landlords, and the Tribals continued to lose their lands. The ruler of Chota Nagpur gave the traders the villages on temporary lease when he could not pay in cash for the goods he purchased from them. This eventually led the traders to become their landlords and finally ousted the Tribals from their villages. This loss of land was to have an effect on the social, political and religious lives of the Mundas and the Oraons.[43] The sudden changes in all aspects of their

[38] During his imprisonment in Gwalior he happened to meet some Hindu Kings and that shaped his ideas seeing the outside world. After his release from prison in 1628, in imitation of the Hindu Kings, he brought in Brahmins, Rajputs courtier and warriors, and a number of other things underlings belonging to various Hindu and Hinduised castes from outside Chota Nagpur. It is probably at this time that the Raja and his descendants became hinduised and through frequent intermarriage with Aryan families became Aryianized. He now began to act as a King. He even assumed, the title Maharaja. Cf., Fidelis De Sa, *Crisis in Chota Nagpur* ..., 34-35.

[39] Fidelis De Sa, *Crisis in Chota Nagpur* ..., 35-37. See also Pashupati Prasad Mahato, "In Search of Roots and Identity: The People of Chotanagpur now Domiciled in North Bengal and Assam," *Religion and Society* 37/3 (September, 1990): 54.

[40] For further treatment on the British administration and the sufferings of the Tribal people under their new administration, see Fidelis De Sa, *Crisis in Chota Nagpur* ..., 41-72.

[41] Joseph Bara, *Colonial Chhotanagpur* ..., 92.

[42] Joseph Bara, *Colonial Chhotanagpur* ..., 92.

[43] Cf., Fidelis De Sa, *Crisis in Chota Nagpur* ..., 38-39.

existences confused the people. The landlords in collaboration with the British colonial forces exploited the people to their best advantage. The Tribals could not bear the loss of land therefore revolted against the landlords in 1789, 1797, 1807, 1820 and 1832. The revolt in 1832 was more severe which was put down with the help of the British colonial power. The suppression actually became an opportunity to ruminate over the efficacy of the mode of violence for cultural rehabilitation and exploration of an alternative.[44] It was in this context when the people were finding difficulty to adjust to the new and changing conditions, the Christian missionaries came to Chota Nagpur.

The early missionaries played a dynamic role towards the uplift of the people by establishing schools, institutions, churches and hospitals. The education imparted by them helped the people understand their present position and the loss of their traditional rights and privileges.[45] The missionaries began to involve in their struggle for freedom and human dignity. The missionaries advised the people to fight legally in the court for their rights and justice which resulted positively in favour of the people. By 1856 the landlords had lost several court cases pertaining to land.[46] This timely help rendered to the people culminated to more people embracing Christianity. The people who became Christian obtained the help and advice of the missionaries in their court cases. The missionaries were regarded by the villagers as their defenders in their struggle. The missionaries began to give serious attention to the socio-economic problem of the people and tried to redefine missionary responsibility and strategy against this backdrop. They felt that it is the obligation of a Christian to involve in the struggle of the people to foster tranquility and social equality. In several ways and in the interest of the mission the missionaries tried their best to help sort out the problems of the people. In support of the people Rev. F. Batsch of the Gossner Mission, wrote to the deputy commissioner of Chota Nagpur explaining to the officials the traditional ideas governing the right of ownership in Chota Nagpur and also the forms of oppression which the landlords practiced on the people – both Christian and non-Christian.[47] Onasch of the same mission assisted the people in their "bodily and spiritual poverty" and took initiative in giving details of the evil inherent in the social condition of the people.[48]

Fr. Lievens the Jesuit missionary also did remarkable work to the struggle and uplift of the people. He himself was a good lawyer. He found that in such a context direct preaching and evangelism could not draw people's attention. Stephen

---

[44] Joseph Bara, *Colonial Chhotanagpur* ..., 92.

[45] Shivaji Koyal, "A Critique of the Missionary Movement in Chota Nagpur 1845-1900," *ICHR* 19/2 (December, 1985): 140-141.

[46] Fidelis De Sa, *Crisis in Chota Nagpur* ..., 84.

[47] The Calcutta Review, 135-136, quoted in Fidelis De Sa, *Crisis in Chota Nagpur* ..., 89-90.

[48] Papers Relating to Chotanagpur Agrarian Disputes, Vol. 1, quoted in Shivaji Koyal, *Missionary Movement* ..., 139.

Neill remarked that Lievens was on the side of the people on their campaign of disobedience to the unjust demands of the landholders and their agents.[49] He considered it his duty to see to both the spiritual and temporal welfare of the people.[50] On some occasion he would loan money to pay for litigation and would direct the people to honorable lawyers, advised the people to pay only the legal amount of rent and to insist on a receipt for the payments of rent, advised the people to take the landlords to court, and told the people to refuse to give bribe to the police officials.[51] Seeing this new positive development and the feeling of solidarity showed by the missionaries encouraged the people which ultimately resulted in large scale conversion. Conversion to Christianity increased rapidly not only in terms of the individual but the village as a whole.

However, there are some instances like losing certain court cases, *Bhuinari* land survey, and *Sardar* Movement where people revolted against the missionaries when they could not meet their aspirations which eventually led to leave the mission, developed suspicion, lost faith on the missionaries and alienated from them.[52] The *Sardars*[53] were active and under their influence some of the Christians lost hope of finding means of adaptation. Due to this reasons the missionaries by 1870 realized that the movement towards Christianity was a social movement. As long as they thought that the new religion was offering them protection and providing a means to adapting to the new conditions they embrace Christianity. The opposition of the landlords and the reaction of the government officials also

[49] Stephen Neill, *The Story of the Christian Church in India and Pakistan, Indian Edition* (Delhi: CLS - ISPCK, 1972), 113.

[50] Fidelis De Sa, *Crisis in Chota Nagpur* ..., 338.

[51] Cf., Fidelis De Sa, *Crisis in Chota Nagpur* ..., 124-127.

[52] A Lutheran missionary by the name Onasch, had done his best to help the people in their court cases but at the end could not meet all their aspiration. Perhaps they expected too much from him. As a result in 1878 three elders accused Onasch for not fulfilling his promise and left the mission. Several of the converts followed the examples of the elders. So also when they lost their lands through their fault they put the blame on the missionaries. This was happen in the *Bhuinari* land survey. The *Bhuinari* lands were the property of the Mundas and Oraons. When these lands fell into the hands of the landlords, the latter charged the aboriginals rent for them. The aboriginals regarded these lands as rent free. Besides, they claimed that they could not be disposed of them. To bring peace, it was necessary to find out which lands were *Bhuinari* and which were not. Therefore, the government ordered to prepare a register of all *Bhuinari* lands in 1858. This came into effect in 1869 by an Act called the *Bhuinari* Survey and Settlement Act or simply *Bhuinari* Settlement. Several of the people lost their lands through this survey. Even the Christians lost their lands. Among the Christians who lost their lands there grew a feeling of suspicion against the missionaries and lost faith on the missionaries. See Fidelis De Sa, *Crisis in Chota Nagpur* ..., 60-61; 99-102; Shivaji Koyal, *Missionary Movement* ..., 143-149.

[53] *Sardar* means a leader. The organizers of the movement called themselves or were called leaders. The movement consisted in collecting money from the Tribals to defray the expenses of sending petitions to the Government. The movement seems to have begun about 1866 or 1867. It is to be noted that, in time, all took part in the movement were called '*sardars*' and not merely the organizer. For detailed explanation see Fidelis De Sa, *Crisis in Chota Nagpur* ..., 111-115.

slowed down the work of the mission. Due to this reasons several missionaries had developed the thought that the Mundas and the Oraons became Christians not so much out of spiritual motives, but for the secular benefits they hoped to attain. This was necessary since the people were seeking a means of readjustment to a new situation created by the landlords and the British Empire.[54] However, when asserting that the spiritual element was present in the conversion movement, Fidelis De argued that: The Tribal people were looking for justice and human dignity in the face of oppression and exploitation. They could only achieve this goal as a community. And so when they were converted to Christianity, they came over either to obtain justice, or because they had already obtained it. And when they came over, they did so in groups – in families, in entire villages. This group movement was an expression of their closely knit social system and an answer to their need for readjustment. Only in such a group phenomenon could there be peace and harmony among the villagers at home; and only then could they find a group answer to the massive problems that surrounded them. Who would say that these were merely 'secular' reasons.[55]

Reading the history, it is evident that the Mundas and the Oraons converted to Christianity because it provided them the pivotal means to readjust in the new socio-economic conditions. People were desperately finding a means to adjusting to the new situation created by the landlords and the Britishers. They lost most of their lands at their hands. This lost brought about a drastic change in their socio-economic, political and religious systems. Christianity provided the required means of adaptation to the people. It is true that as long as the people felt that the mission was helping them to save their lands they joined the mission and when they felt that the mission is not protecting them they left the mission and sought aid from other means. Though the Christian missions did not offer the people the full means of adaptation to the new situation since by the time mission entered to their land people had lost most of their lands. However they played a significant role in helping the Tribals to readjust to their new conditions.[56] At times the government also asked the missionaries for their advice in formulating the laws. Joseph Bara opined that, "Christianity became a means for cultural restoration that would yield them their rights and human dignity. Their effort for recovery of the lost rights and dignity led them to the idea of autonomous status in the region."[57] Therefore, the conversion movement among the Mundas and the Oraons can be best explained in terms of Christianity providing them the means to adapt themselves to the new socio-economic situation.

---

[54] Fidelis De Sa, *Crisis in Chota Nagpur* ..., 159.

[55] Fidelis De Sa, *Crisis in Chota Nagpur* ..., 160.

[56] Fidelis De Sa, *Crisis in Chota Nagpur* ..., 332.

[57] Joseph Bara, *Colonial Chhotanagpur* ..., 94.

Conclusion

The study of the Christian conversion movements in the selected areas among the Dalits and Tribals in India was to find out the motives and theories behind the conversion history. This is to situate the conversion history among these people from their social context. As stated above several scholars and historians have undertaken this subject and construed it with several reasons and factors pertaining to conversion. Analyzing the theories on conversion movements among the Dalits and Tribals in India we find that it is very much integral to their struggle for social improvement. Most of the historians who have dealt with this issue like John C.B. Webster, G.A. Oddie, Dick Kooiman, Duncan B. Forrester, George Oommen, Fidelis De Sa, and J.W. Gladstone, agreed to it. In fact while investigating the conversion movement history their outcome were divergent within a specific social structure and people but without ignoring the spiritual and psychological forces their consensus is that they all advocated upward mobility, justice and identity as important factors in conversion movements among the Dalits and Tribals in India.

W.T.

Chapter 8

Theories and Motives of Conversion Movement Among the Nagas in Nagaland

It was Edward Winter Clark who introduced Christianity to the Nagas[1] - first among the Ao-Nagas in 1872. The dawn of Christianity not only ushered in transformation and development but also led to a large scale conversion. The Ao-Nagas were receptive to the new religion brought by the missionaries. As a result there was a massive conversion movement among the people. Due to political unrest in Nagaland, the missionaries were asked to leave by the Government of India in 1954. This chapter therefore is confined up until 1955 - the year the last missionary left the Ao-Naga Hills. The history of Christian conversion movement among the Ao-Naga people in Nagaland is being construed and credited by several writers to the Christian mission from the West. It was indeed due to the efforts made by the American Baptist Mission that a high degree of conversion movement took place among the native people. But the question is, were there any substantial contributions from the native people towards the conversion movement? Or was it purely through the works of western missionaries? These questions demand an in-depth investigation. The attempt here is to locate the contribution of the Traditional Ao-Naga Religion to conversion to Christianity.

[1] This chapter is restricted to the Ao-Nagas. Though it deals with just one Naga community in Nagaland, it can be inferred to the other communities also since all the Naga communities have certain affinities and similarities in their religious belief systems and practices.

Christian Mission

The Christian mission reached the Ao-Naga people in 1872. Historically, it was in 1839 that the American Baptist Missionary could establish contact with the Nagas through Mr. & Mrs. Miles Bronson. However, this mission was short-lived. The resumption of Naga Mission started only after the arrival of Rev. Edward Winter Clark to Sibsagar (Assam) in 1869. Therefore, it was Clark who re-introduced Christianity to the Nagas, first among the Ao-Nagas in 1872. Permanent mission station was established only in 1876. For more than eighty years the missionaries in turn served the Ao-Nagas. Since its inception until 1954, when the missionaries were forced to leave the Nagaland by the Government of India, nineteen (fourteen couples and five single ladies) American Baptist missionaries worked among the Ao-Nagas. The new religion brought by the Christian mission from the West was well accepted by the Ao-Nagas as well as the neighbouring tribes in Nagaland. Very soon there was massive Christian conversion movement among the people. The number of converts began to grow in most of the villages culminating to establishing several local churches. The native evangelists and pastors also played a significant role in the conversion history. The history of the Christian conversion movement is but a subject to ponder with wonder and admiration. Therefore, it is right to assert that the Nagas experienced the most massive movement to Christianity in all Asia, second to the Philippines. It is imperative at this point to ascertain the theories and their motives of conversion. The Christian mission played a dynamic role and made an immense contribution to the uplift of the Ao-Nagas. The establishment of schools, medical services, literature and reducing the native language to a written form were some of the notable contributions to the people.

Interrogating the Term Religion

The definitions and opinions on religion advocates that the essence of religion lies in the human inner experience. There is a realization that there is an absolute power which is superior to man. Therefore, there exists a sense of human dependence manifested in terms of prayer, sacrifice and ceremonies. The word religion in Ao-Naga is '*Yimsu*'. 'Yim' means 'village,' 'Su' means 'shawl.' Thus, *Yimsu* is something that covers the whole village and its inhabitants.[2] This definition gives the idea and concept that religion occupies a prominent central place in the total life of the Ao-Nagas. It is disheartening that the traditional Ao-Naga religion was characterized as animism by social scientists and scholars ignoring the very essence and structure that composed and held together the traditional Naga society from time immemorial. Two prominent western anthropological writers who worked among the Nagas commented on the Ao-Naga religion were J.P. Mills, who

---

[2] O. Alem Ao, *Tsungremology: Ao Naga Christian Theology* (Mokokchung: Clark Theological College, 1994), 2.

observed that "the religion of the Aos does not have a moral code but it is a mere system of ceremonies"[3] and also W.C. Smith stated that "the propitiation of the evil and capricious spirits is practically the sum and substance of their religion. There is no idea of worship or reverence; there is neither joy nor a feeling of religious consolation, as in Christianity. There is very little of morality attached to this religion."[4] These statements are incorrect and unjustified.

Religion for the Ao-Nagas is the guiding principle of the moral, ethical, cultural and social life of its people in terms of an individual's immediate relation to society and a cohesive force for the whole community.[5] In fact, the Ao-Naga religion had no written scripture, no texts, no creed, no doctrine but it was transmitted logically from generation to generation through oral tradition as part of her culture. On this line, Thanzauva rightly opined that the tribals do not depend on a written Scripture but on the experience of the peoples' encounter with their environment in their day to day life. Rather than reading written Scripture, tribals read nature and what happened to their own life in order to understand God's intention for them.[6] Text based religious traditions or in other words highly well written literature and document cannot be taken as a measuring rod of a people or religion. The Ao-Nagas cannot think of an external world separate from religion. For an Ao the whole being of a person comes under the purview of religion. There is no distinction or separation between secular and sacred. It is therefore, not justifiable to term the Ao-Naga religion as a religion without any moral code or does not have the idea of worship or reverence as was thought by the early scholars and writers. The religion of the Ao-Nagas can be best understood when taken into consideration the whole aspect of human existence in relation to political, social and cultural systems and not only on one aspect of emotional, spiritual or social life. The social, cultural and political organizational set-up of the people is depicted in their idea of God. It would be wrong to think that only the emotional or spiritual aspects of human are religious.

Ao-Naga Understanding of God and Incarnation: Conceptual Categories and Ideas

In the traditional Ao-Naga religious beliefs and practices the concepts of cosmology; God; Human Spirits and Souls; Heaven and Hell; Angel; Life after Death; Incarnation; Priesthood; Sacrifice; Salvation; Sin and Absence of

[3] J.P. Mills, *The Ao Nagas*, 2nd Edition (London: Macmillan & Co., Ltd., 1926; London: Oxford University Press, 1973), 215.

[4] W. C. Smith, *The Ao Naga Tribe of Assam: A Study in Ethnology and Sociology* (London: Macmillan and Co., Ltd), 76.

[5] Panger Imchen, *Ancient Ao Naga Religion and Culture* (New Delhi: Har-Anand Publications, 1993), 8.

[6] K. Thanzauva, *Theology of Community: Tribal Theology in the Making* (Aizawl: Academy of Integrated Christian Studies, 2004), 115.

Forgiveness of Sin, Eternal Life, etc., were there. In this chapter, we shall deal only the concept of God and Incarnation to situate as an example in understanding its conceptual categories and ideas in relation to Christianity.

God (*Tsungrem*)

In the traditional Ao-Naga religion the existence of God called *Tsungrem* was never been questioned. It is believed that God existed from time immemorial and humankind was at the mercy of God. For them *Tsungrem* is unique and incomparable, hence utmost reverence has to be bestowed on him. In the presence of *Tsungrem* an Ao stands in fear and reverence and yet, turns to him for protection, security, well-being and blessing. The existence of something supernatural, and something more than an impersonal power was being recognized as *Tsungrem* in the Ao-Naga traditional religion. Renthy Keitzar rightly observed that the tribal people's belief in High God, who is both personal and a Creator, and its similarity to biblical thinking makes it easy for them to accept Christian idea of God.[7] He further stated that the Nagas have a belief in a High God or Supreme Being (or some High Gods in some cases) who is believed to be the creator and dispenser of everything.[8] For the Ao-Nagas there is only one Supreme Being, though people addressed him by different names according to the different roles he plays - this means seasonal god/s. This subscribe to the idea that the Ao-Nagas belief in the existence of one God and hence monotheism like Christianity.

For more clarity on the understanding of a monotheistic God we can infer the following ideas. For instance, when people speak of the Supreme Being in relation to the heavenly elements such as the sun, the moon, rain, lightening, air and the solar system, they called him *Lungkitsungba* whose dwelling place is secured permanently in heaven above. When he is referred to in connection with the fortune of a person, he is called *Tiaba*, and when referred in relation to judgement in life after death, he is called *Meyutsungba/Motsungba*. These are different names but represent various manifestations of one *Tsungrem*, i.e., God. When the Ao-Nagas talked of the Supreme Being in relation to creation, the earth and vegetation, they called him *Lijaba*. The word *Tsungrem* is used for all that which manifests the supernatural be it animate or inanimate. It is because of this vague usage, descriptive or functional names were given to all supernatural manifestations in order to differentiate one deity from the other.[9] Therefore, the Ao-Nagas believed in a God above all creatures who is the provider, protector, sustainer and a righteous judge.

---

[7] Renthy Keitzar, "Tribal Cultural Ethos and Christianity in North East India," *ETC Journal*, No. 2 (January – May, 1988): 51.

[8] Renthy Keitzer, *In Search of a Relevant Gospel Message* (Guwahati: Christian Literature Centre, 1995), 21.

[9] O. Alem Ao, *Tsungremology* …, 15.

Evangelist Godhula's first preaching to the native people was also based on to firmly believe in the creator of all human beings who is the dispenser of all blessings. He preached that God the Father is Jehovah, the creator of both the heaven and earth.[10] The idea of one God who is in heaven or above the sky (*Anung Tsungrem* which means God of the sky) which was preached by the missionaries was not totally a new concept to the native people rather it was offering the same thing to them but in a new systematic form.

Conceptual Category of Incarnation vis-à-vis Christianity

Lijaba the God of Creator once visited *Chungliyimti* (name of a village) in a disguised form of a poor old man, unwanted, with sores over his body. In fact, the visitation of *Lijaba* to the people in a human form has a historical and theological significance. The mythology of *Lijaba*, though it is not fully developed can be used as a type for the incarnation of God in human form in Jesus Christ. In a strict sense therefore, God becoming man or God coming to the world in human form was totally not a new concept in the understanding of the Ao-Nagas about God. *Lijaba* is a God who brings prosperity and blessings. On the other hand cursed people for not giving due attention to him. Similarly in the teachings of Christianity the coming of Jesus Christ brought blessings, prosperity and eternal life to those who accepted him and condemned to those who rejected him. There is a striking similarity between Jesus Christ and *Lijaba* at least in its concept of coming to the humanity in a human form.

At the initial stage the missionary taught the native people the simple story of Jesus of Nazareth. The story of Jesus and his life and work was the main thrust of their preaching. The native people in fact eagerly accepted the good news of Jesus of Nazareth and even in their prayers they would enthusiastically pronounce *Yehovah Yeesu Kreesta* (Jehovah Jesus Christ).[11] Hence, when the missionaries started teaching about how God revealed himself in Jesus Christ to the humanity - the native people would not be surprised as this concept of incarnation was there in their philosophy of religion and mindset. The only difference in Christian teaching between the incarnate Christ and *Lijaba* was: Christ gives eternal life while *Lijaba* gives plenty of harvest and blessings of wealth and opposite to those who refuse him. Jesus of the Christians is what *Lijaba* is to the Aos, the only difference is that Christianity has a clearer teaching about the latter.[12] It is therefore, not impossible for an Ao-Naga to accept that God is incarnated in human form.

---

[10] *A Light to the Nagas* (Jorhat: Molungkimong Baptist Church, 1972), 13.

[11] Mary Mead Clark, *A Corner in India*, Reprint (Philadelphia: American Baptist Publication Society, 1907; Gauhati: Christian Literature Centre, 1978), 57, 104.

[12] Cf., Panger Imchen, *Ao Naga* ..., 76; O. Alem Ao, *Tsungremology* ..., 66; Takatemjen, *Studies on Theology and Naga Culture* (Mokokchung: Published by the Author, 1997), 65-71.

If a synthesis has to be drawn between the teachings of the gospel and the traditional Ao-Naga religion in regard to the understanding to humility, God becoming human, concept of poor, and acceptance of others there is no better instance than this mythology. The wisdom provided by the story of *Lijaba* to the people through their encounter had a bearing in their acceptance to the gospel. It could be because of these conceptual categories and ideas on the native people that the gospel could have had an easy penetration in the minds, thought and philosophy of the native people.

Conversion Movement: Theories and Motives

As noted, in the traditional Ao-Naga religious beliefs and practices the conceptual categories and ideas corresponded to the Christian teachings and doctrines. Many of these beliefs and practices are now abandoned and no more being practiced and observed in the community. Before the advent of western mission these beliefs and practices were the binding factors that kept the community alive and sustained. Looking at the traditional Ao-Naga religion, their understanding about God-Human-World relationship was very strong and firm in their philosophy of religion. These concepts and ideas are embedded in myth, oral history, folklore, traditional songs and rituals. They have their own construction of worldview which in the process weakened by the coming of Christian mission.

The coming of Christianity in the later part of the 19th century made a drastic reversal in the whole life aspect of the native people. The changes and progress impacted by Christianity to the people was significant on an individual, social and religious level. They found their old faith was not the ultimate goal in search for truth. However, there is a strong assertion that there were certain significant contributing factors for the conversion of the people, and this must be attributed to the native people's religious conceptual categories corresponding to the Christian religious categories. This conceptual categories and ideas are found in the traditional Ao-Naga religion. In no way whatsoever, it is the intention to legitimize the traditional religion and their belief and practices but to bring out its essence and philosophy in their religion that could have played a vital role in their conversion movement. It was due to their belief system and practices that they could develop certain concrete conceptual ideas in their mindset and philosophy which corresponded to the Christian teachings and understanding. In several ways they both complemented well in their interaction. No doubt, the traditional Ao-Naga religion lacks in several ways. They were not materially and ideologically sophisticated in modern sense. However, the deep religious philosophy of the people cannot simply be ignored when taking the task of conversion movement.

In fact, it was an encounter and interaction between the traditional religion and Christianity that culminated to the native people's conversion to Christianity. It would be appropriate to begin with the following statement: Upinder Singh states, "History is not one but many stories; only a few have been written. The challenges to build on the advances so far are many."[13] This statement calls the attention to look for the role and contributions of the ordinary people in writing an objective history. Richard Eaton viewed that "in most cases, conversion history has so far been looked from the perspective of the agent, i.e., the missionary who goes out and "converts" the "native" to his or her religion – rather than from that of the society undergoing change"[14] Immanuel David also rightly commented, "Too much history of Christianity has been from the standpoint of the 'shepherds' and too little from that of the 'flock'. However, it is in studying the activities of ordinary people that we can see most clearly the history of a past age."[15] These statements advocates to locating the role and contribution of the native people in the process of conversion and not from the stand point of the agent - the missionaries. Hence, this chapter intends to look the history from the perspective of the society that had contributed in the process of conversion to Christianity. Therefore, the traditional Ao-Naga religion has been taken as the focus of study to investigate its contribution in the conversion history.

As against the views expressed by others, it has been argued and substantiated that the traditional Ao-Naga religion was not a mere system of ceremonies but a distinctive religion, having all the phenomenal aspects of a 'true' religion.[16] However, it is important to note that when compared to the religion of Christianity the traditional religion falls short in its articulation and sophistication. The religion of Christianity was no doubt far superior in all levels of understanding. But the question is why such a large scale of Christian conversion movement occurred in this tiny and isolated land far from the modern civilization. At this point the contribution of their traditional religion becomes indispensable. Pre-Christian religious conceptual categories and ideas contributed to their conversion to Christianity. In this line of thought C. Lakra also opined that "there is a symmetrical relation between tribal religion and Christianity. There are elements of God the Father as creator, protector and redeemer from whom all blessings flow over the tribe, family, children, cattle, crops, fields and jungles."[17] The life of the Nagas or for that matter the Ao-Nagas as mentioned are so holistic and integrated that it is difficult to separate religion, culture, and nature from their very lives. For them religion is but life itself and not a dogmatic

[13] Upinder Singh, "Changing Interpretations of Early Indian History," *The Hindu*, 30 June 2008, 10.

[14] Richard M. Eaton, "Comparative History as World History: Religious Conversion in Modern India," *Journal of World History* 8/2 (1997): 244.

[15] S. Immanuel David, "History of Christianity in India: Changing Perspectives," *ICHR* 30/1 (June, 1986): 8.

[16] Renthy Keitzar, "A Study of the North-East India Tribal Christian Theology," in *Good News for North East India: A Theological Reader*, edited by Renthy Keitzar (Guwahati: The Christian Literature Centre, 1995), 34.

[17] C. Lakra, "Christianity and Tribal Identity," *Religion & Society* 36/2 (June, 1989): 36-37.

affirmation. Their construction of cosmology is that everything is interrelated and self-sustaining whole in the cosmos. Be it living or non-living thing, nature or creatures all are but interrelated and interdependent. This understanding affirms a symbiotic relationship in their existences. Even if it affects only one aspect of the structures it subsequently affects the whole system of structure. Downs therefore aptly remarked that "Tribal societies with their closely interrelated social, economic, political and cultural elements are particularly vulnerable to change, even when it affects only one aspect of their life."[18]

For a considerable period of time the Ao-Nagas as well as the other Naga tribes were living in isolation from the outside world. There was neither distinction nor classified category in the society – a casteless society. All were treated equally before the law. Since all are treated equally there were hardly any economic and social exploitations or disparities in the society. Therefore, the Nagas have never suffered from exploitation by merchants and money-lender which has beggared the lives of other Indian tribal groups.[19] They were also never having been intruded or proselytized by any text based religions. To this effect Frykenberg noted, "These were people who, for ages untold, had never been Sanskritized or Islamicized."[20] Nagas were perhaps content with their lives and existed independently though with limited options. The world for them was a restricted one – confined to their village. It was at this point both the Christian mission and colonial domination ventured into their domain. Their arrival re-structured the whole socio-religious and cultural set-up. This resulted in disruption of order in the traditional society. Nevertheless, it initiated the process of change and transformation. Christian mission and British administration brought the people into contact with liberal ideas of the west and eventually re-shaped their worldview and their ideological construction of life.

The Christian mission viewed conversion to Christianity as a transformed life. This means to adopt a new way of life preceding the old ways like the traditional belief system, culture and societal structure. This ideology amounted to the theory of social change. As a result, to become a Christian was to abandon their mentality, tradition, culture and customs. This is the reason why traditional cultures and customs had to be discarded that eventually led to weakening their whole social structure. Hence W.C. Smith rightly remarked "Christianity has weakened their taboos and their system of social control."[21] In the case of the British administration they introduced the new value system by introducing modern

---

[18] F.S. Downs, "Administrators, Missionaries and a World Turned Upside Down: Christianity as a Tribal Response to Change in North East India," *ICHR* 15/2 (December, 1981): 102.

[19] "Some Notes on Religious, Social and Cultural Change in Nagaland," *Religion & Society* 8/3 (October, 1961): 38.

[20] Robert Eric Frykenberg, *Christianity in India: From Beginning to the Present* (New York: Oxford University Press, 2008), 444.

[21] W.C. Smith, *Ao Naga...*, 190.

communication, transportation, trade, administration, money economy, etc. It touched the whole structure of political, social, economic, culture and religious realm of the people. These developments affected the worldview of the native people. It is to be noted that the social, cultural and political organizational set-up of the people is depicted in their idea of God. Since all the system is interrelated, a change in any of the aspects would adversely affect the whole societal and religious structures. Religion therefore, was the determining causative factor in their whole realm of existence. This was their established philosophy wherein in the process encountered with the modern world that initiated the whole process of change. They have their own established traditional construction of cosmology. But with the coming of the Christian mission and the British administration this established cosmology was reconstructed and initiated the process of social and cultural change through modernization. In the process, conversion to Christianity became inevitable.

They found themselves in a completely new social order. The whole fabric of traditional society had been reshaping for the first time in years. They have now felt and experienced the dynamics of change in their societal and cultural structure. In the process of this sudden change they found that their aged-long traditional cosmology was inadequate to explain the whole process of development and philosophy of life. Christianity presented to them a highly articulated cosmological conception. Downs rightly commented on the point in which the old order could not cope with new order:

> It could not provide the people with a sufficiently advanced and flexible ideology to accommodate themselves to the new order. All peoples required a world-view that provides them with an explanation, a rationalization of their life. The traditional primal world-view simply was not large enough for the new situation in which they were increasingly brought into contact.[22]

They have by now conceived of themselves as part of a larger whole, which had mostly been regarded as something alien and separate, and with the affairs of which they had little concern.[23] They became acutely conscious of the world at large. A shift from the old society to a new one emanated through the encounter with the West created a space for cultural, socio-economic and political re-adjudgement. It was in this context that they found a more advance and satisfactory cosmology in Christianity. Downs therefore, aptly remarked that "Christianity provided an ideology that helped the tribal people maintain their

---

[22] Downs, *Administrators, Missionaries…*, 110.

[23] Alemchiba Ao, "Problems of Re-adjudgement to a New Situation with Special Reference to the Naga Tribe," in *Tribal Situation in India*, edited by K. Suresh Singh (Shimla: Indian Institute of Advanced Study, 1972), 480.

identity in the face of serious erosions of their traditional religious, social and political institutions."[24]

Downs statement is certainly and undisputedly true. He advocates the theory of acculturation in relation to the whole process of change and conversion to Christianity in the Naga society. Christianity in fact became the primary agent of acculturation. He further states, "Under the circumstances (this means socio-cultural change) it was inevitable that Christianization appeared to be most attractive option."[25] In fact, since there were no other religions it was obvious that they embraced Christianity. But the point is, Downs had ignored or did not give much attention to the religious dimension and its contribution in the conversion movement. He gave more emphasis and attention to the factors leading to conversion thereby ignored the aspect of religion which was an important component to their conversion history. It has been made clear that in the tribal society all the structures are highly interrelated and has religious connotations and significance. Everything comes within the parameter of religion. Therefore, the aspect of religious belief and system should be given importance in analyzing the conversion movement of the native people. In fact, Religious change or for that matter the conversion movement cannot be purely the monopoly of social or cultural change. The dynamics of Ao-Naga religious belief system and practices should be considered in the study of the conversion movement since it permeates the whole human existence. The traditional religious conceptual ideas and categories indeed facilitated conversion to Christianity. Therefore, Richard Eaton rightly argued that it would be wrong to see Naga conversions simply as a function of social change.[26]

It is therefore, imperative to see the perspective of the society which is undergoing change and in the process what exactly is changing. A particular society or a social group though at times was being imposed does not merely accept a new religion without a concrete reason. There are certainly several reasons for accepting a new religion. That reason/s needs to be analyzed to determine as to why they accepted the new religion. History is being constructed many a time from the view point of the deliverer/agent/shepherd rather from that of the receiver or flock. So, looking the history from the point of receiver or flock will give a clearer picture of reciprocity in the interaction between the deliverer and the receiver. We should therefore, adopt the perspective of the society actually undergoing change and see conversion not as passive acceptance of a monolithic,

---

[24] Downs, *Administrators, Missionaries…*, 105.

[25] Downs, *Administrators, Missionaries…*, 111.

[26] Richard M. Eaton, "Religious Conversion in Nagaland," in *Encounter Between Gospel and Tribal Culture*, edited by A. Wati Longchar (Jorhat: Tribal Study Centre Eastern Theological College, 1999), 14.

outside essence, but as creative adaptation of the unfamiliar to what is already familiar, a process in which the former may change to suit the latter.[27]

Since all the structures are interrelated and the religion binds all those structures in the Ao-Naga society, the role and contribution of the traditional religion becomes apparent and pertinent in the movement of conversion to Christianity. The Christian mission came with a set of well established doctrine to convert the receiver. All the process of change in the societal structure comes within the purview and scheme of the Christian missionizing since they viewed conversion to a theory of social change. Their sole objective was therefore to baptize the new converts[28] and to introduce a new way of life style. As stated, for the missionaries conversion should find expression in a transformed life which means a new mode of life. The outlook changes were therefore became inevitable for the native people. This ultimately initiated the whole process of change in the Ao-Naga society. Conversion in a strict sense was essentially a religious issue but it encompassed the whole aspect of one's or community's life.[29] The point to underscore here is that, it was the encounter between Christianity with the traditional religion that ignited the changes in the society and concurrently ushered a new movement towards Christianity.

It was in such a context in which religious change or for that matter conversion to Christianity took place that emanates through the changed experience of social relation and structure. When a community is widening its social contacts, relationships and boundaries due to social change[30] it would take the form of conversion since religion permeates the whole aspect of life. In the case of the Ao-Nagas it is Christianity that facilitated the basic tools and religious quest for them. Hence, it is right to advocate that it was an interaction between the Christian religious categories and the traditional Ao-Naga religious categories that facilitated the change and concurrently the conversion process. A society or an individual responds or acts according to their constructed worldview. This worldview constitutes people's reflecting upon life itself. The cognitive realm developed through the existential situations paved them to formulate their conceptual categories and ideas. In the process this facilitates them to explain, predict and control the immediate phenomenal world. However, their encounter with the advanced world weakened their whole worldview and philosophy. In Christianity they found a more refined and defined worldview. The encounter

---

[27] Richard, *Religious Conversion*..., 1.

[28] Cf., J.P. Mills, *Ao Nagas*..., 412.

[29] Cf., Lal Dena, *Christian Missions and Colonialism: A Study of Missionary Movement in North East India with Particular Reference to Manipur and Lushai Hills, 1894-1947* (Shillong: Vendrame Institute, 1988), 86.

[30] Cf., Richard, *Religious Conversion*..., 5; George Oommen, "Re-reading Tribal Conversion Movements: The Case of the Malayarayans of Kerala, 1848-1900," *Religion & Society* 44/2 (June, 1997): 67.

broadened their perspective in perceiving the world beyond their limited construction and acknowledged the role of the Supreme Being in all its dynamics. Nevertheless, it should not be overlooked that the Ao-Naga conceptual categories and ideas corresponded with the Christian categories and ideas and found fuller expression in the Christian religion.

Conclusion

The subject in question is to analyze the contribution of the traditional religion to conversion movement. It has been analyzed comprehensively that in the traditional Ao-Naga religion, their perception about God (Supreme Being), the world (origin of the universe), the concepts of the belief in an individual soul, life after death, sin, salvation, sacrifice, incarnation, evil spirits, Lord's Day, heaven and hell, etc., were upheld firmly. In fact, these are some of the important conceptual categories and ideas of the native people that facilitated to respond positively to Christianity. These traditional religious categories were continuous in its essentials with the Christian religious categories. It has therefore, a strong historical and theological implication which finds its expression in the history of the conversion movement without much resistance. They do not have a written scripture, dogma or creeds that facilitate a systematic exposition about these. But the whole concepts and ideas are embedded in the myth, oral history, folklore, traditional songs and rituals. There were indeed differences in specific details in their interpretation and exegesis of theological ideas and concepts, yet both (i.e., Christianity and traditional religion) presentations found significant similarities. They both found a place of convergence in their religious interaction. In Christianity the native people found more adequately relevance in their quest for life and for the hope of the future. Thus, in the context of the changing scenario their traditional religious belief system became inadequate to respond effectively. It was Christianity that played the role of a facilitator in presenting the required means and methods to the native people. The material comfort, benefits and advancement which the new religion had brought with it were also really crucial in the minds of the native people. Christian mission indeed accommodated and identified with the religious categories, ideas and concepts of the traditional religion. This gives us a clear idea that the traditional Ao-Naga religion contributed positively to their conversion to Christianity.

W.T.

Chapter 9

Christianity and its Impact on the Tribes of NEI

Whether the record of location is a mistaken one or not, the earliest record of Christian presence in NEI is dated back to the 17th and 18th Centuries. According to Milton S. Sangma, "the earliest Christian contacts with North-East India were made by the Roman Catholic missionaries and the first Christian Communities in North-East India were also the Roman Catholics."[1] It has been recorded that there was flourishing community of 7,000 Christians at a place called Rangamati in Goalpara District of Lower Assam.[2] The second earliest record of the presence of a Christian (Catholic) community is at Bondashill in the Cachar District of present Assam,[3] and a very little known Catholic community of Mariamnagar in

[1] Milton S. Sangma, *History of American Baptist Mission in North East India* (1836-1950), vol. I (New Delhi: Mittal Publications, 1987), 16-17.

[2] For different records on this, see F. S. Downs, "Rangamati: A Christian Community in North East India during the Seventeenth and Eighteenth Centuries," *Indian Church History Review* XII/2 (Dec. 1978): 88-99.; Sangma, *History of American Baptist Mission*..., 15. Here one must make a note that whether the place called "Rangamati" of those days was in Assam proper is a matter of dispute. According to David R. Syiemlieh and Menamparampil, this place is not Goalpara of Assam but of Cooch Bihar in present North Bengal. Cf. David R. Syiemlieh, *A Brief History of the Catholic Church in Nagaland* (Shillong: Vendrame, 1990), 36.; Thomas Menamparampil, *Church in North-East India: A Study* (n.p., 1974), 17. It is in fact surprising that such a great moment of history which might have threatened the culture of Assam was not recorded anywhere in the Assam *Buranjis*. Therefore, from the various stories and folk songs of the Bangladeshi cultures in relation to a place called "Ranga-mati" (colour-soil or coloured soil), it is more likely that the place was not in Assam but the Chittagong Hill Tracts of Bangladesh.

[3] According to Sangma, the Catholic community of Bondashill exists till today. For further account of the origins, development and remnants of this community, see Becker, *Early History of*

Agartala of present Tripura.[4] Surprisingly, these communities did not leave any trace and Christianity did not spread. Downs assumes that "these communities seem to have been preoccupied with their own affairs and took no initiative in the later spread of Catholic Christianity in the North East."[5] Moreover, they were all remnants of Christian soldiers of Portuguese origin[6] who were under the service of Mughal Emperor and being outsiders they could not make any impact on the local inhabitants.[7]

Arrival of the Modern Mission in NEI

The entry of Christianity and its growth in the region has to be understood from the perspective of relationship between British Administration and Christian mission, in a broader sense, the Church and State relation in British India. Christianity entered the NEI particularly the hills through the shadow of British Administration. It was the British Administration that first entered the difficult terrain with certain political and economical gains.[8] When the administration had smoothed the surface, the Church went into action and sowed the seeds of Christianity in the name of civilisation. According to Barpujari, "the Cross not unoften followed the British flag."[9] It has been observed that in different capacities,

---

the Catholic Missions…, 99-108.

[4] Syiemlieh notes that the Church historians have made no mention of this community. The only reference to them till date is found in Sambhu C. Mookerjee, *Travel in Bengal: Calcutta to Independent Tipperah* (Calcutta, 1887), 213-237. Syiemlieh, *A Brief History of the Catholic Church in Nagaland,* 36. Also see David R. Syiemlieh, "Mariamnagar: An Ancient Christian Settlement in Tripura," *Indian Church History Review* 28/ (1994): 15-21.

[5] F.S. Downs, *History of Christianity in India: Northeast India in the Nineteenth and Twentieth Centuries,* vol. 5, part 5 (Bangalore: The Church History Association of India, 1992), 65.

[6] Not only soldiers, but there were also two Portuguese Jesuit travelers, namely Fr. Stephen Cacella and Fr. John Cabral, who came to Pandu and Hajo in 1626 A.D. A letter written by Cacela on 4th October, 1627 mentions that they came searching for a route to an unknown kingdom called "Cathay" later identified as Potente (Bhotana or Bhutan) or Tibet and China where Portuguese missionaries introduced Christianity in about 13th century and by the next century the number of Catholic Christians were so great that even an Archbishop was appointed for Cambaluc (Khan-Balig or Khan's town). This letter was originally published in Edward Maclagan, *The Jesuits and the Great Moghul* (London: Burns Oates and Washbourne Ltd., 1932). The same was reproduced in C. Wessels, *Early Jesuit Travelers in Central Asia, 1603-1721* (Hague: Martinus Nickhoff, 1924), 136 f.; K. Barua produced the English translation of the old Portuguese by Araujo in his article, "Seventeenth Century Portuguese Travelers in Assam," in T*he Journal of the Assam Research Society 3* (Oct., 1937), 87-91, which is reproduced in a compiled book, *Studies in the Early History of Assam,* 154-160. For further details, see Barua, 154 ff. Downs, "Rangamati: A Christian Community in North East India during the Seventeenth and Eighteenth Centuries," 89.; Sangma, *History of American Baptist Mission…*, 14.

[7] Cf. Downs, "Rangamati…," 89.

[8] In fact, political, economic developments and Christianity went together into the frontier people. Cf. Syiemlieh, *A Brief History of the Catholic Church in Nagaland,* 34.

[9] Barpujari, *Assam in the Days of the Company (*1826-1858), 300.

both administration and Christian mission have contributed towards the development and civilisation of various tribes. Chaube categorises the contribution of the British Administration into four sectors: the establishment of law and order, improvement in communication, introduction of money-economy in the remote areas and the creation of vested interests. But "the government contribution to the material culture of the hills peoples was almost nil.... Consequently, the hills people got only half-educated. The task of acculturation, on the subjective level, was almost entirely left to the Church of various denominations."[10] In a way, the lack in administration was filled by mission. Though both had their own interests, in certain limited areas they complemented each other. In Downs words, "Government found the missions useful, or so they hoped, in pacifying the hills tribes and providing education at minimal cost to itself; the missions found the government useful in underwriting, in many cases, their educational work and in providing security for both themselves and their converts."[11]

Nevertheless, the entrance of missionaries into the hill areas was controlled by the British administration, particularly through the Inner Line regulations. As per the general rule of the Government, only one mission was allowed to work in each Hill District. The Government always kept a watchful eye on missionary activity and their permission had first to be sought before evangelisation works were started. For which mission agencies had generally agreed "not to encroach upon each other's fields."[12] This policy consequently worked in favour of the older Protestant missions, the American Baptist, Welsh Presbyterian and British Baptist.[13] The American Baptists were allotted the Naga Hills, the Brahmaputra valley and the Garo Hills; the Welsh Presbyterians were entrenched in the Khasi Hills and the North Lushai Hills and the Roman Catholics missionaries were permitted only to work in the hills areas of present Meghalaya. Chaube sates that "the Catholics were, however, in the British days, confined mainly to Shillong, and could enter deeper into the hills only after independence" and interestingly even "the London Baptist Mission somehow lost Government patronage in Assam, and could enter only the South Lushai Hills which had been with Bengal at the beginning of administration."[14] Further, as regards such control over the field of mission work, Chaube comments that "it appears that Government both of British India and of independent India have followed a discreet licensing policy in respect of the Church."[15] Amidst such circumstances, the NEI was exposed to six

---

[10] S. K. Chaube, *Hills Politics in North East India* (Calcutta: Orient Longman, 1973), 42.

[11] Downs, *History of Christianity in India: Northeast India in the Nineteenth and Twentieth Centuries,* 30.

[12] Cf. Indian Statutory Commission, XIV, 106-107. As found in Syiemlieh, *A Brief History of the Catholic Church in Nagaland,* 35.

[13] Cf. Downs, *History of Christianity in India...*, 21-22.

[14] Chaube, *Hills Politics...*, 42.

[15] Ibid.

different streams of Christian Mission during 19th century – Serampore, American Baptist, Welsh Presbyterian, Roman Catholics, Anglican and Lutherans. All these missions entered into the region at the backdrop of political situation.

The Serampore Mission

Right after the passing of the Charter Act to permit missionaries to preach the Gospel in India in 1813, the Serampore Mission began to take an interest in the Khasi hills. The very same year, Carey received a letter from W.N. Garrett, the Judge of Sylhet suggesting of sending someone to evangelise several hundred Khasi tribes who were told to be the refugees from inter-tribal warfare in the adjoining hills. Garrett proposed that "two or three hundred of the fugitives should be made Christians at once by baptism and instructed afterwards."[16] Accordingly, Carey agreed to send a missionary – not a foreign missionary but a local man, Krishna Chandra Pal, the first Serampore convert. He took along Gora Chand, a local Christian as his assistant and landed to Pandua, Cherrapunjee of present Meghalaya via Sylhet. As per his letter to a man in England, within 18 months he baptised seven members, in his own words, "four Sepoys, two natives of Khasis and one of Assam"[17] were brought to believe in the Lord Jesus. However, Pal's mission and Serampore mission as a whole sustained only for a short period (1811-1837/38). It was ineffective without much impact on the lives of the people as it was expected by the British administration and missionaries. Nevertheless, one of the good things the mission did was the translation of the New Testament into Assamese (1819), Khasi (1824), Manipuri (1827) languages and the entire Bible into Assamese in 1833.[18]

The American Baptist Mission

The misfortune of the Serampore mission led the American Baptist Mission to break through in Assam. Though it was a bypassing mission,[19] the ABM occupied the region in 1836.[20] The ABM missionaries first set their feet on this land with the arrival of Nathan Brown and Oliver Cutter with printing press on 23 March

---

[16] Baptist Missionary Society, "Periodical Accounts related to Serampore Mission," IX (Jan-March, 1822), 7. As cited in Sangma, *History of American Baptist Mission*...,17.

[17] John Hughes Morris, *The History of the Welsh Calvinistic Methodists' Foreign Mission, to the end of the Year 1904* (London, Carnarvon: 1910), 71. As cited in Sangma, *History of American Baptist Mission*...,18.; Downs, History of Christianity in India..., 66.

[18] Downs, *History of Christianity in India*...,17-22.

[19] The missionaries were not prompted to plunge into the mission work in this region but only as a means of entering into Northern Burma and china. Cf. Sangma, *History of American Baptist Mission*...,28.; Also see Barpujari, *Assam in the Days of the Company* (1826-1858), 301. According to Downs, "the first American Baptist stations in the North East were not established in order to evangelize the peoples of that area, but as strategic outposts for reaching the Shan tribes of Northern Burma and Southern China". Downs, *History of Christianity in India*..., 70.

[20] Cf. Sangma, *History of American Baptist Mission*..., 23.

1836.[21] Invited by the commissioner, Francis Jenkins, to undertake a work among the Khamtee and Singpho tribes, the first missionaries arrived at Sadiya at the eastern extremity of the Brahmaputra valley.[22] Initially, they stationed in Namsang – a Naga village in the Tirap District of present Arunachal Pradesh, but the missionaries turned their attention to the Assamese people of the Brahmaputra valley. The mission succeeded in baptising the first Assamese convert, Nidhiram on 13th June 1841.[23] A Baptist Church was established in December 1945 and the two branches were organised in the same year in Nagaon and Sibsagar.[24] However, "the Assamese for whom the mission had yielded Sadiya and Jaypur...failed to accept Christianity."[25] Yet, with persistent spirit, the missionaries founded some of the unfamiliar institutions of the time, like orphanages, hospitals, schools, literary and vocational centres for both boys and girls that invaluably contributed to the Assamese society. Later, two Garos, namely Omed and his nephew Ramkhe were baptised on 8 Feb, 1863 at Gauhati[26] which marks as beginning of ABM mission among the hill tribes.

Welsh Presbyterians

Thomas Jones and his wife arrived at Cherrapunji on 2nd June, 1841 and with much difficulty they succeeded in converting two Khasis – U Amor and U Rajon. They were baptised on 8th March, 1846 and the Nongsawlia Church was established.[27] The mission was extended to Mizo Hills. D.E. Jones accompanied by a Khasi, Rai Bhajur arrived at Aizawl in 1897. The first two Mizo Christians – Khuma and Khara were baptised in the summer of 1899.[28]

---

[21] Gammel William, *History of the American Baptist Mission* (1850), 21-3. As referred in Barpujari, *Assam in the Days of the Company (1826-1858),* 301.; Swarna Lata Baruah, *A Comprehensive History of Assam* (New Delhi: Munshiram Manoharlal Publishers, 1985), 12.

[22] Downs, *History of Christianity in India...*, 69.

[23] F. S. Downs, *The Mighty Works of God. A Brief History of the Council of Baptist Churches in North East India: The Mission Period, 1836-1950* (Gauhati: CLC, 1971), 31.

[24] Downs, *History of Christianity in India...*, 70.; Barpujari, *Assam in the Days of the Company* (1826-1858), 302.

[25] Victor Hugo Sword, *Baptist in Assam: A Century of Missionary Service (1836-1936)* (Chicago, 1935), 119. As cited in Barpujari, *Assam in the Days of the Company (1826-1858),* 302. In fact, the Christian missionaries miserably failed in their mission among the Assamese. A.K. Gurney observed that, "Assamese are apparently unimpressive; preaching and talking to them seem to no effect on them.... In fact they have an accommodating theory that all religions are true 'for the European's they say Christianity is good; for the Hindoo, Hindooism; for the Mussalman, Muhammedanism'". "Hindoos in Assam," The Baptist Missionary Magazine, (August 1877). As cited in Barpujari, *Assam in the Days of the Company (1826-1858),* 305. For further reasons of failure in Assam mission, see Barpujari, 305ff.

[26] For detail account about their conversion, see Downs, *The Mighty Works of God...*, 47-53.

[27] Cf. Morris, *The History of the Welsh Calvinistic Methodists' Foreign Mission...*, 116-7.

[28] Downs, *History of Christianity in India...*, 84.

Roman Catholics

Though the oldest Christians who existed in the region belonged to the Catholic community which dated back to early 17th century, the entry of the modern Catholic mission is much later than the Protestants. Syiemlieh writes that "it is ironic that the Catholics, the first Christian Church to have come into the Northeast took as long as it did to join the Protestant missions in taking Christ to the people."[29] One of the reasons is that their mission to the NEI was a by-passing and unintentional mission.[30] Fr. Otto Hopfenmueller along with Fr. Angelus Muenzloher and Bro. Marianus Schumm and Bro. Joseph Bächle set foot in Gauhati, Assam on 21 February, 1890 which marks the beginning of modern Catholic Mission in North East India.[31] There was a phenomenal growth of Catholic Church in entire NEI after the independence. The independence of India opened door for the Catholic Church to penetrate even to some of the dominant Protestant areas such as Nagaland.[32]

Anglicans

Although, the Anglican clergy were the first to come to Assam with political support and financial grants, they showed very little interest in the evangelisation of the native people for a long time.[33] In fact, there were no Anglican missionaries as such in the North-East. But the Anglican Church, as per Wyld, has been working in Assam since 1951,[34] through the chaplains in the tea gardens and military camps. But there was no success story of evangelisation by this mission agency. Till the close of the century there were hardly 500 local Christians.[35] However, one of the most remarkable works done by this mission is the translation of the New Testament into Kachari language and production of a major anthropological study by Sydney Endle[36] who arrived as a tea garden chaplain in 1864.

---

[29] Syiemlieh, *A Brief History of the Catholic Church in Nagaland...*, 35.

[30] Cf. C. Becker, *Early History of the Catholic Missions in Northeast India (1598-1890)*, ed. F. Leicht and S. Karotemprel, trans., F. Leicht and S. Karotemprel (Shillong: Vendrame, 1989), 94-99.

[31] For detail study on this, see C. Becker, *History of the Catholic Missions in North East India, 1890-1915*. Translated by G. Stadler and S. Karotemprel, edited by G. Stadler and S. Karotemprel (Calcutta: Firma KLM Pvt. Ltd., 1980), 5-10.; George Kottupallil, "A Historical Survey of the Catholic Church in Northeast India from 1627 to 1969," in *The Catholic Church in Northeast India,* 1890-1990 (A Multidimensional Study), ed. S. Karotemprel (Shillong/Calcutta: Vendrame/Firma KLM Pvt. Ltd., 1993), 35.

[32] Cf. Syiemlieh, *A Brief History of the Catholic Church in Nagaland*, 38.

[33] Cf. Mathew Muttumana, *Christianity in Assam and Inter-Faith Dialogue: A Study on the Modern Religious Movements in North East India* (Indore/Pune: Satprakashan Sanchar Kendra/ Ishvani Kendra, 1984), 124.

[34] Cf. Downs, *History of Christianity in India...*, 88.

[35] Cf. Ibid., 89.

[36] Sidney Endle, *The Kacharis (Bodo)* (Originally published in 1911, reprint. Delhi: Low Price Publications, 1990).

Lutherans

The Lutheran mission in Assam faced unfortunate circumstances caused by other late-comer missions. Lutheran mission in Assam was started by Mr. Hesselmeyer, the first Lutheran missionary, at Tezpur in 1860. However, within two years, it came into end as the founder himself joined the SPG Mission in 1862.[37] Many of the Adivasi tea garden workers were Lutherans. But due to lack of care, many of them went back to their traditional faiths and many have joined other Churches.[38] The two Lutheran Churches – Gossner Evangelical Lutheran Church (GELC) and Northern Evangelical Lutheran Church (NELC) were at work in Assam at the close to 19th century. The later Church belongs to the Scandinavian mission.[39] Both the Churches are basically from Bihar which came following the Santhal immigrants in Assam. The Churches were established in various tea gardens. Along the tea gardeners, the local tribes – Boros and Garos also embraced Christianity propagated by the Lutheran mission.[40] At present, there are more than five hundred Lutheran congregations in NEI altogether.[41]

One of the notable phenomena at this point is that Christianity entered in the region with multi-denominational backgrounds. Apart from the above-mentioned mother denominations, there were numerous new missions[42] and sectarian groups,[43] as they are called, which flocked into the region after World War

---

[37] M.E. Gibbs, *The Anglican Church in India, 1600-1970* (Delhi: n.p., 1972), 241.

[38] In fact, the other Churches such as Baptist and Anglican established their own Christian communities at the expense of the Lutherans, although the Lutherans under the Gossner Mission had practiced great tolerance towards the other Sister-Churches. Cf. Hans Lokies, *Hundert Jahre Gossnersche Mission* (Berlin-Friedenau, 1936), 11.

[39] A Norwegian missionary, Lars Olsen Skrefsrud and a Danish missionary Hans Peter Boerresen opened the first mission station in Koroya near Dumka, Santhal Parganans in 1867. Three Santhals were baptized in 1869 namely, Sriram, Jogot and Raghu. Cf. M.M. Tudu, "Evangelisch-Lutherische Kirche im Nordlichen Indien," in *Evangelische Kirche in Indien*, ed, H.Grafe (Erlangen,1981), 250-51.

[40] The first Boro convert into Lutheran Church in Assam was Tekhla Boro who was baptized on 7th January, 1888. N. Borgoary, *Souvenir, First Centenary Jubilee 1888-1988* (Bongaigaon: Bongaigaon Diocese, 1988), 70.

[41] This includes all the Lutheran Churches within Northern Evangelical Lutheran Church (NELC) and the recently (2003) organised Evangelical Lutheran Church in the Himalayan States (ELCITHS).

[42] Such as Australian Baptist Mission, the General Conference Baptist Mission, the Baptist Mid-Mission and Salvation Army. Cf. Lal Dena, *Christian Missions and Colonialism: A Study of Missionary Movement in North East India: With Particular Reference of Manipur and Lushai Hills, 1894-1947* (Shillong: Vendrame Institute, 1988), 65-68.

[43] For instance, Seventh Day Adventists and various streams of Pentecostals such as Assemblies of God, the Unitarian Pentecostal Church and the resultant indigenous Pentecostals. For their activities, particularly in Mizoram, see C. L. Hminga, *The Life and Witness of the Churches in Mizoram* (Serkawn: Literature Committee Baptist Church Mizoram, 1987), 198, 199-201, 228-30, 256-61, 339 and 340-1.

II. The Christian missions were established not only in line with denominations, but also in line with ethnic groups. In the early stages, Christianity even played a divisive role among the tribes. Due to denominational loyalties, Christianity could not transcend the ethnic loyalties as well. One can observe two kinds of divisions. The first kind involved division between different ethnic groups and the second kind is between Christians and non-Christians that interrupted the traditional tribal society. As the number of Christian increased, the first kind of division got intensified.[44] The replica of the former is realised today in various inter-ethnic conflicts in the region.

Resistance

The entry of Christianity into the region in the initial stages was not free from resistance. The British rule as well as the introduction of Christianity to the hill tribes was viewed as a threat to the traditional way of life and social order in its initial stage. History records reactions to these changes even through violent resistance.[45] One of the first manifestations of resistance came from the chiefs of the various tribal societies. In Manipur, this resistance to the spread of new faith was sometimes even supported by the British officers.[46] As far as the chiefs were concerned, Christianity caused a social and cultural dislocation among the people. In tribal society, the chiefs had position and temporal powers through performing indigenous customary rites. If the people embraced Christianity, it automatically led to the loss of their ritualistic privileges and real temporal power. For instance, in the Lushai Hills, where Christianity has achieved the highest record of success in India, "the chiefs, the traditional rulers", according to McCall, "who being, on Lushai standards, comparatively rich, were less ready to give up their standards, their *Zu* (rice beer), and their sacrifices. The main mission impact fell upon the ordinary people."[47]

---

[44] For instance, the American Baptist Mission in Nagaland has formed 14 Baptist Associations as per the 14 different Naga tribes. 1. The Ao Baptist Association, 2. The Angami Baptist Association, 3. The Lotha Baptist Association, 4. The Chakhesang Baptist Association, 5. The Sema Baptist Association, 6. The Kuki Baptist Association, 7. The Rengma Baptist Association, 8. The Zeliangrong Baptist Association, 9. The Sangtam Baptist Association, 10. The Konyak Baptist Association, 11. The Chang Baptist Association, 12. The Phom Baptist Association, 13. The Yimchunger Baptist Association, 14. The Kheamungan Baptist Association. For exhaustive study on the Baptist Missions in Nagaland, see Downs, *The Mighty Works of God...*,; P. T. Phillip, *The Growth of the Baptist Church in Nagaland* (Guwahati: CLC, 1976), 73-172.; Sangma, *History of American Baptist Mission...*, 218-272.

[45] For instance, there were major armed conflicts such as Anglo-Khasi War (1829-33), the Jaintia Resistance (1860-62), the Khonoma Uprising (1878), the Kuki Rebellion (1919-20), and the Heraka Cult rebellion (1930).

[46] Cf. Downs, *History of Christianity in India: Northeast India in the Nineteenth and Twentieth Centuries,* 110.

[47] Anthony Gilchrist McCall, *Lushai Chrysalis* (reprint, Aizawl: Tribal Research Institute, Dept. of Art & Culture, Govt. of Mizoram, 2003 [1949]), 208.; In Assam plains Christianity

Similar is the reason for the belated success of Christianity in the Naga Hills. Among the Eastern Nagas, particularly the Konyaks, who were under the greatest amount of authoritarianism, resistance to Christianity was very strong. So also among the Khasis, who did not embrace the new faith until the beginning of 20th century. Till today, few Siemships are non-Christian. The traditional religious rites are so strongly attached to the Khyrim Siemship that the incumbent cannot afford to change his/her faith even though most of his/her close relatives might have done so.[48] In the Garo Hills too, many *Nokmas* (chiefs) are yet non-Christian. Robbins Burling writes that when a *Nokma* adopts Christianity, *Nokma* ship should pass on to another, but Government continued to recognise the former.[49] This created dislocation in the traditional system, but not necessarily in the social plane for usually a wealthy non-Christian took over the ritual responsibilities of the *Nokma*. Thus, a distinction developed between *Aking-Nokma* (Chief of the village-land) and *Nokma-Ganna* (Chief for the religious purposes).[50]

In the plains of Assam and Manipur, the resistance was in a great proportion due to the influence of Hinduism upon tribals. As it is noted, the resistance was against the challenge that the Church was posing to the structure of authority.[51] Though the British administration tried not to disturb the social equilibrium, the challenges posed by the Church went deep into them and upset the traditional relations of authorities. Referring to "a Hill District" (but implying the Lushai Hills), Government of Assam reported to the Indian Statutory Commission that the area had been peaceful, since the surrender of the chiefs, until 1911 when "the attempt of a missionary to undermine the authority of the chiefs in a matter which is considered uncivilised led to apprehensions of disturbances" as a result of which the missionary had to be expelled from the District.[52] Thus, there was a strong resistance from the allies of Government – the chiefs and officials with some vested interest in fact.

---

attracted the lower castes/tribes.

[48] Chaube notes that in the religious ceremonies of Khyrim in which Siems' youngest sister acts as the chief priestess, the Christians are not permitted to take part. Cf. note 28 in Chaube, *Hills Politics…*, 60.

[49] Cf. Robins Burling, *Rengsanggri* (Philadelphia: n.p., 1963), 67.

[50] Chie Nakane, *The Garo and the Kashi* (Paris, 1967), 62.

[51] For instance, in the Khasi Hills, the leadership of the resistance was assumed by Babu Jeebon Roy, member of a Dkhar clan (originating from a non-Khasi), son of a trader at Cherrapunji and the first self-educated hill-man to have become an Extra-Assistant Commissioner by virtue of which he became the biggest landowner of the District. He was an avowed enemy of the Welsh Presbyterian Church and never accepted Christianity. Besides patronization of a Brahmo Primary School at Shillong and leading to the establishment of a Government High School at Shillong free from missionary control for some years, he founded the Seng-Khasi (Khasi Association), a revivalistic, anti-Christian organisation in 1893which earned the blessings of some of the powerful Siems in the Khasi Hills. Cf. Chaube, *Hills Politics…*, 58.

[52] *Memoranda of the Assam Government*, 106. As cited in ibid.

However, in the long run, the hill tribes accommodated themselves to British rule and began to see it, as well as Christianity, as a defence against the greater threat of dominance by and absorption into the more advanced Hindu community of the plains.[53] Perhaps of limited success, however, by the close of 19th century, one could see the mission work spread all over the NEI region, except the present Assam and Manipur plains, Tripura and Arunachal Pradesh. And by the first half of the 20th century, almost whole of NEI was covered by the Christian missionary activities. At the beginning of the century, Lushai Hills (Mizoram) witnessed rapid growth[54] followed by Nagaland.[55] Including all denominations, there are about 4.5 million Christians in NEI as per the Census of 2001.[56]

The Impact of Christianity

Christianity in NEI faced a great challenge of inter-relationship with tribal society. In the process of its interaction with religious beliefs and practices of tribals and bringing radical changes, Christianity appeared good as well as bad, helpful as well as useless, liberating as well as enslaving, to the people according to time and situation.[57] It is good to start here with the positive results wrought by Christianity. In fact, it cannot be disputed that the credit for the change in primitive society goes to the Christian missions. Though it was situational, the emphasis on social dimension was great which otherwise the society might not have been as it is now. Writing on the mission work among Lakhers, Parry writes that "a more active instrument of change than government is the Christian Mission."[58] Undoubtedly the tribal society in North-East India has undergone immense changes in its

[53] Downs, *History of Christianity in India...*, 15.

[54] For comprehensive history of Christianity in Mizoram (Missiological Perspective), see *The Life and Witness....*

[55] Cf. Downs, *The Mighty Works of God...*, Sangma, *History of American Baptist Mission...*, 218-72.

[56] The state-wise Christian population of NEI is as follow: Arunachal Pradesh - 89,013 (10.29%), Assam – 7,44,367 (3.32%), Manipur – 6,26,669 (34.11%), Meghalaya – 11,46,092 (64.58%), Mizoram – 5,91,342 (85.73%), Nagaland – 10,57,940 (87.47%), Tripura – 46,472 (1.68%). As per record given in Basic Statistics of NER 2006 and Registrar General of India, Census of India, 2001, Series-1, Paper-1 of 2001. Final Population Totals.

[57] For a variegated views and reviews on the impact of Christianity upon the tribes of NEI, particularly see, O.L. Snaitang, *Christianity and Social Change in Northeast India* (Shillong, Calcutta: Vendrame Institute, Firma KLM Private Limited, 1993).; J.J. Roy Burman, "Impact of Christianity among the Tribes of North-East India," in *Tribal Situation in North-East India*, ed. Sartak Sengupta, [Tribal Studies in India Series T 170] (New Delhi: Inter-India Publications, 1994), 165-83; Sebastian Karotemprel, "The Impact of Christianity on the Tribes of North-East India," in *Tribal Situation in North-East India,* ed. Sartak Sengupta (New Delhi: Inter-India Publications, 1994), 134-64.; J. Puthenpurakal, ed. Impact of Christianity in North East India (Shillong: Vendrame Institute of Publications, 1996).; and T.B. Subba, Joseph Puthenpurakal, and Shaji Joseph Puykunnel, eds., *Christianity and Change in Northeast India* (New Delhi: Concept, 2009).

[58] N. E. Parry, *The Lakhers* (Calcutta: Firma KLM Pvt. Ltd., 1932 [1976]), 19.

psychology, world-view, languages, cultures, social habits, economic activity, etc. as a result of its interaction with Christianity. The momentum of change has been extraordinary, given the psychology of the tribal society, its democratic ways, aspirations for a new life, simple socio-cultural, theological and philosophical thought patterns favouring quick social transition.[59]

One of the most significant positive impacts of Christianity is on *language and literature*. Dr. Chhangte Hminga, a Mizo Christian, wrote that

> The British government for its own convenience, was intending to impose the Bengali language on the Mizos. . . . Had that materialised, it might have meant the dying out of the Mizo language. . . . Indeed, evangelisation of the whole tribe in such a short span of time would never have taken place if the Gospel had not been communicated in the language of the people. . . . The missionaries gave to the Mizo people the supreme gift of a written language and literature.[60]

The civilising impact through education and literatures was indeed immense. In many areas, Christianity appears to have served the role of filling up the intellectual and spiritual vacuum caused by the growing scepticism among the tribal population, about their traditional faith and world-view.[61] In other words, it provided intellectual and emotional equanimity.

Although in a limited way, secondly, Christianity could control some of the social evils and prescribe *social behaviour*. It could instil a sense of valuing human life, role in the society, role to the world of nature and other living creatures and relation to fellow human beings. While reporting on the Khasis, Mills pointed out that

> However their moral character may have deteriorated, the advantages they have derived and are deriving from their connexion with our Government is great, and numerous civil wars, which continuously distracted the country have been put down...there is a striking improvement in the condition of the people, to say nothing of the benefits which they have derived from the attempt, feeble though it has been, to diffuse amongst them the advantages of education. We have also reaped the benefits of our position in having obtained an entire

[59] Cf. Karotemprel, "The Impact of Christianity on the Tribes of North-East India," 134-35.

[60] C. L. Hminga, "The Life and Witness of the Churches in Mizoram" (D.Missiology Dissertation, Fuller Theological Seminary, 1976), 47.

[61] Cf. B.K. Roy Burman, "Integrated Area Approach to the Problems of the Hill Tribes," in *Tribal Situation in India,* ed. K.S. Singh (Shimla: IIAS, 1972), 80.

> cessation of the murderous inroads which these mountaineers constantly made into the plains.[62]

It was reported that "Men (*sic*), who had been accustomed to decorate their houses with skulls, felt almost content in using pumpkins for this purpose."[63] Similar reports on the Nagas read:

> For centuries the Naga had been living in a world of their own leading a traditional life constantly warring against one another and more often than not hunting human heads. After their conversion to the new religion, wanton killing was realised as a sin in the light of the teaching of Christ and hostility was replaced by love. Some of their evil practices like head-hunting and blood warfare amongst them virtually ceased and the Naga by and large settled down to peaceful living devoting themselves to agriculture and trade.[64]

All this implies that they have realised the necessity of peace, toleration and co-existence with their own people and neighbours in the plains. As noted earlier, this was indeed the exact motif behind the invitation of the missionaries particularly Serampore Mission in Khasi Hills and the American Baptist Foreign Mission society by Jenkins in North East Frontier Agency (NEFA). In the case of the later, it was thought that the task of pacifying the Singphos and the Khamtees, could be effectively done by the spread of the Gospel.[65] Indeed, the British rule through the power of the Gospel if not totally stopped, reduced the inter-village warfare, raids on plains village and the traditional practice of head-hunting.

Another explicit expression of behavioural change can be seen in the following words of Clark, the pioneering missionary among the Naga tribe:

> During the last year cows stolen from the plains and taken into Deka Haimong Song, been returned to their owners in the plains. By the same Christian influence goods have been returned to Assamese traders in the Song, which had been stripped from them in revenge for their abusive language.

---

[62] A. J. M. Mills, *Reports on the Khasis and Jaintia Hills* (Reprint, Shillong, 1901), 5-6. As cited in Chaube, *Hills Politics...*, 46.

[63] J.B. Fuller, *Introduction in L.W. Shakespear History of the Assam Rifles* (London, 1928), vii.

[64] *Bengal Judicial Proceedings,* No. 21 (January 1873).; *Foreign Political Proceedings (External A),* No. 37 (September, 1885), 9. As cited in S. K. Barpujari, "Christianity and Its Impact on the Nagas," in *The Tribes of North East India,* ed. Sebastian Karotemprel (Shillong: Vendrame Missiological Institute, 1984), 107-8.

[65] Gammel William, *History of the American Baptist Mission* (1850), 212-23. As referred in Barpujari, *Assam in the Days of the Company* (1826-1858), 301.; also in Sangma, *History of American Baptist Mission...*,24-26. Each missionary agencies had similar motifs behind their mission work.

> At one time in the year, the Nagas burning under what they seemed a great wrong and having hope of redress through Commissioner of Assam, were strongly determined to take the law into their own hands in the way of a vindictive raid. They were only restrained by the native Christian portraying to them in the strongest terms the suicidal folly of such a course and the terrible punishment Government would be sure to inflict upon them.[66]

Thirdly, one of the most remarkable impacts having relevance to contemporary NEI is *identity elevation*. Christianity could instil a sense of status and dignity among the tribes. The Church strengthened a sense of tribal identity for the first time at a level higher than that of a village or relatively small cluster of villages. Downs observes that "one of the functions of Christianity, sociologically speaking, was to help the hill tribes preserve their identity in the face of the perceived new threat of assimilation into the Hindu societies of the plains."[67] This new identity was to become the basis of modern political movements, though this was not the conscious objective of the missionaries or Church leaders.[68] While writing on Khasis' acceptance of Christianity as the alternative to their survival, Kottupallil states that "Christianity seemed to offer them dignity, recognition and hope of salvation both on this earth and in eternity."[69] Christianity provided a means of preserving tribal identities and promoting their interests in the face of powerful forces of change. Through Church polity, new structures of tribal identity were created and through education and literature, Christianity provided the people with skills necessary to function self-reliantly within the new order.[70]

---

[66] Barpujari, "Christianity and Its Impact on the Nagas," 108. Of course this may not be the total picture of change in social behaviour. Michael Scott had quite different view on such metamorphosis of tribes through Christianity. He wrote: "Out of the religion brought by American Missionaries, who loved them (Nagas) and were welcomed amongst them as friends, they (Nagas) have made something of their own and in no way incompatible with their own zest for life and for the songs and dances, animated by beings and beliefs which they have not discarded and see no incongruity in retaining along with their beliefs in the powerful reality of God, the driving force of creation and of purpose in their lives and all life – *yet no one could possibly describe them as a pious or even a moral people. There is a fierce quality in them which is capable of terrible retaliation….* There is also a streak of cruelty which is part of the texture of their life as it has come to be woven into a pattern out of the hard and harsh raw materials of existence. It is as visibly there, as the qualities of gaiety, friendship and generosity, however the preachers may deplore it". D. R. Mankekar, "Understanding the Tribals on the North-Eastern Border," in *Tribal Situation in India*, ed. K.S. Singh (Simla: Indian Institute of Advanced Study, 1972), 113. [*italic* added]

[67] Downs, *History of Christianity in India…*, 4.

[68] Cf. Ibid., 209.

[69] Kottupallil, "A Historical Survey of the Catholic Church in Northeast India from 1627 to 1969," 37.

[70] Cf. F. S. Downs, "Christianity and Cultural Change in North East India," in *Christian Faith and Multiform Culture in India,* ed. Somen Das (Bangalore: United Theological College, 1987), 97.

The fourth important impact was *culture preservation.* Over against the accusation – "Christian missionaries Westernising the tribal cultures", it is counter-argued that "Westernisation was inevitable in independent India, and Christianity saved the Mizos from losing their tribal identity in the process."[71] It is contended that "the adoption of Christianity did not in a fundamental way affect the culture of the Naga people. This was due to the fact that the British administrative officers had appealed to the missionaries to uphold the tribal cultures as far as possible.[72] One of the local persons also said: "Christianity is not spoiling our tribal selfhood, as is sometimes alleged. When we become Christians we do not get detribalised. Instead of Christ's teaching taking away anything of value from our tribal life, it is enriching it in many ways."[73] Kottupallil makes a statement which seems acceptable, viz., that

> Most tribals were happy to see that the Catholic Church rather than the Protestant in general cared to *preserve their culture*. The Catholic missionaries, compared to the Protestants, were more sympathetic to tribal customs traditions, to tribal music, dance, and architecture and to tribal cultural values like respect and veneration of the dead and their ancestors.[74]

Among the Mizos, the missionaries are given credit for being *sensitive to their culture* and viewpoints. Even Hminga compares the missionary activities in Mizoram with the 19th century movement called "the broad Christian humanitarian movement" in Britain saying that these missionaries had no formal missiological training, yet they made good use of its principles. Finally, he concludes saying, "most normal missionaries have considerable anthropological insight."[75]

Fifthly, one of the widely accepted reasons for successful story of Christianity is that it gave *hope of bright future* to the hill tribes. This is why Christianity was successful in hills area than plains. According to Dena Lal's assessment,

> The phenomenal success of Christianity in the hill areas was largely due to the specificity of the new faith and the 'modern' world from which it came. The tribals saw in the new religion elements of radicalism and it offered them hopes for the future. Apart from spiritual gains, the process of conversion should also be seen in terms of the technology

[71] F. S. Downs, *Christianity in North East India* (Madras: CLS, 1976), 279.

[72] Cf. V.C. Kanito Sema, "A Critical Assessment of Christianity Acculturation of North-East India," in *Religion and Society of North-East India*, ed. S. Miri (New Delhi: Vikas Publishing House, 1980), 78.

[73] As reported in M. M. Thomas and R.W. Taylor, eds., *Tribal Awakening* (Bangalore: Christian Institute for Study of Religion and Society, 1965), 48.

[74] Kottupallil, "A Historical Survey of the Catholic Church in Northeast India from 1627 to 1969," 55.

[75] Hminga, "The Life and Witness of the Churches in Mizoram," 247.

> the missionaries involved for the material well-being of the people. The development of written forms of various of languages, printing of books, medical work and opening of schools were some of the important introduction into the tribal area.[76]

Finally, perhaps the most significant impacts of Christianity was *tribal ecumenism*[77] or *inter-ethnic alliance.*[78] The tribal society was divided into numerous small groups. From time immemorial, not only the tribes but even the clans and in certain cases, the villages have led a separate existence. Various factors have had driven these tribes, clans and villages into isolation. But with the appearance of British administration and Christian mission, many of the tribes were brought together into one umbrella. The Church organisations, associations, synods, councils, conventions, assemblies, circles and dioceses served as a forum for corporate identity as Naga, Mizo, Garo, Khasi and so on. Among the Nagas, Christianity was perceived as cement which would bring together the various sub-tribes. J. H. Hutton in his report claimed that: "In some villages, perhaps most villages, the different clans dwell normally in peace and unity together, but this is probably much more the case under British rule than it was aforetime."[79] F.S. Downs, one of the most authoritative modern historians of the region argues with vivid historical evidences that

> Christianity has been one of the most powerful integrating agencies within the tribes, districts and states of the region, as well as between the peoples of the hills and those of the plains. It has also played a significant role, popular notions to the contrary notwithstanding, in the process of integrating the hills people in the North East with the rest of the country.[80]

Similarly, this fact has been even observed by B. K. Roy Burman. Christianity, he said, "has also tended to serve as the vehicle for unification of the isolated small

---

[76] Lal Dena, *Christian Missions and Colonialism*, 25.

[77] Downs for the first time used the term "tribal ecumenism" in an appendix written in C.B. Firth's book, *An Introduction to Indian Church History.* He actually used the term to refer to the development of new relationships at the intra-tribal, inter-tribal and extra-tribal levels. Cf. Appendix in C. B. Firth, *An Introduction to Indian church History* (Madras: CLS, 1976).; Also see F.S. Downs, "Tribal Ecumenism in North East India: The Christian Role in Solidarity Movements," *Eastern Theological College Journal* 2/2 (Jan-May 1989): 48 ff.; *ICHR* XXVIII/1 (June 1989): 23ff.

[78] S.M. Dubey, "Inter-Ethnic Alliance, Tribal Movements and Integration in Northeast India," *Tribal Movement in India* Vol. I/ (1982): 13ff.

[79] Hutton, *The Angami Nagas: With Some Notes on Neighbouring Tribes* (London: Oxford University Press, 1969 [1921]), 109.

[80] Downs, *History of Christianity in India: Northeast India in the Nineteenth and Twentieth Centuries,* 131.

communities into a larger entity."[81] Not only did it unified the tribes but it also opened up a wider ecumenism in later days. Both the Church and theological education and institutions served as medium that connected the isolated tribes with the wider India and world.

However, alongside the positive impacts, the Christian mission left some of the dangerous legacies for present-day conflicts in the tribal society in NEI. First of all, Christianity or Church as an identity elevator tended to be reinforcing traditional animosity between the hill tribes and people of the plain as well as feeling of regionalism. To a certain extent, Christianity seems to be misappropriated in political movements by the Christian mass particularly in Nagaland and Mizoram. According to Datta Ray, "Christianity has emerged as a strong factor of modernisation, and has given tribals a sense of Identity.... The phenomenal rise of Christianity in all North-Eastern states except in Arunachal Pradesh, during 1961-1981 became a symbol of tribal regionalism."[82] In his Presidential address in the Sixth Session of NEI History Association held at Agartala in 1985, H.L. Gupta expressed that

> After Independence the role of the foreign missionaries was highly dubious, if not positively and openly anti-Indian. It is said that they encouraged secessionist tendencies among the tribal leaders and incited them to claim free tribal states by exciting their fear that in the Indian Union their identity would be lost and their cultural heritage would be destroyed.[83]

The Naga and Mizo Movements had close association with Christianity both in the minds of their leaders and supporters. It was therefore a prominent element in their Naga identity in contrast to what was seen as neo-colonialism by Hindu India. In particular, Christianity and the Gospel provided ideology for liberation among the Nagas and Mizos. It is clear that the Naga insurgency movements in India, like the comparable Chin and Karen independence movements in Myanmar, do have to a degree a Christian ideological base.[84] For instance, the first Naga independence leader, Phizo was a convinced Baptist. In the earlier period a

---

[81] B. K. Roy Burman, "Integrated Area Approach to the Problems of the Hill Tribes," in *Tribal Situation in India*, ed. K. S. Singh (Shimla: Indian Institute of Advanced Study, 172), 80.

[82] B. Datta Ray, "Anatomy of Regionalism in North-East India Hills: A Preliminary Observation," in *Tribal Transformation in India: Ethnopolitics and Identity Crisis,* ed. Buddhadeb Chaudhuri (New Delhi: Inter-India Publications, 1992), 475.

[83] *Proceedings of the Northeast India History Association, Sixth Session*, (Agartala, 1985), 19. As cited in Downs, *History of Christianity in India: Northeast India in the Nineteenth and Twentieth Centuries,* 117-18.

[84] Cf. John Parratt, "Christianity, ethnicity and structural violence: The North-east India Case," available at: http://www.kanglaonline.com/index.php?template=kshow&kid=8& (accessed July 9, 2007).

substantial number of pastors joined the underground. Even the cadres did not fight on Sundays unless attacked.[85]

The slogan "Nagaland for Christ" was a recognised rallying cry, and to some extent, still it is. Overtly Christian elements have appeared in official statements. The Constitution of the Federal Government of Nagaland, while it guaranteed free profession and practice of any religion, declared that Christianity would be the religion of the Naga state.[86] It was not averse to using religion as propaganda tool either, when it claimed that the "Hindu government" of India had adopted a policy of stopping Nagas eating meat. In the earlier days of the movement volunteer Gospel teams preached under armed guard which one might almost say "gun in one hand Bible in the other" and the conduct of the jungle camps was ordered by Christian spiritual activities. As with the non-Christian Meitei movements, the NSCN tended towards puritanical life style, banning alcohol and drugs, and discouraging sexual immorality. Provision of social amenities, like schools and clinics, goes hand in hand with religious teaching.[87]

Secondly, alongside the positive impact of education, British administration and Christian mission left dangerous legacies for present-day conflicts over language and ethnicity. There is much evidence to show that, though administration and the Church were functioning in the hills with the same objective, namely, the consolidation of British rule, the results of their operations were not complementary in all respect. The strategy of administration was least interference with the existing order while the activities of the Church were undermining their foundation, by providing the new elite with intellectual ammunition.[88] The inevitable result was a social imbalance that not only lingered but also became aggravated after independence.

Such metamorphoses resulted from the imposition of the Rules for Administration of Justice which vested the village chiefs and headmen with judicial authority. The application of the Rules, at the same time created some formal stereotypes for the hills administration that affected the traditional set-up of the hills societies so long based on unwritten customs. Hutton stated that "... Assam hill tribe taken before annexation and administration have had time to modify its primitive customs and mode of life...and their customs and outlook have been modified...to the extent of causing them to conceal customs which they have discovered to engender disapproval on the part of the stranger."[89]

---

[85] Cf. M. Horam, *Naga Insurgency: The Last Thirty Years* (New Delhi: Cosmo Publications, 1988), 77.

[86] Ibid., 61.

[87] Cf. Phanjoubam Tarapot, *Insurgency Movement in North-Eastern India* (New Delhi: Vikas Publishing House Pvt. Ltd., 1993), 125.

[88] Cf. Chie Nakane, *The Garo and the Kashi* (Paris, 1967), 64-65.

[89] J.H. "Hutton Introduction," in Parry, *The Lakhers*, ix.

It was in accordance with the Administration's aversion to considerable involvement in the hills that education in the hills was almost entirely left to the Church, subsidised by Government.[90] But, beside government's definite reservation about elementary education for the hill tribes, even the primary objective of the missions was to collect good preachers, not educate citizens. Their teaching was biased toward religion and literature of the West.[91]

Another consequence of the excessive reliance of Government on the Church as an agency of education and other social services was the growth of vested interest of the Church. The Church was not only "the only religious and cultural agency" in the remotest parts of a District, but also an employer of the educated people who took to teaching and preaching as a black-coated occupation. Referring to the Lushai Hills McCall wrote, "Local educational practice soon gave rise to the belief that education and Christianity were the passport to "salaried job", relief from the wearisome toil of cultivating a hard land. Education has constituted a means to a dead end, the salaried post."[92] He adds, "Black-coated occupations became synonymous with progress. Christianity led towards blackcoatism."[93] For a talented young man, the favour of a Church could mean financial assistance to enable him to reach the threshold of higher education in the plains. The Church, thus, became a centre of power and patronage in the Hill Districts.[94] The result was the creation of an oligarchy, privileged, salaried, and therefore, materially powerful Church-Executives. Christianity and the oligarchy, according to McCall, bred individualism, flourishing in the headquarters in towns and naturally imbued with the thrill of seeking independence of the Chiefs and freedom from customary communal discipline,[95] which the British administration had always tried to retain, in its own interest.[96]

In short, Christianity in the NEI happens to be the cultural dimension of the political process. It became a symbol of tribal identity and produced organised middle class leadership in tribal society. Christianity or at least Christians have played a prominent role in the process of political and social adjustment. Church spread education in tribal society and helped the birth of elite dominant class in the hills' urban centres. The towns have become fortified centres of wealth and middle class solidarity.[97] But the dependent rural people still remain in utter poverty under semi-feudal social set up in all the hills of NEI.

S.B.

---

[90] Cf. Chaube, *Hills Politics...*, 56.; Parry, *The Lakhers,* 19.

[91] Cf. Chaube, *Hills Politics...*, 43 & 56.

[92] McCall, *Lushai Chrysalis,* 205.

[93] Ibid.

[94] Cf. Chaube, *Hills Politics...*, 57.

[95] Cf. McCall, *Lushai Chrysalis,* 216-217.

[96] Cf. Chaube, *Hills Politics...*, 57.

[97] Cf. Ray, ""Anatomy of Regionalism in North-East India Hills...," 478.

Chapter 10

Ao-Nagas, Christianity and Administrators: Issues and Conflicts

The arrival of the American Baptist mission to the Ao-Nagas and subsequently to the other parts of Nagaland and the contribution they have had made to the people will be remembered in the history of Christianity in Nagaland. The missionaries laid the foundation for development and change in the society – a change that transformed the whole aspects of society. Hence, we may say that the dawn of the 19th century initiated the process of change and transformation among the Ao-Nagas and the Nagas. In the meantime the presence of British administration also ushered in the process of creating space for civilization and modernization of the Ao-Naga society. However, it should be noted that the coming of both the Christianity and the British administration created both positive and negative impact in the society. Therefore, an attempt is made here to investigate some of the major issues and conflicts confronted by the converts, missionaries and the British administration in the course of their interaction.

Socio-Cultural, Political and Religious Issues: Problems and Conflicts

The coming of Christianity and the British administration to the Ao-Nagas created social-political, religious and cultural re-adjustment. In the progress created perplexity in the whole structure of the society and also the newly formed church. Christianity introduced a new religion to the existing traditional religion and ushered a new social order that broadened their consciousness. Their interaction resulted in progress, transformation and changes. In the process confronted with rejection and compounded with differences of opinion. This resulted in socio-religious issues, problems and conflict within the church and also between the British officials and the missionaries. Some of the outstanding major problems and conflicts were:

Strained Relationship between Missionaries and British Administration

As stated the coming of Christianity and the establishment of British government created a new epoch in the history of Christianity in Nagaland. The methods applied by the missionaries in evangelizing the native people were at times very radical. The native people found it difficult to fit-in in their imposing attitude towards the new culture. This was a crucial period wherein the missionaries prohibited most of the cultural practices and belief system of the people. For instance, the missionaries began to oppose to most of the existing traditional tenets like, food, festivals, dress, ornaments, religious beliefs, communal institutions (*Ariju/Morung*), and living style, etc. As Downs noted, the missionaries opposed to traditional activities simply because they did not fit in with their own rather solemn Evangelical notions of Christian propriety.[1] In regard to the attitude of the mission towards the tribal culture and religion Alemchiba aptly remarked that:

> As religion played a part in every Naga ceremony and as that religion was not Christianity, they felt every ceremony should be abolished. The tendency was to abolish abruptly the old thing and substitute individualism for the strong community feeling which had enabled the tribes to survive for so long. Not only was this individualism wrapped up with strong emphasis on person salvation, it induced a direct and natural reaction against all the old things that mattered in the village life and social genius of the tribe. The result was a conflict not necessarily a conflict of arms but of culture, a conflict between the interest of community and individual which caused cultural tension in the society.[2]

Therefore, from 1880-1940 they were confronted with socio-religious issues, problems and conflict of re-adjustment to the new order. The relationship between the British government and the missionaries became ambiguous and tense. Thus Sanyu commented, the Britishers who were mostly Anglicans, Methodists or Presbyterians with their colonial cause and the American Baptist missionaries with their missionary zeal were not always in good terms with each other in the Naga Hills.[3] The greatest difficulty which the missionary had to face

---

[1] F.S. Downs, "Christianity and Socio-Cultural Change in the Hill Areas of North East India," *ICHR* 26/1 (June, 1992): 55.

[2] Alemchiba Ao, "Problems of Re-adjudgement to a New Situation with Special Reference to the Naga Tribe," in *Tribal Situation in India*, edited by K. Suresh Singh (Shimla: Indian Institute of Advanced Study, 1972), 479-480.

[3] V. Sangyu, *A History of Nagas and Nagaland: Dynamics of Oral Tradition in Village Formation* (New Delhi: Commonwealth Publications, 1996), 116.

at one time was perhaps over-cautiousness on the part of the British officials, as they were opposed to the missionaries.[4] The methods applied by the missionaries in converting the people in relation to opposing to traditional and ethical tenets of the native people were viewed as disruptive and destructive by the British officials. The British administration did not temper with the traditional relationship, tribal laws, tribal leadership, tribal council, etc., or in other words, tribalism based on cultural and ethnic unity was left undisturbed.[5] On the attitude of the British Administration towards the tribal people, Alemchiba opined that:

> The Britishers knew that on the preservation of customs developed exactly to fit the environment and tested by centuries of use depended upon the whole fabric of the tribal society. They took great pains to preserve them to the utmost limit possible and to ensure that such change as would inevitably come should not be destructive in its suddenness.[6]

The attitude of the missionaries to the tribal culture was therefore, being questioned by several western writers also. Among them J.P. Mills argued:

> Of all the mistakes made by the Mission, the gravest, in my opinion, and the most fraught with danger for the future is their policy of strenuously imposing an alien Western culture on their converts. I think I am right in saying that no member of the Mission has ever studied Ao Customs deeply, but nearly all have been eager to uproot what they neither understand nor sympathize with, and to substitute for it a superficial civilization.[7]

From the perspective of the missionaries we have the opinion of M.M. Clark. She states:

In our work it has been church and state .... Some are disregarding the injunction of the missionary to keep the Sabbath; some are looking to English officials for an example, rather than to the missionary .... English Government failing to see eye to eye with the missionary .... A crisis in our work seems to be upon us, and we need at this juncture the continued, earnest, faithful prayers which have hitherto helped us.[8]

---

[4] H. Bareh, ed, *Nagaland District Gazetteers Kohima* (Kohima: Government of Nagaland, 1970), 190.

[5] S.K. Barpujari, "Christianity and its Impact on the Nagas," in *The Tribes of North East India*, edited by Sebastian Karotemprel (Shillong: Center for Indigenous Cultures, 1998), 122.

[6] Alemchiba, *Problems of Re-adjudgement...*, 479.

[7] J.P. Mills, *The Ao Nagas*, 2nd Edition (London: Macmillan & Co., Ltd., 1926; London: Oxford University Press, 1973), 420-421. (Hereafter referred to as J.P. Mills, *Ao Nagas*).

[8] *BMM*, July 1890, 268 in A. Bendangyabang Ao, *History of Christianity in Nagaland: A Source Material* (Mokokchung: Shalom Ministry, 1998), 119.

It is clear that the British administration did not wish to tamper the cultural values of the people but on the other hand the missionaries regarded them as valueless culture. They could not find a convergence to this issue. We see here the conflict of ideology between the mission and the Britishers. It was therefore, a period of debate, interference, orders and notices between the missionaries and the British officials. Thus, with occasional exception like in the case of desirability to imparting education to the Nagas, wherein the missionaries and British administration were of one mind - the relation between the missionaries and the British officials were not at their best resulting to tension and confusion.

Conflict between Converts and Non-Converts: Reformation of the Church

In the process of the conversion movement misunderstanding gripped in between the converts and the non-converts. By this time there was a spectacular growth of conversion movement sweeping the whole land. This prompted the non-converts to dictate certain conditions which they thought would be for the benefits of the community. One of the reasons was that the new converts were abandoning the long established traditional belief and practices, which the non-converts thought that it would affect the whole system of order in the society. Thus, at times despite its best endeavor the Christian conversion movement was waning. The missionaries in the process saw the deteriorating situation in spiritual discipline among the Christians. According to the view of the missionaries: "There were no churches in the strict sense of that term, and even at Molung where there were some fifty members, there was no semblance of an organization, although Mr. Clark always referred to the teacher as the Pastor."[9]

Therefore, the missionaries at any cost wanted to impose strict rule of Christian discipline to the new converts: Thus according to the report of Haggard:

> Mr. Clark had long felt that there were some things which he would desire to have eradicated from the church but he had not thought it wise to undertake the task until he was reinforced. With three of us on the field, however, there was no longer any occasion for delay; and hence we began at once to consider the details of the steps to be taken. Among other things, a covenant, which will serve both as a standard for individual churches, and also to define the position of the Mission before the people on the great questions of idolatry, liquor drinking and opium eating, Sabbath observance, marriage relation, and the giving to the Lord's work, etc., was formulated. As was anticipated, it did not meet the approval of the members; but the time had come to rid the

[9] Clark to JNM, 21 March 1877, Box 40 Gr 1, ABHS R NY, 4, quoted in Joseph Puthenpurakal, *Baptist Missions in Nagaland: A Study in Historical and Ecumenical Perspective* (Calcutta: Firma KLM Private Limited, 1984), 109.

> Mission of certain grave evils connected with the questions mentioned above; and a determined stand was necessary.[10]

As stated Clark, Perrine and Haggard with this objective resolved to re-organize and reform the Molungyimsen church by applying a radical solution. They resolved that the basis for church membership should be based on teetotalism. The Ao-Nagas were very fond of consuming rice-beer, which was also central to their traditional feasts. The converts were strictly warned to abstain from such practices. Anyone therefore who transgresses this law was expelled from the community. Abstaining from drinking rice-beer was considered as an outstanding sign of Christianity.[11] The converts found it difficult to forbid drinking and therefore, completely rejected this demand except for two members namely Bendanglemba and Molungba. As a result the church at Molungyimsen was officially disbanded on 19 August 1894. Perrine in his report in 1895 recorded that before the Church at Molungyimsen was disbanded there were 68 members.[12] However, in a strict sense Clark was not in favour of abstinence as the basis of church membership. In the later part, the missionaries approach to this rigid attitude was changed. Along with Bendanglemba and Molung supported by Zilli and his wife joined to reform the church. Mr. Kilep who was then not baptized decided to join the reformed group. They together decided to lay down some resolutions to be followed by the Christians who wished to join the church. This was done under the leadership of Perrine on 19 August 1894.[13]

In 1896 Mr. Kilep became the pastor of Molungyimsen Church. With this reformed attitude and message Mr. kilep played a very important role to spreading the new religion. The picture of Molungyimsen church being reformed gave a clear view on the position as to how the church should be spiritually transformed and disciplined. This was the very intention of the missionaries. As a result the religious and social reform was beginning to take deep root among

---

[10] Haggard, "Molung," *BMM*, LXXV/7 (July, 1895), 307-309.

[11] Cf., J.P. Mills, *Ao Nagas* ..., 416.

[12] The following shows the status of Church membership: 1) Deka Haimong (Molungkimong) - 13 members; 2) Wameken - 3 members; 3) Molung (Molungyimsen) – 40 members; 4) Yajang - 7 members; and 5) Merangkong -5 members. See S.A. Perrine, "Report from the Ao-Naga Field," *Assam Baptist Missionary Conference Report* (1896), 43.

[13] The Resolutions were: 1) Resolved to faithfully obey and adhere to the teachings of the Bible; 2) Resolved to worship no other gods but only God of Jehovah; to whom we would pray unceasingly; we would not seek the help of sorcery and witchcraft but seek the help of God of Jehovah; to observe the Sabbath day; 3) Resolved to join the reformed community and not to offend but to love God, to propagate the good news, to expand the Christian church, to help people, to forgive fellow beings, to abstain from fornication and adultery, etc; 4) Resolved to abstain from taking opium, drinking, etc., and to help fellow beings to abstain from these practices; and 5) Resolved to walk in the fear of the Lord and to live a life worthy of the calling. May God be with us and bless us. L. Kijung Ao, *NokinketerMungchen* (Gauhati: Ao Baptist Arogo Mungdang, 1972), 68-69.

the people. In regard to the reformed group M.M. Clark wrote: "Every form of demon worship, open or suspected, was attacked – Sunday breaking, rice beer drinking, licentiousness, and all social vices ... Congregating promiscuously at different houses at night, singing objectionable songs, telling doubtful stories, and engaging in lewd conversation, these young reformer built a dormitory for their own accommodation, in which purity and holiness should reign. Here at morning and evening time the voice of prayer and songs of praise are heard."[14]

Socio-Cultural and Religious Conflict

The religion of Christianity demanded certain moral standards from the people. The missionaries without proper articulating the deep philosophy beneath the cultural and religious practices termed all the practices of traditional religion as 'heathen practices'. Within their limited presumption they tried to prohibit most of the cultural and religious practices. As a result of their radical attitude many age-old customs have to be prohibited forcefully. These prohibitions were the very antithesis of the Ao-Naga way of life. From a positive angle, the missionaries cannot be blamed altogether for their attitude towards the practices of the native people. The context in which they were situated was harsh which was totally in contrast to their culture and theology which is defined by 19th century evangelicism.[15]

Therefore, it is to be noted that the 19th century protestant missionaries understanding of Christianity was the idea that becoming a Christian meant a new mode of life.[16] They saw conversion as a conscious moral turnabout.[17] Hence, began to oppose the tribal socio-cultural and religious practices by terming it as hidden practices without any moral code. Their whole idea therefore, was to convert as much as they can and to report the success story of their labour among the lowly-cultured people. The missionary attitude and its presupposition towards the native people are clearly evident in the writing of M.M. Clark. She wrote, when we entered "A Corner of India" the darkness seemed impenetrable. She continues "Mine album is the savage breast, where darkness broads and

[14] Mary Mead Clark, *A Corner in India*, Reprint (Philadelphia: American Baptist Publication Society, 1907; Gauhati: Christian Literature Centre, 1978), 138-139.

[15] The term evangelicalism usually refers to a largely Protestant movement that emphasizes and conceptualizes their Christian faith on: 1) The bible was understood as authoritative and reliable; 2) Eternal salvation was possible only by regeneration (being "born again"), involving personal trust in Christ and in his atoning work; 3) A spiritual transformed life marked by moral conduct and personal devotion, such as Bible reading, prayer; and 4) Zeal for evangelism and mission. See George M. Marsden and William L. Svelmoe, "Evangelical and Fundamental Christianity," *Encyclopedia of Religion*, Vol. 5, Second Edition, edited by Lindsay Jones (U.S.A: Thomson Gale, 2005): 2887.

[16] Frederick S. Downs, "Faith and Life-Style: How Christianity was Understood by Nineteenth Century Converts in North East India," *BTF* 14/1 (January-June, 1982): 22.

[17] Richard M. Eaton, "Religious Conversion in Nagaland," in *Encounter Between Gospel and Tribal Culture*, edited by A. Wati Longchar (Jorhat: Tribal Study Centre Eastern Theological College, 1999), 12.

tempest rest without one ray of light...."[18] Their weakness was the failure for an in-depth analysis of the people's age old practices and the ethical, moral and philosophical thought enveloped therein. Hence culminated in disputes, hostility and misunderstanding between the converts and the non-converts who were the custodian of traditional customs and practices. After assessing this development W.C. Smith in his book criticized Christianity that was presented to the Nagas as little more than the adoption of another set of taboos, and taboo is no new element in the life of any group on a preliterate cultural level.[19]

The position of Christian mission towards the new converts therefore, was to imbibe them to desist from what they called 'heathen practices'. Since the conversion to Christianity was massive it led to the disappearance and discontinuance of such practices which created cleavage between the converts and the non-converts. The whole structure of community life was in new order and was in a situation which was never having been experienced before. At this point in 1905 issues and conflict arose on the question of observation of festivals, ceremonies and sacrifices involving the whole village. The non-converts forced the converts to observe all festivals and *geenas* and pay for the expenses for these rituals. The converts on the other hand refused to subscribe to their forceful demand. Often the new converts were driven out of their villages, and even those who remained on were denied many facilities in the village as pressure tactics on them.[20] This issue was eventually taken to the court and the Deputy Commissioner issued orders declaring 'Liberty of Conscience' to all and thus relieving the Christians from the payment of village taxes for false worship and for the entertainment of the visitors.[21]

Later a more serious crisis arose on the question of celebration of '*Among*' (it is a traditional Sabbath of the Ao-Nagas i.e., a day of rest). Literally there were numbers of *among* to be observed in the traditional religion. The Christians were forced to observe these restricted *among* and asked to pay for the sacrifices. They were compelled to comply with the village council's orders. At times the Christians were fined for breaking the traditional laws of the Ao-Nagas.[22] This was a clear nature of persecution meted out to the early Christians. This imposition

---

[18] M.M. Clark, *A Corner in India* ..., vii, 162.

[19] W.C. Smith, *The Ao Naga Tribes of Assam: A Study in Ethnology and Sociology* (London: Macmillan and Co., Ltd., 1925), 224.

[20] Cf., Hokishe Sema, *Emergence of Nagaland: Socio-Economic and Political Transformation and the Future* (Delhi: Vikas Publishing House Pvt Ltd., 1986), 50.

[21] F.W. Dowd, "Impur," *Assam Baptist Missionary Conference Report* (1907), 51. See also W.F. Dowd, Report from Impur Field, Gauhati, January 5-12, 1907, quoted in Milton S. Sangma, *History of American Baptist Mission in North-East India (1836-1950)*, Vol. 1 (Delhi: Mittal Publications, 1987), 233; Clark, 92nd Annual Report, American Baptist Missionary Union, 1906, 156, quoted in P.T. Philip, *The Growth of Baptist Churches in Nagaland*, Second Edition (Guwahati: Christian Literature Centre, 1983), 71.

[22] Cf., R.B. Longwell, "Impur," *Assam Baptist Missionary Conference Report* (1910), 87.

created apprehension among the people and affected the growth of conversion movement. Later the issue was taken to Mr. J. Needham, the then Sub-Divisional Officer (SDO) at Mokokchung. In 1910 on 15 March, J. Needham gave the ruling that in Ao-Naga country the Christians should participate in all the 17 regular *Among* and 4 irregular *Among.*[23]

Many Christians were summoned to the court for violating the *Among* and were prosecuted.[24] They were also threatened with expulsion from the village, from clan inheritance and restricted from cultivation of their common lands, etc. The then Deputy Commissioner (DC) also made it clear in his letter that, "If it was impossible for the Christians and the non-Christians to live together, the only way of the difficulty is for the Christians to form a separate village where land is available probably somewhere on the outer range."[25] Fortunately not many villages formed a separate Christian village except in the case of Khensa and Changtongya who had to move out to form new villages in the manner of Molungyimsen. Rev. Longwell in one of the annual sessions in 1910 reported: "One of the greatest hindrances to our evangelistic work is the persecution which has been inflicted

---

[23] The Regular Among were: 1) Moatsu mong (Rest at the change of seasons) – for 3 days; 2) Tsungrem mong (rest and worship to deity) – 3 days; 3) Jameja mong (Worship to secure good crops) – 1 day; 4) Tenden mong (Worship and sacrifice at sowing time) – 1 day 5. Chiden mong (Consecration of growing crop) – 1 day; 6) Lijaba mong (Demon worship to avert calamity) – 1 day; 7) Lung Kulem mong (Worship accorded to rocks/sacred rocks) – 1 day; 8) Tzu kulem mong (Worship of large water/sacred water) – 1 day; 9) Tzubu Kulem mong (Worship of village spring/pond) – 1 day; 10) Tokong Kulem mong (Worship of the mountain/hill) – 1 day; 11) Yim Kulemshi mong (Worship of the village deity) – 1 day; 12) Talen Busong (Worship of the path to the new cultivation/new village path) – 1 day; 13) Talen Meshi mong (Sacrifice to consecrate cultivation path) – 1 day; 14) Talen walok mong (A second consecration after burning) – 1 day; 15) Aobi mong (a rite to ward off fire) – 1 day; 16) Mangkotrong Mulem mong (a rite celebrated to the skull tree on the behalf of the youg men wishing to wear boars' tusks, and also on behalf of the villagers) – 1 day; 17) Alu rong mong (worship of the cultivation after burning) – 1 day. Cf., L. Kijung Ao, *Nokinketer Mungchen* ..., 90-91; Tajen Ao, *Christianity Versus Ao Nagas* (Mokokchung: Tribal Gospel Mission Publishers, 1984), 82-83.

The Irregular Among were: 1) Keyii Sua Aoba mong (among for a man killed by tiger) – 6 days; 2) Sungdong nungi tsuka asuba mong (death by falling from a tree) – 6 days; 3) Nura agi asuba mong (death of a woman at child birth) – 3 days; 4) Keyi lepsetba mong (when villagers kill a tiger) – 2 days (In the above four Among the Christians were supposed to observe the Among according to the court order); 5) Pungzu lepsetba mong (On occasion of killing wild hog) – 1 day; 6) Su lepsetba mong (On occasion of Mithung killing) – 1 day; 7) Ki rong mong (on occasion of house burning) – 1day; 8) Among sungdong kosuk mong (on occasion of tree falling near the village gate) – 1 day; 9) Tsungsang tajung meshiba mong (worship to secure good weather) – 1 day. L. Kijung Ao, *Nokinketer Mungchen* ..., 91; Tajen Ao, *Christianity* ..., 84.

[24] L. Kijung Ao, *Nokinketer Mungchen* ..., 92.

[25] Wood Letter, Dated April 1, 1910, quoted in L. Kijung Ao, *NokinketerMungchen* ..., 92; Tajen Ao, *Christianity* ..., 85.

with the increasing rigor for a few years. If this persecution were at the hands of the un-Christian native alone, it would not be so hard to overcome."[26]

In the midst of persecution a meeting was convened in 1912 from 10-12 February under the leadership of Rev. R.B. Longwell. The outcome of this meeting was that the Christians firmly resolved not to observe *among*, not to help construction and sleep in the *Ariju*, not to pay contribution for heathen worship, etc. They resolved to put forward a memorandum to the DC Kohima containing the meetings decision.[27] In response to the memorandum, the DC granted some of the request made by the Christians. A Christian Dobashi (Interpreter) by the name Mr. Tekasosang of Changki village was appointed to be a mediator in times of disputes in consultation between SDO Hutton and Rev. Longwell. By 1916 on 16 September the issue of *Among* came to an end with this resolution: "Thereafter, case cropping up for *Among* would be decided by the local courts on merits and any aggrieved person may prefer an appeal to the higher courts. Thenceforth, the missionaries were not allowed to interfere in any case between the Christians and the Ancients. In case of disputes cropping up between the Christians and the Ancient were to be tried in a local court."[28]

In the later part of the mission it has been found that the Christians after having been discontinued to participate in the traditional practices there have been no serious calamities on their lives, and that the Christians villages was found to be more evidently prosperous than the others. This had resulted in embracing Christianity. However, the point is that the Christian missionaries' vigorous attempt to abolishing those ancient traditional cultural features was on the assumption that most of them were connected with the traditional religious practices. It is imperative to note that for the Ao-Nagas there was no dichotomy between secular and sacred. This is the point wherein the whole issue was bounded. Both the missionaries and the native people failed to examine and distinguish between what was actually connected to the ancient traditional practices and what were customary and a traditional part of life.[29] In the light of the above mentioned problem the Ao Mundang formed a strong Committee called the Ao Committee

---

[26] Rev. R.B. Longwell, "Impur," *Assam Baptist Missionary Conference Report* (1910), 87.

[27] The memorandum contained the following objections among others: 1) Objection against Sub-divisional Officer's order compelling people including Christians to attend Bazar on Sunday at Mokokchung; 2) Objection against Sub-Divisional Officer's order forbidding Japu village to send pupils to school at Impur; 3) Objection against contribution to heathen religion rites and ceremonies; 4) To exempt the Christians from labour for government works on Sundays; 5) To discontinue the custom of the Christian boys sleeping in Ariju; 6) To reconsider the matter of the Christians who are compelled to abstain from working in the fields on Among days. Tajen Ao, *Christianity* ..., 85-86; See also L. Kijung Ao, *Nokinketer Mungchen* ..., 92-93.

[28] Tajen Ao, *Christianity* ..., 90.

[29] Cf., Panger Imchen, *Ancient Ao Naga Religion and Culture* (New Delhi: Har-Anand Publications, 1993), 159.

for smooth functioning of the churches and to maintaining peaceful relation within the Ao-Naga society and also with the British administration.

Socio-Political Issue and the Role of the Church

The impact of World War I had some indirect bearing and influence on the life of the Ao-Nagas and the Nagas as a whole. This gave birth to a strong Naga National Consciousness. During the War, a Naga labour force consisting of 200 Ao-Nagas went to France to support the allies. It was a time of encounter with the modern world that would shape their whole perspective in their long history of political struggle. For the first time they saw the mighty civilization of the outside world. The civilization they saw and encountered enhanced their horizon of rationality. According to AsosoYonuo:

> The Nagas who went to France brought back horrified accounts as to how the great civilized nations fought for their ends and interest while Nags were condemned as barbarous for their head-hunting. Second, the intercourse among the different Nagas of different tribes in France, far from home fostered mutual love, service and a sense of political unity which manifested itself in their verbal resolution that on their return to their land they would work for friendship and unity among themselves … It was this spirit which spearheaded an upsurge of the Naga Nationalist Movement.[30]

After their return these Nagas decided to form a Naga Association in 1918, which was called 'Naga Club'. This Club sought to solve the problems of the Naga people with the British through talks and consultations. In the beginning this Club consisted of old soldiers, government officials and Dobashis.[31] The spirit of nationalism was slowly gaining ground in Nagaland. The purpose of Naga Club in its inception was social rather than political in character but later it developed a political outlook and raised its will against the British imperialism. When the Simon Commission[32] visited Kohima on the 10 January 1929, the Naga Club, the only Naga organization existing then, submitted a memorandum underlining their demand for the independence of the Nagas. This memorandum was signed by as many as 20 persons representing the different tribes. The memorandum states:

---

[30] Asoso Yonuo, *The Rising Nagas: A Historical and Political Study* (New Delhi: Vikas Publishing House, 1974), 125-126.

[31] Hokishe Sema, *Emergence of Nagaland* …, 80.

[32] This was a Statutory Commission consisting of six English Members of Parliament that formed under the chairmanship of Sir John Simon in November 1927 during the Baldwin Government to study the Indian situation for future policy.

> We pray that the British Government will continue to safeguard our rights against all encouragements from other people who are more advanced than us by withdrawing our country from the reformed scheme and placing it directly under its protection. If the British Government, however, want to throw us away, we pray that we should not be thrust to the mercy of the people who could never have conquered us themselves, and to whom we were never subjected; but to leave us alone to determine ourselves as in ancient times.[33]

Though the memorandum contained the request to exclude Nagaland from the proposed reform, it certainly has had political significance and bearing. It indicated the restoration of independence which the British had forcefully taken over from them. But the Commission did not consider the Naga memorandum since it lacked the requisite qualifications for a separate state. Later they were included in the list of 'Excluded Areas' of India under the Government of India Act 1935 under the direct responsibility of the Governor of the province of Assam on 3 March 1936.

During the Second World War (1939-45), the Nagas worked consistently for the Allied troops to defeat the Japanese forces marching along with the Indian National Army led by Subhas Chandra Bose. Nagaland's capital, Kohima became a battle ground. Many Ao-Nagas were also recruited to the battle field. The war brought them closer to the modern world which for centuries was isolated. Their direct contact with the different nationalities enhanced their worldview and began to conceive of themselves as part of a larger world. They were galvanized within a transient span of time into the modern streams and conceptions of life, humanity and made known to outside world.[34] The society began to transform in all the areas of political, social, economic, moral and cultural life. In the process of their interaction and encounter with the people and to the alien culture which was superior to them resulted in degrading their moral condition. The church was not immune by this moral corruption. In this regard Rev. Temjen comments: "There were many who started drinking and disobeyed the discipline of church. The spiritual life of the Church began to decline and turned cold. Gambling, robbery and adultery became a common feature. People lost interest in the teaching of the word of God. There were more backsliders in the church than genuine believers."[35] For this reasons many Christians were excommunicated from the

---

[33] M. Alemchiba, *A Brief Historical Account of Nagaland* (Kohima: Naga Institute of Culture, 1970), 164.

[34] Cf., Asoso Yonuo, *The Rising Nagas* ..., 149.

[35] Temjen Ao, *Tsungremer Tsunglu* (God's Rain) (Mokokchung: ACYE Press, 1979), 12.

church. The immoral spirit continued in the church so there was only a slight growth during the 1940s.[36]

Sensing the Nagas aspiration and in the light of the political development the then Deputy Commissioner of Naga Hills C.R. Pawsey, with the aim of uniting the Nagas established an institution in April 1945, which was called the 'Naga Hills District Tribal Council' to bring political unity of all the Nagas for national freedom. The following year on February 2, the name was changed to the Naga National Council (NNC), which ultimately emerged as the only political organization in Naga Hills.[37] The NNC until this time was seeking local autonomy of the Naga people within India. However, the demand for independence of Nagaland was officially voiced first in June of 1947 by the NNC. They voiced that Nagaland should become a sovereign independent state when British rule in India ceased on 15 August 1947.[38]

Following the policy of the NNC, an armed struggle between the Nagas and the Government forces was ensued and the supporters of the NNC were subjected to great torture and harassment by the Government forces. Agitation for independence seemed to gain momentum. People resorted to Civil Disobedience movement and arms to achieve their goal. In the process there had been the tragedy of burning houses, terrorizing of villages with atrocities and threats from both the India side and the underground Nagas. The Nagas extremely suffered during this national crisis. Many innocent lives were lost and there were deaths on both sides.[39] The evangelization work was also affected. In this line Anderson noted: "The agitation among the Nagas for independence is affecting the workers in our Churches also as their attendance at various and frequent committee meetings takes time and energy and other work suffers."[40]

The years between 1954-1974 were the most serious political disturbances in the political history of the Nagas. The Church suffered deeply during these periods of political unrest and therefore simultaneously hindered the work of the missionaries in several ways. For instance, during the operations of the Indian Army, many churches were burned down, ransacked and violated its sanctity.

---

[36] Cf., Nuklu Longkumer, *The Growth of Baptist Churches among the Aos of Nagaland* (Jorhat: Changtongya Baptist Church, 1988), 72-73.

[37] M. Alemchiba, *Historical Account* ..., 165.

[38] Asoso Yonuo, *The Rising Nagas* ..., 200. They declared Independence on August 14 1947 and on September 18, 1954 they declared "Free Nagaland" as Sovereign Republic. They also re-organized their government and formed the "Federal Government of Nagaland" (FGN) on October 16, 1956. After three decades due to long unfulfilled aspiration, another organization emerged as the National Socialist Council of Nagaland (NSCN) on January 31, 1980. But later split into two as NSCN (I-M) and NSCN (K) in 1988, just after eight years of its formation. See A. Lanunungsang Ao, *From Phizo to Muivah* (New Delhi: Mittal Publication, 2002), 67, 97.

[39] Puveyi Dozo, *The Growth of the Baptist Church in Chakhesang Naga Tribe* (Calcutta: The Statesman Printing Press, 1978), 60.

[40] Anderson, "Impur Mission Field Report," *Annual Baptist Mission Field Report* (1947), 2.

The movement of missionaries and evangelists were also restricted. This however, did not weaken both the church as well as insurgency movement. Rev. Kijung remarked in his report in 1955 and 1958 the position and vision of the church:

> Our Churches have had to undergo many hardships because of political unrest in our area; however we have been able to keep politics out of the church circle[41] .... In trials, sufferings, and difficulties, churches are conscious of the voice of God, speaking to us today, challenging us to go forward to proclaim the gospel of Jesus Christ not only to the Nagas but to the world. God has His own way to prepare His people for a purpose for the glory of His kingdom. Whatever may come for the Naga people, the churches in Nagaland have taken their stand to be with Christ who is the hope of the World.[42]

Despite visits by dignitaries and exchange of visits of Good-will Missions the situation remained unabated. The NNC remained firmed in its stand for a sovereign and independent Nagaland. On the other hand the Government of India was also firmed on its stand that while it was prepared to allow the Nagas to enjoy maximum autonomy within the Indian Union, it was not prepared even to discuss the issue of complete independence. Thus, the political situation became day by day worse and worse and eventually led to open arm conflict.[43] Therefore, when the movement launched by NNC was offing, American missionaries and the Church were suspected by the Indian Government for abetting secessionist movement. As a result, the Government of India issued orders against the missionaries to leave Nagaland. Thus the missionaries were forcefully evacuated from Nagaland.[44] On the departure of the missionaries, the responsibilities were transferred to the native missionaries. However, the Church continued to achieve great results amidst political instability. For instance there were 1234 members in 1956 and 2500 in 1958; in 1961, the Christian community was roughly estimated to be 51,520 out of the total population of 53,576.[45]

Amidst the political turmoil Nagaland was granted statehood on 1 December 1963. But this did not solve the aspiration of the Nagas for the assertion to become an independent and sovereign Nagaland. Sensing the deteriorating political conditions of the Naga people the Church began to take active role with a view to solving the problem. As a result, under the initiative of the Nagaland Baptist

---

[41] Kijungluba, "Ao Church Association," *Annual Report Council of Baptist Churches in Assam and Manipur Minutes* (Dec, 1955), 50.

[42] Kijungluba, "Ao Church Association," *Annual Report Council of Baptist Churches in Assam and Manipur Minutes* (Dec, 1958), 70.

[43] M. Alemchiba, *Historical Account* ..., 179.

[44] Cf., Tajen Ao, *Christianity* ..., 457; A. Bendangyabang. Ao, *History of Christianity in Nagaland; Social Changes, 1872-1972* (Bangalore: Shalom Ministry Publication, 2004), 208.

[45] P.T. Philip, *The Growth of Baptist Churches in Nagaland* ..., 77.

Church, a Peace Mission was formed in 1964 and the peace negotiation began the same year. On 6 September 1964 an agreement to cease-fire was signed between the Government and the Nationalist leaders. Among the native missionaries, late Rev. Longri Ao occupies a unique position in the history of missionary for the role he played in bringing about ceasefire between the Naga Federal Government and the Government of India under the aegis of the Peace mission in 1964.[46] It is poignant that even after more than 60 years the problem of the Naga National movement has not been solved. This is an acute problem in Nagaland. However, the church in its own capacity is playing a vital role in ushering reconciliation and peace process between the Government and the nationalist groups.

Conclusion

Evidentially, coming of Christianity and British administration weakened and re-shaped the Ao-Naga traditional worldview as the worldview and value system presented by Christianity was seen to be highly articulated and superior to their traditional value system. Hence, in Christianity they have found a more refined worldview. In the process of their interaction the old cultural, social and religious values began to disintegrate in order to give a new meaning to it. In the process the missionaries based on their strong conviction of evangelical theology opposed the traditional socio-cultural and religious beliefs and practices. Consequently the new converts began to abandon their traditional beliefs and practices. As a result hostile opposition and persecution followed due to the wide acceptance of the new religion since it began to demean the traditional belief system and practices which at one point of time was a binding factor for the community. Seeing this alarming change sizable non-convert began to opposed to the mission activities. This resulted in socio-religious issues, problems and conflict within the church; the native people and the missionaries and also between the British officials and the missionaries. The British administration was in against of the attitude of the missionaries towards the tribal culture. This development strained their relationship. However, despite certain difficulties and issues the impact of Christianity was tremendous on individual, social and religious levels. This level of interaction led to a new route for change and transformation. The progress of the people was made possible through the introduction of Christianity. Social and religious disillusion were removed and gave them a new social status. The moral standard and values of life was positively affected and improved. It provided space to develop consciousness in matters relating to individual, community and in their spiritual lives.

W.T.

[46] Tajen Ao, *Christianity* ..., 47.

Chapter 11

Trends of Tribal Awakening in North East India Since 1947

There are three major trends of tribal awakening one could observe in North East India (NEI) since colonial times. The first one is a consolidated spirit of various tribal organisations to fight for their rights during pre-independent India (1933-1947). The second one is a consolidated political movement for separate political units (1947-1980s). Thirdly, a new turn of tribal awakening since late 1980s, which is very much exclusive in nature and fragmented one based on ethnicity.[1] The first one was against the British colonialism on the issue of Tribal land; the second was against the Indian state and dominant communities on the issue of economic and political neglect and domination; and the third one is within the ethnic communities over the issue of land and ethnic identity.

This chapter is an attempt to analyse and present the positive and negative aspects of tribal awakening in NEI with an objective of finding way forward towards ethno-ecumenism and peaceful co-existence among all ethnic communities.

An overview of Tribal Awakening process in NEI

As it is already introduced, the tribal awakening in NEI underwent micro to macro level shift in focus. It moved from tribal consolidation to ethnic consolidation and then finally ethnic fragmentations. No doubt, unlike the tribals

[1] For this reason, and the very nature of people's awakening in ethnic line, the phrase "ethnic awakening" is used here rather than the "tribal awakening." Also this is deliberately used for the fact that many of the ethnic communities in the region are not included under "tribal" category as political usage of the term is concerned. However, the "tribal awakening" also is used as general category to mean all marginalised indigenous people groups of India.

of mainland India, every ethnic communities of NEI have become conscious of their identity, dignity and status, and awakened to fight for their due rights. There is great amount of awakening and forward movement in all aspects of life and to a large extent achieved their aspirations of self-determination and self-rule, especially in the Hills. However, not only the tribal communities as a whole, but also the indigenous communities of the region have completely got fragmented because of exclusive ethnic self-awakenings. The trend of consolidated tribal awakening during pre-independent India as well as the ethnic consolidation after Independence is no more visible.

At the wake of state reorganisations (1960s-1980s) and creation of various autonomous councils and districts based on ethnic composition the trend of tribal awakening completely changed from micro to macro movements with very exclusive claims and demands, particularly over the issue of land and ethnic identity. In other words, it has shifted from tribal to ethnic; from tribal consolidation movement to separatist ethnic movement; or from inclusive tribal movement to exclusive ethnic movements over land and identity. Instead of raising voices together, various ethnic groups raised their voices in isolation to each other. The common concern of tribal communities to fight for the preservation of respective ethnic identifies through a common political platform have completely disappeared. The very focus of fight against the centre's neglect, and the social, economic and political oppression, exploitation and discrimination meted out by the dominant people of the region got shifted to fight among each other and to its worst, an internecine and fratricidal conflicts. One can perhaps consider this negative awakening as dark side of tribal awakening in NEI.

The Process of Ethnic Awakening in NEI

The ethnic awakening in the form of movements uses the "primordial" and "instrumental" elements,[2] which have deep-rooted historical, social, economic and political foundations in them. Ethnic identity, considered in the positive sense of the term, involves a subjective and symbolic use of certain cultural elements by a group of people whereby they differentiate themselves from others. Hence, initially the primordial identification marks are consolidated for ethnic mobilisation by utilising them for formulation of ideologies and determination of ethnic boundaries. However, since much of the anxiety which has characterised the ethnic groups of NEI has been associated with the identity crisis which

---

[2] There are several alternative approaches that have been articulated to explain the persisting ethnic conflict in the modernised world. "Primordial" and "Instrumental" are two important dimensions that prominently figure in the context of NEI. The concept "primordial" is used here to refer the ethnic solidarities that prompt people to mobilise in defence of their culture; and the "instrumental" to refer to the cultural identity which is invoked as an instrument to attain political and material goods. Cf. Debasish Bhattacharjee, "Hmar-Dimasa Conflict in Assam: A Historical Perspective," in *Inter-Ethnic Conflict in Northeast India*, ed. Girin Phukon (New Delhi: South Asian Publishers, 2005), 124.

they had been facing due to various factors – economic, socio-cultural and political – and with their search for roots,[3] those groups which have reached a level of self-awareness tend to articulate their own criteria for inclusion into and exclusion from the other. As a consequence, in the subsequent phases, the same identities are used as "instrumental" with a view to seeking political and economic advantages.[4] These, in their turn are eventually used for political goals – "politics of recognition"[5] as vehicles for psyche emancipation and political empowerment.

A rightful fight against economic and political neglect, and cultural hegemony by the dominants, on the one hand, and the increasing importance given to the assertion of identities, self-determination and the upsurge of ethno-national[6] movements, on the other, constitute two contrasting reality of ethnic awakening in NEI. The former attempts to de-legitimise the notion of exclusive national-territorial domains, the later, instead, envisages the state or other legitimate territorial arrangements as the only route to liberation, democracy and development.[7] The later trend has occupied centre stage in NEI, leading to a crisis point as different groups of ethnic communities within the region assert their specific claims for what they consider to be, legitimate political power and share of resources, particularly, the land.

In the process, the different ethnic groups have passed through three stages of identity formations. The *first stage* is ethnicity, involving an existence of cultural markers easily recognisable, but whose political significance is generally unnoticed. The *second* is community awareness, involving the evolution of cultural identity into a political consciousness with the attendant urge to employ it for furthering community interests. And the *third* is of nationality formation involving the right

[3] Cf. B. Datta, "Ethnicity, Nationalism and Sub-Nationalism with Special Reference to North-East India," in *Nationality, Ethnicity and Cultural Identity in North-East India,* ed. B. Pakem (New Delhi, Guwahati: Omsons Publications, 1990), 39.

[4] Cf. M.N. Karna, "Ethnic Identity and Socio-Economic Processes in North-Eastern India," in *Dynamics of Identity and Intergroup Relations in North-East India,* ed. Kailash S. Aggarwal (Shimla: IIAS, 1999), 29.

[5] Charles Taylor, "The Politics of Recognition," in *Multiculturalism: Examining the Politics of Recognition,* ed. Amu Gutman (Princeton, NJ: Princeton University Press, 1994), 25.

[6] The term was originally used by Walker Connor for whom nationalism in its pristine sense is integrally related to ethnicity. Cf. W. Connor, *Ethnonationalism: The Quest for Understanding* (Princeton: Princeton University Press, 1994), xi. Taking this sense, Pachuau argues that that is how most "tribals" of Northeast India understand their "national" identity; and from this perspective, India is a multinational country. Lalsangkima Pachuau, "In Search of a Context for a Contextual Theology: The Socio-Political Realities of "Tribal" Christians in Northeast India," in *In Search of Identity and Tribal Theology,* ed. A. Wati Longchar (Jorhat, Assam: Tribal Study Centre, ETC, 2001), 32-33.

[7] Cf. Akhil Ranjan Dutta, "Globalization and Ethnic Movements: A Synoptic View," in *Inter-Ethnic Conflict in Northeast India,* ed. Girin Phukon (New Delhi: South Asian Publishers, 2005), 40-41.

to self-determination.[8] Most of the ethnic groups in the region seem to have reached the *third stage* of evolution in which the *nations from below*[9] are launching movements against the State machinery with a view to offset the State dominance.

Two category of resultant movements have emerged though such process of ethnic awakening – ethno-cultural movements and ethno-political[10] movements with the objectives of defending their livelihood, protecting their identity and propounding a cultural specific sub-nationalism.

Ethno-Cultural Movements

In general, there were two diametrically opposite processes that was in operation among various tribes of NEI – first, trying to emulate the traditional Hindu way of life, the second, making a conscious effort to reinforce their own traditional socio-cultural systems.[11] The former is more visible among the Plains tribes and the latter among the Hills tribes. Whatever, the case may be, the ethno-cultural movement is the first clear pointer of ethnic awakening among various tribes of NEI. In most of the ethno-cultural movements, the tribes try to revitalise their traditions and cultures in order to stand against the hegemonic dominant cultural milieu.[12] There has been conscious attempt of reviving the socio-cultural traditions among the tribes. This process perhaps interestingly resembles with the "Revitalisation Movement" of Wallace[13] and the "Nativistic Movement" of Linton.[14]

---

[8] Analyzed and interpreted based on Paul Brass's theory and comparison on ethnicity and nationalism. See, Paul R. Brass, *Ethnicity and Nationalism: Theory and Comparison* (New Delhi: Sage Publications, 1991), 18-23.

[9] For the elaboration of this concept, see Prasenjit Biswas, "Nations from the Below and Rebel Consciousness: The 'New Subaltern' Emergence of North East India'," in *Human Rights and Insurgency: The North-East India*, ed. R. R. Dhamala and Sukalpa Bhattacharjee (New Delhi: Shipra, 2002), 140-69.; Prasenjit Biswas and Sukalpa Bhattacharjee, "The Outsider, The State and Nations from Bellow: North East India as a Subject of Exclusion," in *Ethnicity, Identity and the State in South Asia*, ed. J. Azam Kousar (New Delhi: South Asian Publisher, 2001), 232-259.; Prasenjit Biswas and Chandan Suklabaidya, *Ethnic Life-Worlds in North-East India* (New Delhi: Sage Publications, 2007), ch. 6.

[10] The political movements in NEI are basically based on ethnic considerations. Therefore, the coined term "ethno-political" is used with the double meaning i.e. ethnic and political.

[11] Buddhadeb Chaudhuri, "Identity Crisis of the Tribals: A Case Study," in *Tribal Transformation in India, Ethnopolitics and Identity Crisis*, ed. Buddhadeb Chaudhuri (New Delhi: Inter-India Publications, 1992), 435.

[12] A vivid example of such self-identity consciousness is seen in their change of names. For instance, *Lothas* and *Semas* in Nagaland adopted *Kyongs* and *Sumi* respectively; known as *Mikirs* in Assam changed their name to *Karbis*; *Pawis* and *Tuikuks* in present Mizoram changed to *Lai* and *Riangs* respectively; some of the *Kukis* in present Manipur came to be known as *Thado* and *Daflas* in Arunachal Pradesh called themselves as *Nishis* and so on.

[13] A. Wallace, "Revitalization Movements," *American Anthropologist* 58 (1956): 264-81.

[14] R. Linton, "Nativistic Movements," *American Anthropologist* 45 (1943): 230-40.

Such awakening is an attempt to define the socio-cultural identity of each tribe in the new context of Independence, especially among the Hill tribes who are not much touched by the Hindu cultures.[15] However, the process had grown in strength even among the once most Hinduised plain tribes of Assam after the Independence. The emergence of Boro nationalism is one of the notable examples of such a movement. Following India's Independence, cultural and social activities were the prime concerns of the Boro movement and their demands were confined to greater educational opportunities and developmental assistance. The establishment of *Boro Sahitya Sabha* (Boro Literature Society) in 1952 led to the demand for the introduction of Boro as an optional language in schools of Assam. In the middle of the sixties, the Boros started demanding the use of Boro language as the medium of instruction at the higher secondary stage. Successful accomplishment of this linguistic struggle was shifted into the demand for Bodoland, a State separate from Assam.[16]

Similarly, two other nativistic movements sought to revive the pristine elements of indigenous culture in Meghalaya and Manipur. The *Seng Khasi* in Meghalaya, a socio-cultural organisation of Khasis was established in 1989 to preserve the Khasi way of life, with its ancient system of clan relationship, which had been disturbed by the large-scale conversion of the Khasis to Christianity.[17] The Zeliangrong, a similar movement, started as a religio-cultural movement under the leadership of Jadonang in Manipur. But it assumed political overtones and became the only movement to have established linkages with the Indian national freedom movement. Later, under the Rani Gaidinliu, it has remained strongly nationalistic and promoted a tribal solidarity and demanded creation of a separate administrative unit to be formed out of territories inhabited by the constituent tribes in the contiguous regions of Manipur, Assam and Nagaland.[18] However, there is a movement for de-Sanskritisation, an impulse to go back to the pre-*Vaishnava*, the pristine form of Meitei culture which essentially consists of rejecting Hindu cultural hegemony in Manipur.[19] The growth of sub-national and sub-ethnic movements such as of Dimasas, Karbis, Kukis, Hmars and others

---

[15] Cf. M.N. Srinivas and R.D. Sanwal, "Some aspects of Political Development in the North-Eastern Hill Areas of India," in *Tribal Situation in India*, ed. K.S. Singh (Shimla: IIAS, 1972), 118.

[16] Cf. Ajit K. Danda, "Ethnicity and Social Transformation in North-East India," *Man in India* 72/2 (1992): 133.

[17] A cultural dimension of the political process has been the phenomenal rise of Christianity in all the hill states particularly during 1961-71 as symbol of tribal identity, as a marker of status. Christianity emerged as the strongest factor of modernisation, and has given the tribals a strong sense of identity.

[18] Cf. G. Kabui, "The Zeliangrong Movement: A Historical Study," in *Tribal Movements in India,* ed. K.S. Singh (New Delhi: Manohar Publications, 1982), 53-66.

[19] B.B. Kumar, "North East India: Crisis of Perception & Credible Action," Dialogue: *(Quarterly) A Journal of Astha Bharati* 1/2 (Oct-Dec.1999). Available at: http://www.nenanews.com/ne.htm (accessed Sept. 7, 2008).

though with different outcomes have followed a similar pattern of ethno-cultural movement.

In short, the trend since Independence is that each indigenous tribes dwelling in the hills or in the plains, wants to retain their customs and traditions, actuated by a strong desire to improve their status in the economic and political realm. Many indigenous people converted either to Christianity, Islam or Hinduism are asking questions about their heritages and early beliefs. The most vivid is from indigenous Christians, particularly the theologically oriented ones.

Such ethno-cultural movements were the result of a gradual ethnic awakening process. However, if the cultural identity is not adequately achieved through the "Cultural Revolution" – a conscious symbolical revival of typical traditional tribal culture, each tribe resort to ethno-political movement for a separate State, which often are violent in their means and political in their end.

Ethno-Political Movements

It was just a year before and a decade after Independence of India that the manifestation of ethnic identity took on vigorous political colour in the region. For instance, with purely political objectives, organisations like the Naga National Council (1946),[20] the Mizo Union (1946),[21] the Karbi Movement for Autonomous District (1946),[22] the Zeliangrong Movement for Separate State (1947),[23] the Tripura Upajati Samiti (1957)[24] and so on surfaced throughout NEI. After 70 years, the number of such organisations and movements have multiplied into hundreds and almost all of these political organisations having underground wings styled as "liberation" or "security" forces. In accordance with this, most of the ethnic groups today have their own political parties, and even militant organisations named after their respective ethnic names[25] with promising agenda of liberating the group they represent.

---

[20] Cf. M. Alemchiba, *A Brief Historical Account of Nagaland* (Kohima: Naga Institute of Culture, 1970).

[21] Cf. B. B. Goswami and D. P. Mukherjee, "The Mizo Political Movement," in *Tribal Movements in India,* ed. K.S. Singh (vol. I. Delhi: Manohar Publications, 1982).

[22] Cf. R. D. Pathak and N. Saha, "Political Developments in the North Cachar Hill Distict," in *Tribal Movements in India,* ed. K.S. Singh (vol. I. Delhi: Manohar Publications, 1982).

[23] Cf. G. Kabui, "The Zeliangrong Movement : A Historical Study," in *Tribal Movements in India,* ed. K.S. Singh (Delhi: Manohar Publications, 1982).

[24] Cf. S. K. Chaube, *Hills Politics in North East India* (Calcutta: Orient Longman, 1973).

[25] For example, Boro Liberation Tigers (BLT), Karbi National Volunteers (KNV), Tiwa National Revolutionary Force (TNRF), Kuki National Front (KNF), Hmar Revolutionary Front (HRF), Dimasa Halam Daogah (DHD), Zomi Revolutionary Voluntary (ZRV) and so on. A detailed report and analysis of such organisations can be found in Apurba K. Baruah, *Youth Organisations in North East India,* Report of the ICSSR, NERC Project on Youth Organisations in North East India, Submitted to NERC, Shillong, 2000.

In fact, the awakening and aspiration for self-determination due to specific historical and separate administrative traditions in the hills has been political in nature since colonial rule. Perhaps, the seeds of identity-consciousness were sown with emergence of a "middle class" through expansion of modern education and entry to the jobs under colonial Administration,[26] But as it is discussed above, such assertiveness started among the plain tribes primarily with an apparent non-political focus such as the safeguarding cultural identity, the preservation of language, the choice of script, the instruction of education through one's mother tongue, the continuance of English as the common medium of instruction in higher education etc. Such demands later culminated into a political demand – a separate political identity. Consequently, some demanded ST status, some a Federal Structure, some an Autonomous State, some a Separate State and even Sovereignty for some. In all this, the middle class and student youth forces play major role to awaken the people of their respective societies for ethno-movements.

All the ethno-political movements primarily have to do with identity issue.[27] Though all of these movements have diverse aims and objectives, the objective of "liberation" and "establishment of identity" are common to all.[28] Those movement are not an insurgency or insurgent movements[29] as it is commonly labelled, but rather considered as a liberation movement.[30] B.K. Roy Burman, a noted anthropologist of the region also of the view that "in their heyday the insurgents are not anti-social. In their subjective-objective concourse they are pilgrims in the turbulent journey towards, what they think to be just society,

---

[26] P.S. Datta, "What Ails Assam? Need for Soul-Searching," *Mainstream* XXIII/50 (Oct. 6, 1990): 15.

[27] B. G. Verghese, *India's Northeast Resurgent: Ethnicity, Insurgency, Governance, Development* (Delhi: Konark Publishers, 1996), 285.

[28] Of course, there is a dilemma between whether "liberation first then identity" or "identity first then liberation." For some it is "how can there be identity without liberation?" and for others, "how can one achieve liberation without proper identity first?" In case of the most of armed struggle movements, it is liberation first, but for most of the social change and transformation movements, it is liberation through identity building.

[29] This is the most common expression used to identify the revolutionary movements in NEI. However, the leaders of these movements never describe themselves as "insurgents" but rather as patriots, freedom fighters, defenders of their people and so on. "Insurgent" is therefore not a self-designation but a term generally applied by their opponents. For detail reports on this, see B. Pakem, ed. *Insurgency in North-East India* (New Delhi: Omsons Publications, 1997), 3.

[30] There are several terms used by the journalists, government officials and some academicians which strongly picture and publicise the negative image about the tribal people in NEI. For instance, *India's North-East Frontier: Fifty Turbulent Years*; *Boiling Cauldron of Insurgency and Terrorism* (S. K. Ghosh); *Insurgency in NEI* (B. Pakem); *Naga Insurgency: The Last Thirty Years* (M. Horam).

good society, liberated humanity."[31] Neither can this be considered as tribalism.[32] Instead, it is tribes of the region trying to resolve the problem of being the fringe of marginal groups in the wider national and oppressive dominant contexts. It is a movement for liberation from various aspects – basically protection of land and liberation from external forces as well as preservation of the distinctive identity, culture, tradition, customs and their own history as a whole.

Factors of Ethnic Awakening and Resultant Ethno-cultural-political Movements

As it already has been noted, the manifestation of ethnic awakening through ethno-cultural and ethno-political movements in NEI emerged out of numerous diverse factors. Those factors perhaps can be analysed under two broad categories – the perceived and factual factors.

First and foremost, the British Colonialism and Christian missions are perceived to be the prime factor of various ethnic awakenings, basically the negative awakenings from the perspective of dominants. The British administrative policies during pre-independent India and conversion to Christianity are considered as the initial factors towards a new consciousness of identity.[33] For instance, it is alleged that the Christian missionaries penetrated deep into many of the ethnic communities. They opened them up to a modern world by providing education and health care.[34] Indeed, a significant changes in the tribal pattern of life and culture resulted from conversion to Christianity, education and other welfare measures introduced by the missionaries. Education, in fact, happens to be the most efficient direct factor for ethnic awakening. The active engagement in literary works and education acted as opinion builders and motivators of socio-political awareness among the hill tribes.[35] This generated a new social and political awareness among the ethnic communities.[36] It has made them more articulate and has given them courage to oppose the exploitation and inhuman treatment meted

[31] B.K. Roy Burman, "Insurgency: Its Dynamics and Vision for Northeast India," in *Insurgency in North East India*, edited by B. Pakem (New Delhi: Omsons Publications, 1997), 21.

[32] For, "the tribalism is deliberate withdrawal and unwillingness on the part of a small community to explore the possibilities of social and political relationship beyond the tribal universe." A.C. Bhagabati, "Tribal Transformation in Assam and North-East India: An Appraisal of Emerging Ideological Dimensions," in *Tribal Transformation in India: Vol. III Ethnopolitics and Identity Crisis,* ed. Chaudhuri Buddhadeb (New Delhi: Inter-India Publications, 1992), 501.

[33] Cf. K. Thanzauva, *Theology of Community - Tribal Theology in the Making* (Aizwal: Mizo Theological Conference, 1997), 54.

[34] "Tenth Business Session (Discussion): Integration and Understanding in the North-east," in *The Tribal Situation in India,* ed. K.S. Singh (Shimla: Indian Institute of Advanced Study, 1972), 19.

[35] Cf. Girin Phukon, "Elite Conflict as a Factor of Ethnic Crisis in Northeast India," in *Inter-Ethnic Conflict in Northeast India,* ed. Girin Phukon (New Delhi: South Asian Publishers, 2005), 87.

[36] Cf. B.G. Verghese, *India's Northeast Resurgent: Ethnicity, Insurgency, Governance, Development* (Delhi: Konark Publishers Pvt. Ltd., 2004 [1996]), 5.

out to them from various quarters.[37] Notwithstanding the negative impacts, one must agree with Mankekar that "India as a whole should however be grateful to the early Christian missionaries for helping these tribals to make the big leap forward from primitive life to modernity and thus taking off the overweighed shoulders of Independent India that gigantic task and preparing them to take their due place in India polity."[38]

Nevertheless, the British colonialism and Christian missions either directly or indirectly cannot be considered as sole factors of ill ethno-awakening in NEI. The impetus behind ethnic awakenings in the entire NEI lies in various factual as well as other perceived factors. The denial of basic human rights or gross violation of human rights, discriminatory economic policy, neglect and non-recognition of peoples' aspiration, non-recognition of their right to protect respective identity and heritage, treatment that they are inferior to the rest of India[39] etc. are some of the direct contributory factors. Besides, the state reorganisations and demographic change on ethnic lines,[40] the issue of land alienation, illegal migration, lack of livelihoods, impact of modernisation and crisis of identity, economic discontentment and competition for limited resources, the perceived feeling of insecurity etc. are some of the prime factors for new turn in ethnic awakening in the region.

No doubt, in nutshell, the ethnic awakening in NEI are due to political subjection, economic and social neglect or lack of action for development from the Centre[41] and state administrations; economic oppression, exploitation and discrimination and cultural hegemony by the dominant communities, which are against their aspirations for better life, dignified identity and better world. But one also cannot overlook the perceptional factors among the ethnic communities which often results in emotional outburst and misplaced anger leading to conflict

---

[37] Cf. Stephen Fuchs, "Liberation Movements among the Tribals of India," in *Towards an Indian Theology of Liberation*, ed. Paul Puthanangady (Bangalore: Indian Theological Association and National Biblical Catechetical and Liturgical Centre, 1986), 216.

[38] Mankekar, D.R. "Understanding the Tribals on the North-Eastern Border," in *Tribal Situation in India.* Edited by K.S. Singh (Shimla: Indian Institute of Advanced Study, 1972), 111.

[39] Cf. B. Datta Ray, "Anatomy of Regionalism in North-East India Hills: A Preliminary Observation," in *Tribal Transformation in India: Ethnopolitics and Identity Crisis*, ed. Buddhadeb Chaudhuri (New Delhi: Inter-India Publications, 1992), 476.

[40] For example, creation of Nagaland 1963, statehood to Manipur and Meghalaya in 1972, Mizoram and Arunachal Pradesh in 1987, and many other autonomous Districts have threatened the other ethic people living in those areas.

[41] Many Northeast watchers feel that the Centre's response to its problems has always been a "knee-jerk reaction". On the one hand, the centre calls them as "problem child"; on the other hand, the tribals feel that they are receiving "step-motherly treatment. See, "Lalsangkima Pachuau, *Ethnic Identity and Christianity: A Socio-Historical and Missiological Study of Christianity in Northeast India with Special Reference to Mizoram* (Frankfurt am Main: Peter Laing, 2002), 29.; Also see Lalsangkima Pachuau, "Towards Overcoming Violence in North East India," in *Overcoming Violence*, ed. Samson Prabhakar (Bangalore: SATHRI/BTESSC, 2004), 32f.

not only with external forces, but also with the perceived enemy within the ethnic communities of the region.

Risk factors in Ethnic Awakening in NEI

Needless to say, ethnic communities of NEI have come of age where they are awakened in every aspects of life with a concerted political consciousness. As it is already stated, there has been great awareness and awakening of ethnic communities after the reorganisation of NEI into various states, autonomous councils and districts. However, such awakening and political consciousness in recent decades, especially late 1980s onwards, has moved from consolidated ethnic awakening to exclusive self-identity consciousness. Looking at the success of some dominant ethnic communities on the one hand, and the experience of neglect and domination by those communities, on the other, have challenged each and every small community characterised with some noticeable cultural markers imagined or real, have started asking for a separate political identity and special privileges.

The current trends of ethnic awakening in the region shows that the perception and consciousness of "Self" and "Other" is on the raise. In fact, as the emancipatory promise offered by identity politics was at its peak during the post - Independence era in India, there was an upsurge in the consciousness of self and recognition of differences. Particularly, since 1980s, the issues of ethnic self-identity and recognition of "other" have multiplied. Several ethnic groups, due to a variety of factors became aware of the necessity of self-identification over against the "others". The ethnic communities saw themselves as being increasingly different from the others. Differentiation became one of the important norms to usher in a new and sharper sense of self-identity. With a view to creating and consolidating its respective identities, every group makes efforts to construct its "other" and this logic of "other" is intensified by the cultural and political consciousness and formation of distinct cultural organisations and political parties in ethnic lines.

Today, every community are conscious of their ethnic identity and take pride in it. Such identity-consciousness is not only taken as pride in respective ethnic tradition, but also as a defence mechanism against the designs of legitimising a system of deprivation. The identity movement is now celebrated as the arena of cultural and political resistance. So, every ethnic community got awakened a latent identity-consciousness and aspire for self-determination. This principle of self-determination perhaps is the guiding proposition of all ethnic movements for liberation. In fact, it is necessary because of the threatening context.

Nevertheless, the process of ethnic awakening are promoting increasingly repressive forms of ethno-centricism. Since the aspirations of certain ethnic communities in the process involve competition, it is leading to conflict and power struggles between members of different ethnic communities.[42] Focused on an unduly restrictive understanding of identity, the ethno-cultural and political movements have, by and large, neglected the fostering of interaction across differences. Instead they have, generally speaking, tended to emphasise separatism, non-conformism and intolerance. The ongoing sporadic inter-ethnic conflicts in the region are predominantly a result of the perception of and differentiation between "native" and "outsider" created by the perception of "self" and "other" in which, the "other" is not just someone different, but the ethnic "other". It never looks at a person as an individual, but always seen in relation to the ethnic groups. The "other" is perceived as one who has come to "dominate and exploit" who is enemy to "self-identity and self-interests", the "cause of problems and suffering."[43] So, what is expected of the "other" is that they should always be submissive to the "natives" or the dominant ethnic communities. If at any time the "other" or "outsiders" refuse to submit or react, they should be eliminated or at least deported to their original land or state.

Contrary to what the postmodernists would have us believe, the experience of NEI shows that identity politics need not necessarily be progressive or a radical politics of the marginalised communities against the domination of hegemonising forces. More often than not, many of the ethno-political movements which initially emerged against the "exploitative Indian State" or "indifferent Central Government" and outsiders, particularly the illegal migrants unfortunately ends up as fratricidal conflicts with the other ethnic communities living within the region. Further, since sustaining self-perceptions inevitably entails crisis, in the process it entails more crisis of potential "detribalisation" from within.[44] Perhaps, what appears out of present plethora of ethnic awakening is that as quest for exclusive ethnic identity dominates and identity politics becomes the norm, it continue to reproduce the ideology of the "other" and the region continue to breed inter-ethnic conflict one or the other kind. The trend also shows that even if the attached underground militants were to lay down arms and surrender to the government, there will always be others taking to arms in the name of protecting their community interests. Even if others are not there, violence is not going to cease, given the reality of ethnocentric differences within one's own self.[45] To put other way around, as long as politicization of economic aspirations and exclusive ethnic identity claims continue, the conflicting situation of internecine ethnic

[42] Cf. B.P. Singh, *The Problem of Change: A Study of North-East India* (New Delhi: OUP, 1987), 33-34.

[43] For critical and illustrative discussion on the issue of self and other, see Biswas and Suklabaidya, *Ethnic Life-Worlds in North-East India,* 238-54.

[44] Eric Lott, ""Who do you think you are?" Christian Faith & Identity in North-East India," *Journal of Tribal Studies* XIII/1 (Jan.-June, 2008): 2.

[45] Cf. Prasenjit Biswas, "Between State and Ethnography: A Paradigm for Everyday," *Man and Society: A Journal of North East Studies* IV (Spring, 2007): 113.

conflicts and fragmentation of communities will continue. The very harmonious living of the tribes in the region will continue to be under serious threat.

Unfortunately one of the ugliest sides of the scene is that many of the conflicting groups on the issue of identity and land are largely Christians as the political development in the hills of the NEI is predominantly led by so to say – the elite or better advanced ethnic groups who are mostly Christians.[46] The following words of V. Xaxa highlights the gravity of such situation.

> The sharpening of ethnic identity has simultaneously sharpened the hostility of the ethnic group against others. This has resulted from time to time in the occurrence of ethnic conflicts culminating in violence, arson, looting and even death. Even people sharing the same faith, but of different ethnic communities have not been spared from such violence. The events of 1987 in Meghalaya are clear pointers in this direction. This shows that faith has not been able to hold the people together, not even those sharing the same faith. It fails to withstand the test when it is confronted with ethnic loyalty. The Christian faith teaches values that transcend caste, race or ethnicity. But it has found itself time and again in a helpless position *vis-a-vis* the ethnic position. And when it has taken a stand the Church has found to be a target of attack even from among the Christians. This is a dilemma which the Church has yet to resolve.[47]

The strategists of the peace process find their hopes repeatedly dashed by unforeseen inter-ethnic tensions among the groups. Although, the Churches in the region have been constantly confronted by this problem ever since its genesis and trying to address the issue through various forums and programmes, no answer has been forthcoming as to why Christians become involved in inter-ethnic squabbling! Why do Christians often adopt an attitude of studied silence when their own "tribe" makes war on another? One of the greatest challenges to the Church, therefore, is:

> How far has the Christianity transformed the values and attitudes of tribals or has Christianity been only a veneer of social refinement? Attitudes of Christian leaders and local clergy during 'anti-outsiders' riots…and the inter-tribal riots…have revealed the extent to which Christians values have or have not penetrated and transformed 'tribalism' in the negative sense of the word.[48]

---

[46] For some evidences, see Downs, *History of Christianity in India: Northeast India in the Nineteenth and Twentieth Centuries,* 28-29.

[47] V. Xaxa, "Sociological Impact of Evangelization in North East India," *Indian Missiological Review* 13/1 (1991): 21.

[48] Sebastian Karotemprel, "Impact of Christianity on the Tribes of North-East India," in *Tribal Situation in North-East India,* ed. Sartak Sengupta (New Delhi: Inter-India Publications, 1994), 158.

Way Forward?

Considering the trend of ethnic awakening in NEI and the innate factors of such awakening, one fact appears clear that there is an utmost necessity of re-looking, re-thinking and re-awakening of the very awakening of various ethnic communities. There is a need of a concerted academic effort and role of civil society in bridging the gaps among the ethnic communities. For the region's ethnic problem in general are "paradoxes of periphery" due to the perceptional psychological gaps and much of the violence in particular seems to be because the perceived "domination-insecurity syndrome". There is a fear psychosis of losing one's identity among all the communities.[49] In many cases, the negative ethnic awakening in the region is due to outburst of emotional and irrational sentiments.[50] There is almost a complete lack of mutual understanding of the psyche of each other. Therefore, it is indeed the unavoidable responsibility of all right thinking members of society to find an answer to the question as to why those who have been friends and neighbours for centuries, are raising accusing fingers against each other and fighting among themselves.

In this regard, it must be acknowledged that the academic community has often not always given the lead.[51] The time has come for new awakening. Not, the external forces, not the perceived "other", the perceived enemy, but one must go to the deeper ground as there are inner forces such as unexplored and immobilised sentiments. The region needs awakening in the inner cave of the heart. There has to be the awakening in different levels of consciousness in people's hearts to value the beauty of ethnic and linguistic diversity, religiosity, gods and rites, customs and behaviour. There is a need of counter consciousness and awakening against the ethnic awakening that have often tended to be exploited and mobilised for bad ethnicity in the region. For ethnic communities in the region are caught up in the dilemma between the necessity of fighting for identity as distinct ethnic groups, and, at the same time, the necessity of striving for identity as human community. In this, what is the way forward? There is certainly necessity of setting the course of ethnic awakening in the region towards a life-affirming conviction for the bewildered and battered communities. The future of ethnic communities in the region lies not in the exclusive claims of identity and survival of self, but in the common struggles for justice, peace and prosperity of all communities.

S.B.

---

[49] Cf. M. Banerjee and R. P. Athparia, "Emergent Ethnic Crisis: A Study of Naga-Kuki Conflict in Manipur," *Anthropological Survey of India* 53/ (2004): 79.

[50] For example, it is conceived that "when people in Delhi think of the Northeast, they think of the distance and that translates into a mental gap. When the people of the Northeast think of Delhi, they think in terms of different levels of developments, and this translates into an emotional gap" S. K. Sinha, "Violence and Hope in India's Northeast," *Faultline* 10 (Jan. 2002): 21.

[51] Cf. B.B. Kumar, "North East India: Crisis of Perception & Credible Action".

Chapter 12

Identity Question and Ethno-Political Movements in North East India

An appropriate and proper identity provides dignity, prosperity and security. An absence of identity pictures a person or people as lower human being. This exactly is the situation of tribals in India as Bishop Nirmal Minz clearly states, "...the tribal person is a strange animal to many in our country even today...."[1] In fact, the ongoing rampant movements in North East India (NEI) are due to such dehumanizing image and treatment given to the first settlers of the region. For, the tribes of this region had a long experience of distinct identities and freedom without any interference from outside forces during pre-colonial period. With the appearance of British administration and Christian mission only, they were brought together into an umbrella which F. S. Downs terms as "tribal ecumenism"[2] and gradually lost their identity and freedom.

Hence, there is a renewed consciousness of their old distinct identities and freedom is emerging again where every ethnic group are aspiring for identity and freedom which has greatly created a flux of identity crisis in particular and national identity issue in general. In the quest of identity anything and everything is happening in the region as well as elsewhere in India. Therefore, the issue is much bigger and deeper than the mere identity struggle and addressing such crucial and sensitive issue is a risky job but helpless due to the demand arising out

---

[1] Nirmal Minz, "Mission in the Context of Diversity – Mission in Tribal Context," *Religion and Society*, 36/1 (1989): 7.

[2] See F. S. Downs, "Tribal Ecumenism in North East India : The Christian Role in Solidarity Movements," *Eastern Theological College Journal* 2/2(1989): 48ff.

of the devastating situation of the region. The crux of this chapter, therefore, is to make a concerted effort to analyze and examine the why and how questions of ethno-political movements in NEI.

Definitions

To fit to the purpose of the chapter, conceptual clarification of two terms is felt necessary i.e. tribal and identity. What is tribal? Indeed, it is difficult to define the term tribe or tribal in the Indian context. For, there is no referable precise and satisfactory definition for the term in the history of social sciences. One of the reasons is that in ancient Indian languages, there was no term equivalent to the term tribe. The term *jati* denoted broadly speaking a community, may be a caste or tribe. There are mentions of many communities which are considered as tribes in the ancient literature of India[3] but without a definition. Even, the Constitution of India does not prescribe any definition or description, but just declares that the Scheduled Tribes are "the tribes or tribal communities." Also, Shimla Seminar,[4] so to be considered as "The Great Congress of Tribal Situation" failed to arrive at a concrete definition except analyzing the tribal situation.[5]

In all laws and literatures, the term is used for denoting certain group of people but not definition. For instance, the anthropologists use the term just to denote,

> a group of people speaking a common language, observing uniform rules of social organization, and working together for some common purposes such as trade, agriculture, or welfare. Other typical characteristics include a common name, a contiguous territory, a relatively uniform culture or way of life, and a tradition of common descent.[6]

According to Dube,

> [it] was used at one time to denote a bewildering variety of social categories that were neither analogous not comparable. The *Rajput* and the *Jat* as well as the aboriginals for example, were categorized as tribes. In later usage it tended to be restricted only to the autochthonous, the

---

[3] D. N. Majumdar, "Ethnicity and Regionalism in North East India," in *Tribal Transformation in India: Ethnopolitics and Identity Crisis*, ed. Buddhadeb Chaudhuri (New Delhi: Inter-India Publications, 1992), 479.

[4] This Seminar was organized by the Indian Institute of Advanced Study in collaboration with the Centre for Advanced Study in Sociology of the Delhi University held in, 1969 (6th to 19th July).

[5] The final statement issued by the seminar does not mention anything about "who they are?" See K.S. Singh, ed., *Tribal Situation in India* (Shimla: Indian Institute of Advanced Study, 1972), 627-632.

[6] Vir Sanghvi, "Can the Twain Meet?," *Sunday*, 13 April 1996, 115.

aboriginal and the primitive groups. At no stage however, did we have a clear set of indicators of tribal-ness.[7]

The commonly used adjective form – "Tribal" is etymologically derived from the root term "tribe" which is foreign in origin[8] that is now used to identify and categorize certain bulk of people groups with attached derogated meanings such as backward, uneducated, uncivilized and so on. Majumdar is right in saying that "[t]hough it was not originally used to indicate small technologically backward communities, the sense of backwardness has accreted to the term tribe only when it came to be used to denote peoples who are at present time denoted by the same term."[9] Thus, the meaning of the term is shifted from appropriate to inappropriate and positive to negative. Such a great shift from original meaning and description, therefore, is a matter of remorse for the people who are called by the name "tribal."

In the case of NEI, as per the racial history is concerned, the so called 'tribal' in the region cannot be identified with the term 'tribal'. For, there is no tribal in the region as per the name is concerned and none of the ethnic groups in the region don't like to be called or identified as 'tribal', except for the claim of constitutional provisions for privileges but by their respective racial name.[10]

Secondly, identity is an undefined expression of the distinctiveness of a person or people that is exhibited by sharing of a common habitat and culture – including language and socio-religious traditions. Identity is so composite that it contains exterior and interior elements in it. The exterior elements are those related to name, term and designation and the interior elements are those related to meaning, attitude and intention. The first kind of identity is by name, by being, by nature, by culture, by occupation by and by location. The second kind is by comparison, by condition and status which more political in nature. Attribution of these elements positively leads to a positive end and the attribution of these elements negatively leads to a negative end. The term 'tribal', a derogatory nomenclature is a mixture of all those elements.

The tribal groups in NEI have acquired the characteristics of ethnic groups as they build up their own identity on the basis of their common language, culture, territory and self-consciousness, a set of common goals and objective and

[7] S. C. Dube, ed., *Tribal Heritage of India. Vol. I. Ethnicity, Identity and Interaction* (Delhi: Vikas Publishing House, 1977), 2.

[8] Originally, the term – "tribe" comes from a Latin word – *tribus* (tri + bhuour or bu = to be) which was basically used to identify or differentiate the three basic divisions of the Roman people, i.e. Tintienses, Ramnenses and Luceres. There was no derogatory connotation as such as it is now. It had a purposeful concept and clear description, basically used for the division of Roman citizens for the purpose of taxation, military conscription and census collection. See , in *Encyclopedia Britannica* (1979), 116.

[9] Majumdar, "Ethnicity and Regionalism in North East India," 483.

[10] Which perhaps is the weakest point of all the tribal groups, especially of NEI.

a sense of pride. Ethnic-cultural identity has been increasingly used as a resource for mobilizing the people in socio-political sphere. Thus, the term identity, here, is used not in connection with any ordinary sign of knowing certain information about things or person, but with the issue of life for the tribals. It means not mere stories of struggle for identity but quest for dignity as human person, in Christian sense, human beings created in the image of God.

Tribal Identity in India

As a whole, what is the identification mark of tribals in India? With what description may their identity today be expressed? Are they be described as - socio-culturally, no permanent land to dwell, no furnished home to live, no pizza to eat, no coca-cola to drink, no suits and ties to wear; economically, no money to use, no bank account to deposit; politically, no politics to play, no politicians to shout; and religiously, no God to believe in and no temple to worship at?

Such is the conception and understanding about tribals that is still prevalent among many non-tribals in India. They are definition-less and identity-less people. Their self definitive name and identities are buried up and clubbed or branded into an artificial superimposed name and considered like some species such as fish, animal, fouls, trees and so on without recognizing their varied distinctive values. Even the main objective of a grand historical Seminar on Tribal Situation in India held in 1969 at Shimla was not for tribal identity but towards integration of diverse tribals in India into a mainstream of national life. One of the three objectives as presented by Niharranjan Ray in his introductory address read as follow:

> Evolving certain policy guide-lines on general problems of national integration of these relatively isolated areas and communities and on specific problems of their economic and cultural development, their health, education and administration, for instance. In other words, as I said as while ago, we should be able to formulate certain policy guide-lines as to how these areas and communities could be drawn into the mainstream of Indian life and society.[11]

Such attempt was perhaps can be seen as a policy for extinction of tribal rather than identifying and defining them as people. The struggle for identity, therefore, is a struggle for existence at the core. It is a quest for life, existence and survival.

Identity Question in NEI

The fateful history of 'tribals' in NEI is a story of rise and fall. They had the experience of wandering Aramean like. Most probably, due to survival means they move out from their original habitats and wandered around the hills and plains

[11] Singh, *Tribal Situation in India*, 4.

of Himalaya's bosom spreading upto present Bangladesh, West Bengal and Nepal. In the later stage due to external aggression their kingdoms were destroyed. Thus, they became people of no land in their own homeland; 'people of the kingdom' became 'people without kingdom'; 'dominant people' became 'dominated'; 'royal citizen' became 'oppressed citizen'; and further at present, the experiencing an internal fractures due to "divide and rule" policy of the Indian state and its mechanisms.

In other words, the tribals in NEI had to resist series of outside forces. Due to inability of cultural resistance many of the tribes lost their distinctive identity and some got extinguished completely, some assimilated to other dominant culture[12] and some transformed to a new clan. Such evidences can be found more among plains tribes than the hills.

How are the people and region as a whole known to the people of mainland India at present? It is a common experience of the Mongoloid tribes of NEI that they are mis-identified as Chinese, Japanese, Nepalese or other people of South East Asia and region as a whole is completely misunderstood. To simplify the point let me quote the following statements.

> … a journalist from Manipur working in Delhi was called 'Bahadur' by his neighbour – the common form of address for a person from Nepal! Another Journalist while checking into a Madras hotel was asked to hand over her passport when she mentioned she was from Shillong. A Catholic priest hailing from Manipur (belonging to the Mo tribe) was returning to Imphal after a trip to Calcutta. He was asked for his passport while checking out at Imphal Airport. It was his own state and the officials, other states, weren't even aware of what the people of the state look like.[13]

> We are dimly aware that India includes several states of people with high cheekbones but we know little else about the region. Ask the average Indian in the plains for information about the North-East and he will mutter something about insurgency.[14]

The people of NEI have three basic liberating quests – identity, equality and respect & dignity.[15] The first and foremost is the claim for distinctiveness in the mosaic of diversified India. Due to this quest for identity, there is a socio-

---

[12] Because, with an expectation of upward social mobility, many tribal groups converted to Hinduism and identified themselves as Hindus.

[13] L. Jeyaseelan, "Conflict Situation in North-East India: The Church's Response. I," *VJTR* 63/6 (June 1999): 436.

[14] Sanghvi, "Can the Twain Meet?" 8-9.

[15] See Peter Haokip, "The Tribal People of the Northeast : A Liberating Quest for Identity, Equality and Respect," in *No More Guns! Peoples Struggle for Justice: Focus on North East India*, ed. A. Wati Longchar (Jorhat, Assam: Department of Tribal Studies, 2000), 5-17.

cultural awakening and mushrooming of movements led by various revolutionary organisations.

Though different ethnic groups existed, there was no problem of ethnic conflicts at all among the tribes during pre-colonial period for which "the tribal movement in North-East India is considered as a manifestation of fight for regional identity although based on ethnic considerations."[16] According to Majumdar,

> it is very clear that in pre-British period though states were based on ethnic identity…like the *Jaintia* state, the *Dimasa* state, the *Ahom* state, the Meitei state or the Manipuri state, there was no tribal consciousness as such. The philosophy behind such ethnic state was not 'a state for an ethnic group' but 'a state which came into power with the ethnic group. Even in those days many of the ethno-cultural groups like the Naga groups, the Khasi, the Garo were not limited by any common political organization."[17]

Only it became problematic when British entered into the region. N. K. Das opines that, "by the encouragement of British officers ethnic identity organizations grew up among many of the major tribal communities in NEI. For instance the Naga Club, which for the first time symbolized Naga unity, came into existence in 1918."[18] Most probably, for either for a compassionate reason or creating division the British government granted some special privileges to the tribes that created a gap between the tribals and non-tribals. This does not mean that such privileges were not granted to other communities, but the problem did not arise because the other communities were part of the Hindu mainstream. The tribals being in the periphery of the greater Hindu society the gap was evident.[19]

Development of Ethno-Political Movements for Identity in NEI

There is a conscious revival of the socio-cultural traditions among the tribes, which resembles with the "Revitalization movement" of Wallace (1956) and "Nativistic movement" of Linton (1943). B. Chaudhuri views that "[i]n the tribal scene, two diametrically opposite processes may operate - one where the tribals are trying to emulate the Hindu way of life, and the other, where the tribals are making

[16] B. Datta Ray, *Tribal Identity and Tension in North East India* (New Delhi: Omson Publication, 1989), vii. ; B. Datta Ray, "Anatomy of Regionalism in North-East India Hills: A Preliminary Observation," in *Tribal Transformation in India: Ethnopolitics and Identity Crisis*, ed. Buddhadeb Chaudhuri (New Delhi: Inter-India Publications, 1992), 476.

[17] Majumdar, "Ethnicity and Regionalism in North East India," 480.

[18] N. K. Das, "The Naga Movement," in *Tribal Movements in India*, ed. K.S. Singh (vol. I. Delhi: Manohar Publications, 1982), 41.

[19] See Majumdar, "Ethnicity and Regionalism in North East India," 480.

conscious effort to reinforce their own traditional socio-cultural systems."[20] After a period of initial contact with dominant cultural milieu, many of them try to revitalize their traditions and cultures.[21]

Then, if the identity is not adequately achieved by the conscious symbolical revival of typical traditional tribal culture, they resort to the later process i.e. demand for a separate state through movements, which are violent in their means and political in their end.

Such a tremendous change among the tribes of NEI during those days is considered as ongoing evolution towards viable identity as S.C. Dube aptly describes,

> A close examination of the tribal situation would suggest that new tribal identities are still in the process of evolution. As new identities emerge, old ones are obliterated. In the process, old tribal names are discarded and new ones adopted (derogatory names given by others were discarded, the original and authentic ones are readopted), mythology and traditions are modified and reversed, and alternative bases of solidarity building are discovered to forge wider links with a view to evolving, articulate, aggressive and viable identities.[22]

This was a gradual process but there is a rapid growth of political movements that are creating upheavals in the society. It was just a year before and after independence of India the manifestation of ethnic identity took political color in the region. For instance, with pure political aims the organizations like Naga National Council (1946),[23] the Mizo Union (1946),[24] Karbi movement for Autonomous district (1946)[25] Zeliangrong movement for separate state (1947),[26]

---

[20] Buddhadeb Chaudhuri, "Identity Crisis of the Tribals : A Case Study," in *Tribal Transformation in India, Ethnopolitics and Identity Crisis*, ed. Buddhadeb Chaudhuri (New Delhi: Inter-India Publications, 1992), 435.

[21] The vivid example of such self-identity consciousness is seen in their change of names. For instance, *Lothas* and *Semas* in Nagaland adopted *Kyongs* and *Sumi* respectively; known as *Mikirs* in Assam changed their name to *Karbis*; *Pawis* and *Tuikuks* in present Mizoram changed to *Lai* and *Riangs* respectively; some of the *Kukis* in present Manipur came to be known as *Thado* and *Daflas* in Arunachal Pradesh called themselves as *Nishis* and so on.

[22] Dube, ed., *Tribal Heritage of India*, 5.

[23] M. Alemchiba, *A Brief Historical Account of Nagaland* (Kohima: Naga Institute of Culture, 1970).

[24] B. B. Goswami and D. P. Mukherjee, "The Mizo Political Movement," in *Tribal Movements in India*, ed. K.S. Singh (vol. I. Delhi: Manohar Publications, 1982).

[25] R. D. Pathak and N. Saha, "Political Developments in the North Cachar Hill Distict," in *Tribal Movements in India*, ed. K.S. Singh (vol. I. Delhi: Manohar Publications, 1982).

[26] G. Kabui, "The Zeliangrong Movement : A Historical Study," in *Tribal Movements in India*, ed. K.S. Singh (vol. I. Delhi: Manohar Publications, 1982).

Tripura Upajati Samiti (1957)[27] and so on emerged. At present, the number of such organization and movement has multiplied. Sharma, in his book, *Insurgency or Ethnic Conflict* lists emergence of 34 insurgent groups[28] including ten inactive in the state.[29] According to an intelligent report, by 2001, there are 19, 590 insurgents and extremists operating in Manipur itself.[30]

All these movements basically have six different kinds of demands. Firstly, movement for complete separation from the Indian nation-state itself ; secondly, a movement for full-fledged states within the Indian Union; thirdly, a movement for autonomy within the Indian states; fourthly, a movements for reservation or special protection within the autonomous structures; fifthly, strives between tribal population/groups for control over land or territorial supremacy; and finally, for certain organisations it is a movement against outsiders or foreign nationals. Though all of these movements have their own aims and objectives, the objective of "liberation" and "establishment of identity" are common to all[31] as B.G. Verghese rightly said, "various movements in the Northeast have all to do with identity."[32] Even all insurgencies, though they are different in expressions, "have common requisites like a favourable homeland, an indigenous population, complex capabilities, catalyst agents and permissive system."[33]

If we observe the every bit of the leading militant organizations,[34] we find certain elements of identity motifs attached into it. Simple example, for instance,

---

[27] S. K. Chaube, *Hills Politics in North East India* (Calcutta: Orient Longman, 1973).

[28] Some of the active groups are: Peoples Liberation Army (PLA), United National Liberation Front (UNLF), Revolutionary Peoples Front (RPF), Peoples Revolutionary Party of Kangleipak (PREPAK), Manipur Liberation Front Army (MLFA), Kanglei Yawol Khnna Lup (KYKL), Revolutionary Joint Committee (RJC), Kangleipak Communist Party (KCP), Peoples United Liberation Front (PULF), National Socialist Council of Nagaland (NSCN-K), National Socialist Council of Nagaland (NSCN-I/M), Naga Lim Guard (NLG), Kuki National Front (KNF), Kuki National Army (KNA), Kuki Defence Force(KDF), Kuki Democratic Movement (KDM), Kuki National Organisation (KNO), Kuki Security Force (KSF), Chin Kuki Revolutionary Front (CKRF), Kom Rem Peoples Convention (KRPC), Zomi Revolutionary Volunteers(ZRV), Zomi Revolutionary Army (ZRA), Zomi Reunification Organisation (ZRO), and Hmar Peoples Convention (HPC).

[29] S. C. Sharma, *Insurgency or Ethnic Conflict* (Magnum, 2000), 217-218.

[30] Phanjoubam Tarapot, *Bleeding Manipur* (New Delhi: Har Anand Publication, 2003), 178.

[31] Of course, there is a dilemma between whether "liberation first then identity" or "identity first then liberation." For some it is "how can there be identity without liberation?" and for some, "how can one achieve liberation without proper identity first?" In case of the most of armed struggle movements it is liberation first, but for most of the social change and transformation movements, it is liberation through identity building.

[32] B. G. Verghese, *India's Northeast Resurgent: Ethnicity, Insurgency, Governance, Development* (Delhi: Konark Publishers, 1996), 285.

[33] Prakash P. D. Singh, *Political Violence in India* (Delhi: Amar Prakashan, 1989), 87.

[34] There are about 40 big and small militant organisations in NEI. To name some of the leading ones are National Socialist Council of Nagaland (NSCN – K & I/M) of Nagaland,

is use of English in naming the organizations. May be it is used as a medium of common communication for certain tribes such as Nagas, or in certain cases it could be a fascination for English but a motif of international publicity seems to be the first reason. The second notable feature is the use of the term 'National' which according to them is a separate nationality with their own culture and social customs that are to be recognized, accepted by the world and preserved by them as a unique identity. The third significant feature is not considering their acts as an insurgency[35] as it is commonly attributed to, but liberation movement.[36] It is a movement for liberation from various aspects – basically protection of land and liberation from external forces as well as preservation of the distinctive identity of each culture, customs religion and their own history as a whole. As a matter of fact, one also must not forget that the harmonious living of the tribes in the region is under serious threat which needs to be addressed along side the identity issue.

Factors behind the Ethno-political Movements

The emerging ethno-political movements[37] in the NEI is mainly inspired by a mixture of several different factors. According to B. Datta Ray,

> On the eve of independence, the situation in North-East [India] was very fluid. The impact of second World War, the policy of colonial administration, the possibility of freedom in near future, the national movement, and the communal riots, a growing sense of ethnic identity

---

National Democratic Front of Bodoland (NDFB), Boro Liberation Tigers of Assam ; Kuki National Organisation (KNO), Kuki National Front (KNF), Kuki National Army (KNA) and Manipur Liberation Front Army (MLFA) of Manipur, National Liberation Front of Tripura (NLFT) of Tripura; Hyniewtrep National Liberation Council (HNLC), of Khasis and Achik National Volunteers Council (ANVC) of Garos in Meghalaya and so on.

[35] This is the most common expression used to identify the revolutionary movements in NEI. However, the term "insurgency" is far from satisfactory, since there is within it the implication of illegitimacy and that the insurgent is an insurrectionist. For, insurgency is a circuit of reciprocal violence, where the players are the state establishment and the challengers of the same. See B. K. Roy Burman, "Insurgency: Its Dynamics and Vision for Northeast India," in *Insurgency in North East India*, ed. Pakem B. (New Delhi: Omsons Publications, 1997), 21. The leaders of these movements never describe themselves as "insurgents" but rather as patriots, freedom fighters, defenders of their people and so on. "Insurgent" is therefore not a self-designation but a term generally applied by their opponents. For detail reports on this See B. Pakem, ed., Insurgency in North-East India (New Delhi: Omsons Publications, 1997), 3.

[36] There are number of terminologies used by the journalists, government officials and some academicians which strongly picture and publicise the negative image about the tribal people in NEI. For instance, *India's North-East Frontier: Fifty Turbulent Years*; *Boiling Cauldron of Insurgency and Terrorism* ((S. K. Ghosh) ; *Insurgency in NEI* (B. Pakem); *Naga Insurgency: The Last Thirty Years* (M. Horam).

[37] The political movements in NEI are basically based on ethnic consideration. Therefore, the coined term "ethno-political" is used with double meaning i.e. ethnical and political.

among different communities in North-East and the fear of losing identity - all these factors combined together contributed to the growth of regional ethno-political movements in North-East India.[38]

Above all, a growing sense of ethnic identity and the fear of loosing identity happen to be the most common factor among the tribals in NEI. However, let me begin with the blame factors. First and foremost, British administrative policies during pre-independent India, conversion to Christianity are considered as the initial factors towards a new consciousness of identity.[39] One of the blames put forward by many of the Indian scholars and other anti-Christian forces that there is a great role of Christianity in all the separatist movements in NEI.
The following statements are explanatory to this point.

- They [Christian missionaries] penetrated deep into many of these communities, converted a good many of them, brought education and health to them and opened them up to a modern world. Naturally, these missionaries, some of them very well-meaning and pious souls determined to save these communities of people from everlasting damnation, as they saw it, were all a part of the great establishment of the foreign rulers, and consciously or unconsciously their mission was directed towards upholding and strengthening that establishment.[40]
- In fact Christian missionaries are there not for advocating a faith but for keeping imperialism alive…missionaries and church leaders are two sides of the same coin, one side crying halt to madness and the other side leading the movement and pronouncing the battle cry.[41]
- They [British] expected that what could not be achieved by military expeditions, which only led to endless wars of revenge and retaliation, could be gained by the powers of gospel.[42]
- No doubt significant changes in the tribal pattern of life and culture resulted from conversion to Christianity and educational and other welfare measures introduced by the missionaries. The colonial administration, however, as a matter of policy refrained from meddling in tribal affairs – so long as its authority was not questioned by the tribals…. The hill tribals, by and large, did not have the scope or the

[38] Ray, "Anatomy of Regionalism in North-East India Hills: A Preliminary Observation," 476.

[39] See K. Thanzauva, *Theology of Community - Tribal Theology in the Making* (Aizwal: Mizo Theological Conference, 1997), 54.

[40] "Tenth Business Session (Discussion): Integration and Understanding in the North-East," in *The Tribal Situation in India*, ed. K.S. Singh (Shimla: Indian Institute of Advanced Study, 1972), 19.

[41] Ibid., 620.

[42] S. K. Barpujari, "Early Christian Missions in the Naga Hills: An Assessment of their Activities," *Journal of Indian History* 48 (1970): 42.

need to conceive their position in terms of a wider national context during the period of British rule.[43]

- Christianity has emerged as a strong factor of modernization, and has given tribals a sense of Identity.... The phenomenal rise of Christianity in all North-Eastern states except in Arunachal Pradesh, during 1961-1981 became a symbol of tribal regionalism.[44]

It is clear from the above criticisms that, at the root, the British government is blamed for problem of distrust and fear among the people of hills and plains[45] and the consequent problems in the region. Christianity as an offshoot of British imperialism is seen as an instrumental agent for ongoing "divide and rule" strategy.[46] The British encouraged active Christian proselytism in the hill region of NEI. It is said that "David Scott, the British commissioner at Rangpur, for instance, proposed a novel plan to the Calcutta Council in 1825, asking permission to invite missionaries to start humanitarian activities among the hill tribes."[47] In short, the mission of civilization to humanization among the wild tribes of north-east frontier region is seen as a hidden agenda of the British imperialist policy.

However, the allegation is just fueling of communal dis-integrity, because, the problem is neither a British imperialistic agenda nor mere religious but an ethnic[48] as well as multiplex geo-political and socio-economical problems. The simple argument is that if Christianity is responsible for the mushrooming movements in NEI, what about in other Christian minority states of the region? The following counter arguments are worth mentioning at this point.

- [t]he causal relationship between Christianity and the secessionist movements, however, lacks historical evidence. The allegations against Christian missionaries have slowly subsided as independence

[43] Ananda C. Bhagabati, "Tribal Transformation in Assam and North-East India: An Appraisal of Emerging Ideological Dimensions," in *Tribal Transformation in India, Ethnopolitics and Identity Crisis*, ed. Chaudhuri Buddhadeb (New Delhi: Inter-India Publications, 1992), 495.

[44] Ray, "Anatomy of Regionalism in North-East India Hills: A Preliminary Observation," 475.

[45] It is said that they are the one who first branded even the vast plains-hills complex among the tribes.

[46] F. S. Downs, "Identity : The Integrating Principle," *Asian Journal of Theology* 6 (1992): 240. This article appeared in *Journal of Tribal Studies* also. See Vol. 1 No. 1 (December 1997): 30-50 [32].

[47] A. Mackenzie, *The North-East Frontier of India* (New Delhi: Mittal Publications, 1884 [reprinted 1995]), 253-254.

[48] See Shantanu Dutta, "Roots of Insurgency in North East India."
http://shantanudutta.sulekha.com/blog/post/2006/06/roots-of-insurgency-in-north-east-india.htm (accessed June 2006).

movements have been taken up by non-Christian communities in the region since the late 1970s.[49]

- [m]issionaries are behind insurgency in North-East" are motivated, childish and ridiculous. Such opinions are spread only by those secularists who are against anything Christian and have contempt for the people of the North-East. They paint a very wrong picture totally unacceptable to the local people.[50]

The ethnic based movements for independence or for greater autonomy in the NEI, perhaps, are outward expressions of inward conflicts. These movements arose out of the conflicting loyalties of the people, the conflict between their ethnic identities and their political identity as citizens of India.[51] The ethno-national feelings are very strong even in places where the movement for independence is over (e.g. Mizoram) or where there has not been such a movement (e.g. Meghalaya). In some ways, the movements may also be seen as the product of the conflict between, what anthropologist Clifford Geertz calls, "primordial and civil sentiments" of the people.[52] The civil sentiment - in this case - should be identified with the national majority's Indic sentiments and the modernisation.

Of course, one cannot deny completely that there is a role of Christianity in augmenting ethno-national[53] feelings within the Christian communities in NEI and some direct or indirect Christian influence as one of the causative factors, and yet one must accept the fact that such movements stemmed out of identity consciousness and realization of their fate. To blame colonial legacy or Christianity as the only root cause of the problem, therefore, is to miss the common thread that binds all the movements together. The impetus behind ethno-politics in the entire NEI lies in the history of racial, cultural differences, political discriminations and other related indirect factors. In short, the political unrest in the region is due to the growing aspirations of the people for better life and dignified identity. VIK Sarin's following words of observation express it clearly.

---

[49] Lalsangkima Pachuau, "In Search of a Context for a Contextual Theology : The Socio-Political Realities of "Tribal" Christians in Northeast India," in *In Search of Identity and Tribal Theology*, ed. A. Wati Longchar (Jorhat, Assam: Tribal Study Centre, ETC, 2001), 30.

[50] L. Jeyaseelan, "Conflict Situation in North-East India: The Church's Response, II," *VJTR* 63/7 (July 1999): 505.

[51] See Pachuau, "In Search of a Context for a Contextual Theology…," 31.

[52] Glifford Geertz, *The Interpretation of Cultures* (New York: Basic Books, 1973), 261.

[53] Originally the term is used by Walker Connor for whom nationalism in its pristine sense is integrally related to ethnicity. See W. Connor, *Ethnonationalism : The Quest for Understanding* (Princeton: Princeton University Press, 1994), xi. Taking this sense, Pachuau argues that that is how most "tribals" of Northeast India understand their "national" identity and from this perspective, India is a multinational country. Pachuau, "In Search of a Context for a Contextual Theology…," 32-33.

> The tribal society is undergoing a cataclysmic upheaval. It is in the process of transition from a primitive community based on shifting cultivation to a society better equipped to grapple with twentieth century ideas, technologies and ways of life. Such a transition was inevitable in a world where faster means of communication are not allowing any area to remain isolated, but it is regrettable that, due no doubt to the long years of neglect and repression, it is happening in series of explosions rather that in a gradual manner. The effect of these convulsions has been to put the tribal society in a state ferment and turmoil, which to a great extent contributed to the insurgency in Nagaland and Mizoram and the current spurt of violence in Meghalaya.[54]

The NEI in general is in fact sharply different from the remainder of the sub-continent. In contrast to the broad Aryan-Dravidian peoples of the heartlands of India, the peoples of the northeast are ethnically Mongoloid, and the bulk of its peoples migrated into the region from the east. Its languages furthermore are not related to Sanskrit, but belong to the quite different Tibeto-Burman language group. Its cultures, despite influence from the Indian subcontinent, in many ways resemble more with those of East Asia.

Geographically, with the creation of present Bangladesh, link between NEI and rest of India was narrowed down to a small corridor[55] between Nepal and Bangladesh near Siliguri. Thus, the NEI is surrounded by five international boundaries, namely, Nepal, Bhutan, China, Myanmar and Bangladesh. It is linked to India only with less than a percent of its boundary. The other problem is being surrounded by the International boundary. As General Kalkat rightly pointed out that, "states on the periphery of a nation get subjected to pulls and pressures of neighbouring countries if there is ethnic similarity with neighbouring country."[56] Indeed this is true in the case of NEI. There is definitely a pulling and pushing pressure from those countries. In the mean time, there is also a kind of "home sweet home" racial consciousness among the tribes in NEI, because, they have more racial similarities with the bordering countries (except Bangladesh) than India.

Therefore, they are even happy to remain isolated from the rest of India in order to preserve their identity. Perhaps, due to this reason the Inner Line Permit introduced in 1873[57] in order to safeguard the region from intrusion of

---

[54] V. I. K. Sarin, *India's North-East in Flames* (Ghaziabad: Vikas Publishing House, 1982), viii.

[55] Some mention the distance by 14 KM and some 20.

[56] Kalkat, *The Hindu*, Wednesday, 5 November 1997, 11.

[57] As per the Inner Line regulation the outsiders, i.e., non-tribal, need to secure a permit to enter into the area. Number of hill areas are enclosed into this regulation in order to prevent British commercial interests from robbing the tribal from their land. However, whether it was for good reason, in effect it virtually cut off the prospect of increasing contact between the hills tribals and the largely non-tribal plainsmen (sic). In fact, the British for good reason or something else wanted the

outsiders and the Government of India Act 1935, conferring most hill areas of NEI to the status of "Excluded Area"; "whereby the elected provincial legislatures ceased to have effective jurisdiction over these tribal tracts"[58] still exists in the hill states of NEI. On the one hand it is not realized by that in the name of preventing an overarching influence of other cultures over tribal cultures resulted in their isolation[59] and the policy of development and aggressive integrationism after 1947,[60] paradoxically, reinforced this isolation. It is also a fact that the people of NEI, as observed by Jeyaseelan, has not realised that "India did not grab the region by foul play as it is now made out by some of the revolutionary groups in the region. A stubborn refusal to accept history stands in the way of the emotional and geographical integration of the North-East with Indian mainstream."[61]

On the other, it is also not realized that in turn the policy of isolation, though it might have been with good purpose, turned into a kind of "Third Newtonian Law of Gravity" and served as an inspiration for ethnic identity consciousness and the resultant attempts to safeguard their ethnic identity through different movements, which often are considered as creating "political turmoil"[62] in the region. At the same time it is also not realised that the incorporation of several special provisions safeguards and protections to the tribals provided them a new political solidarity that "the political status has made them come together for their development and the reservation of seats and services have further increased their political consciousness"[63] and thereby to deduct from Indian nation-state. In short, the constitutional provisions are also a major factor for the ethno-political movements in NEI.

---

hill tribes to be disconnected and so excluded and isolated from the other developed parts of India and world or to keep the area as their expedition centres. And indeed it was one of the root causes of backwardness of tribals in NEI.

[58] G. S. Ghurye, *The Scheduled Tribes* (Bombay: Popular Prakashan, 1963), 122-124.

[59] Kalkat, *The Hindu...*,

[60] B. K. Roy Burman, *Demographic and Socio-Economic Profiles of the Hill Areas of North-East India* (Census of India 1961, monograph. New Delhi: Office of the Registrar General of India, Ministry of Home Affairs, 1970), 113.

[61] Jeyaseelan, "Conflict Situation in North-East India: The Church's Response. I," 441.

[62] For instances See S.M. Dubey, "Inter-Ethnic Alliance, Tribal Movements and Integration in Northeast India," in *Tribal Movement in India*, ed. K.S. Singh (New Delhi: Manohar Publications, 1982), 16. ; S. K. Chaube, "Ethnicity and Political Development in North-East India," in *Tribal Development in India: Problems and Prospects*, ed. Chaudhuri Buddhadeb (Delhi: Inter-India Publications, 1982), 144.

[63] Sixth Business Session held on 12th July, 1969 on the theme: "Economic Development and Social Change," in *Tribal Situation in India*, ed. K. S. Singh (Shimla: Indian Institute of Advanced Study, 1972), 597.

Besides these, there many indirect factors such as, education,[64] communication or exposure to other developed communities, sharing of a common territory and cultural elements, the compelling need to come to terms with the demands of modernization, globalization trends, and determination of political status.[65]

S.B.

[64] This happens to be the most efficient indirect factor. Time and again the Church has been accused of promoting separatist tendencies especially in present Jharkand and in NEI. However, the truth as viewed by Fuchs is that the Christian education…has made them more articulate and has given them courage to oppose the exploitation and inhuman treatment meted out to them from various quarters. See S. Fuchs, "Liberation Movements among the Tribals of India," in *Towards an Indian Theology of Liberation*, ed. Paul Puthanangady (Bangalore: Indian Theological Association and National Biblical Catechetical and Liturgical Centre, 1986), 216.

[65] Cf. Bhagabati, "Tribal Transformation in Assam and North-East India…," 498.

Chapter 13

Christianity and Public Sphere in India: A View from North East India

Religion may be private affair but the Christian faith is not.
For Christ did not preach a private religion but proclaimed the kingdom of God.
Freedom of belief does not mean being allowed to cultivate one's own personal faith;
it means making public use of that faith, and practicing it.[1]

While talking about Christianity and public sphere in India, a question may arise as to what can the tiny Christians do against the giant public space of India? And it is understandable indeed! But what about North East India (NEI) with above 80% Christians in some of the states? A natural question indeed! Why is Gospel value and Christian voice not visible and audible in public spheres? Why is Church silent over structural and rampant open violence and gross injustice, denial of human rights, open corruption etc. all around? Why is Christianity so weak to address such burning issues and public concern?

Perhaps, it is sad to note that Christianity and public sphere in NEI is almost a divorced couple. Both appear to be in their own worlds. Apparently, the Church does not worry about what is going around in the public sphere and the public sphere does not know what is happening inside the Church. Certainly, there no is easy answers to the questions. Yet, the Church and Christians as community of faith cannot easily escape from being responsible. Christianity or Christian faith or the Church has no option but meet open face with the issues in public

---

[1] Jurgen Moltmann, *God for a Secular Society: The Public Relevance of Theology*, trans., Margaret Kohl (London: SCM Press, 1999), 43.

spheres and engage in life affirming mission. For, there is no Christian identity and witness outside public space.

Considering such challenging aspect of Christianity, an attempt is made in this chapter to diagnose and bring into a critical scrutiny the public-ness of Christianity in NEI. The chapter is structured into three sections. The first is an introductory note on the Advent of Christianity, public spheres in NEI, conceptual clarifications of key terms and brief theological note on the publicness of Christianity. And the second is test on the publicness of Christianity in NEI. The third and final one is Further Challenges and Prospects for Publicness of Christianity in NEI.

I. Advent of Christianity in NEI

Though there are early record of Christian presence in NEI which dates back to the seventeenth and eighteenth centuries,[2] Christianity sets its presence only during nineteenth century. The region was exposed to six different streams of Christian Missions – Serampore Mission (1811-1837/38), American Baptist Mission (1836),[3] Welsh Presbyterian Mission (1841), Anglican Mission (1851) and Lutheran Mission (1860) and Roman Catholic Mission (1890). Apart from these main denominations, there are also numerous new missions[4] and sectarian groups[5] which flocked into the region after World War II and post-independence India.

The advent of Christianity in NEI as a whole has to be seen from the perspective of the dynamics of relationship between the colonizing British

---

[2] It has been recorded that there was flourishing community of 7,000 Christians at a place called Rangamati in Goalpara district of Lower Assam. The second earliest record of the presence of a Christian (Catholic) community is at Bondashill in the Cachar district of present Assam. Also, there is a very little known Catholic community of Mariamnagar in Agartala of present Tripura. For detail information see, F. S. Downs, "Rangamati: A Christian Community in North East India during the Seventeenth and Eighteenth Centuries", *Indian Church History Review* XII/2 (Dec. 1978): 88-99.; Milton S. Sangma, *History of American Baptist Mission in North East India* (1836-1950), Vol. I & II. (New Delhi: Mittal Publications, 1987 & 1992), 16.; C. Becker, *Early History of the Catholic Missions in Northeast India (1598-1890)*, trans., F. Leicht and S. Karotemprel, ed., F. Leicht and S. Karotemprel (Shillong: Vendrame, 1989), 99-108.; David R. Syiemlieh, "Mariamnagar: An Ancient Christian Settlement in Tripura," *Indian Church History Review* 28/ (1994): 15-21.

[3] Sangma, Milton S. *History of American Baptist Mission in North East India...*, 23.

[4] Such as Australian Baptist Mission, the General Conference Baptist Mission, the Baptist Mid-Mission and Salvation Army. See See Lal Dena, *Christian Missions and Colonialism: A Study of Missionary Movement in North East India: with Particular Reference of Manipur and Lushai Hills, 1894-1947* (Shillong: Vendrame Institute, 1988), 65-68.

[5] For instance, Seventh Day Adventists and various streams of Pentecostals such as Assemblies of God, the Unitarian Pentecostal Church and the resultant indigenous Pentecostals. For their activities, particularly in Mizoram, see C. L. Hminga, *The Life and Witness of the Churches in Mizoram* (Serkawn: Literature Committee Baptist Church Mizoram, 1987), 198-201, 228-30, 256-61, 33 and 340-1.

Administration and conquering Christian Missions. It was the British Administration that first entered the difficult terrain with an agenda of certain political and economic gains.[6] When the Administration had smoothed the surface, the missionaries sowed the seeds of Christianity. The former found the latter useful in pacifying the hills tribes and providing education at minimal cost. The latter too found the former useful in underwriting, in many cases, their educational work and in providing security for both themselves and their converts.[7] In this, the missionaries are seen as agents of colonial powers. It is accused that Christian missionaries are not for advocating a faith but for keeping imperialism alive.[8] However good their intentions might have been, the Christian missionaries are part of great establishment of the foreign rulers that upheld and strengthened the British establishment.[9] Due to such dynamics, the Churches were established by missionaries in line with denominations as well as according to the ethnic groups. Consequently, the Baptist and the Presbyterian Church forms the major sunk of Christianity among the Nagas, Khasis and Mizos. A substantial number of Catholic, Lutheran, Anglican and other Churches are also there among various tribes. There are close to eight million Christians in NEI at present.[10]

Public Spheres in NEI?

While talking about Christianity and public sphere yet another question arises as to what is public sphere? The term "public" of course has its origin in Latin *publicus* (also *poplicus*) from the root "*populus*", which denotes some mass population (the people) in association with some matter of common interest. Thus, a public, in political science and history is a population of individuals in association with civic affairs, or affairs of office or state. Public is something relating to or involving people where social experience determines the configurations of public, rather than a particular set group of people.[11] As a result there are four publics according

[6] See R. A. David Syiemlieh, *Brief History of the Catholic Church in Nagaland* (Shillong: Vendrame, 1990), 34.

[7] F.S. Downs, *History of Christianity in India: Northeast India in the Nineteenth and Twentieth Centuries* (Bangalore: The Church History Association of India, 1992), 30.

[8] K.S. Singh, ed., *Tribal Situation in India* (Shimla: IIAS), 1972), 620.

[9] Niharranjan Ray "Introductory Address," in K. S. Singh, *Tribal Situation…*, 19.; Yangkahao Vashum, "Colonialism, Christian Mission, and Indigenous: An Examination from Asian Indigenous," http://biblicalstudies.org.uk/pdf/jcta/07-03_vashum.pdf

[10] The total Christian population according to 2011 Census is 78,32,533. The state-wise distribution of Christian population is as follow: Arunachal Pradesh – 4,18,732 (30.26%), Assam – 11,65,867 (3.73%), Manipur – 11,79,043 (41.28%), Meghalaya – 22,13,027 (74.59%), Mizoram – 9,56,331 (87.16%), Nagaland – 17,39,651 (87.92%), Tripura – 1,59,882 (4.35%).

[11] Samuel Mateus, "The Public as Social Experience," *Comunicação e Sociedade nº19* (2011), 275-286. https://www.academia.edu/3248817/The_public_as_social_experience "Public as Social Experience"

to situational theory of public[12] – the nonpublics (who have no problem), the latent publics (who have a problem), the aware publics (who recognize that they have a problem), and the active publics (who do something about their problem).[13] The public therefore is fundamentally a non-static open sociological phenomena of the *Öffentlichkeit* (public sphere).[14] It is events and occasions which are open to all, in contrast to closed or exclusive affairs.[15]

The German term *Öffentlichkeit* encompasses a variety of meanings and it implies a spatial concept, the social sites or arenas where meanings are articulated, distributed, and negotiated, as well as the collective body constituted by, and in this process, "the public."[16] The notion of the public is related to the notion of the common.[17] Thus, "the public sphere", according to Hannah Arendt, "is "the common world" that "gathers us together and yet prevents our falling over each other."[18] Habermas defines it as a "society engaged in critical public debate."[19] The public sphere according to him are the formation of public opinion, all citizens have access, conference in unrestricted fashion (based on the freedom of assembly, the freedom of association, the freedom to expression and publication of opinions) about matters of general interest, which implies freedom from economic and political control, and debate over the general rules governing relations.[20]

To bring the matter home, "the public" in this chapter refers to a common group of people comprising Christians of private religious sphere and the citizens of secular state with concern and commitment for common good, and "the public sphere" a common space of publics. The "public sphere" is used to mean two horizons – the open public sphere and the institutionalized public sphere. The first is the unbound spaces and the latter is the places where institutions

---

[12] John Dewey defined (Dewey 1927) a public as a group of people who, in facing a similar problem, recognize it and organize themselves to address it. Dewey's definition of a public is thus situational: people organized about a situation.

[13] Gabriel M. Vasquez and Maureen Taylor, "Research perspectives on "the Public," in Robert Lawrence Heath and Gabriel M. Vasquez, eds., *Handbook of Public Relations* (SAGE, 2001), 140.

[14] Heath, Robert Lawrence, ed. (2005). "Public sphere (Öffentlichkeit)," *Encyclopedia of Public Relations*, 707.

[15] Jürgen Habermas, *The Structural Transformation of the Public Sphere: An Inquiry into a Category of Bourgeois Society*, trans. Thomas Burger (Cambridge Massachusetts: The MIT Press, 1989 [1962]), 1.

[16] Oskar Negt and Alexander Kluge, *Public Sphere and Experience: Toward an analysis of the Bourgeois and Proletarian Public Sphere* (Minneapolis: University of Minnesota Press, 1993), 19.

[17] Jürgen Habermas, *The Structural Transformation of the Public Sphere...*, 6.

[18] Hannah Arendt, *The Human Condition* (Chicago, Illinois: University of Chicago Press, 1958), 52.

[19] Jürgen Habermas, *The Structural Transformation of the Public Sphere...*, 52.

[20] Jürgen Habermas, *The Structural Transformation of the Public Sphere...*, 27.; "The Public Sphere: An Encyclopedia Article," in *Critical Theory and Society: A Reader*, ed. Stephen E. Bronner and Douglas Kellner (New York: Routledge, 1989), 136.

and political bodies operate. There may be multiple public spheres in NEI, but keeping in mind the key objective of bringing into scrutiny the public relevance of Christianity in NEI, the chapter refers only to few spheres of civil society.

Public-ness of Christianity

Christianity by nature is a public religion. Perhaps whole Bible is a public discourse between divine and human. Biblical God is the God of the public squares. God of Israel was not a God of heaven or God in the temples, but through and through God of public and always in public squares. The Old Testament God did not take delight in worship, rites and rituals in the holy sanctuaries, but in the acts of justice and righteousness in the public squares. Belief in God always was connected with the life in public.

The very incarnation of God in Jesus is out of public concern and for public good. Jesus' earthly life and ministry was through and through at public squares for common good of public. Jesus lived and associated with the publicans and stood for justice in religious, political and socio-economic realms of society. Many of his interactions and radical teachings of Old Testament laws show the public-centric life and mission of Jesus. The description of his mission in Nazareth Manifesto is a crystal clear indication of the publicness of *Imago Dei*. Similarly, the life and witness of the apostles and the early church was through and through public in nature.

Christianity emerged out of public concerns and it exists for public good. However, perhaps unfortunately, the doctrines and dogmas have made Christianity a pietistic private religion detached from the world here and now. The publicness of the Mission of God and Christianity is completely hijacked by the pietistic other worldly vision and mission where the concern is how to go to heaven rather than how to bring heaven down here and now in the public sphere.

II. Test on the Public-ness of Christianity in NEI

As described above, Christianity was brought in NEI by various streams of Mission agencies as purely as doctrinaire religion and predominantly with sole agenda of winning souls and transporting them to heaven. Of course, one of the objectives of British Administration as well as Missionaries along with their selfish motif of political and economic gain was civilization. The civilizing impact of Christian mission in form of social change perhaps cannot be denied. It is because of Christianity and its various humanitarian services, many of the tribes of NEI are as who they are now. The impact of Christianity towards transformation of the tribes of NEI to a great extent is appreciable.

One of the most significant positive contributions is on *language and literature*, which even non-Christian orthodox Assamese Hindus acknowledge. The **second** is the change in social life. The power of the gospel if not totally stopped, reduced the inter-village warfare, raids on plains village and the traditional practice of head-hunting. The wanton killing was realized as sin in the light of the teaching of Christ and hostility was replaced by love. It was reported that "Men (*sic*), who had been accustomed to decorate their houses with skulls, felt almost content in using pumpkins for this purpose."[21] Also Christianity provided a means of livelihood with skills necessary to function self-reliantly within the new order.[22] By and large people settled down to peaceful living devoting themselves to agriculture and trade.[23]

The **third** important contribution is *preservation of culture*. The adoption of Christianity did not in a fundamental way affect the cultures. The British administrative officers had appealed to the missionaries to uphold the tribal cultures as far as possible.[24] It is contended by a native social scientist that "Christianity is not spoiling our tribal selfhood, as is sometimes alleged. When we become Christians we do not get detribalized. Instead of Christ's teaching taking away anything of value from our tribal life, it is enriching it in many ways."[25] Here I must acknowledge that the Catholic Mission and the Church care most to preserve the traditional cultures than the Protestants. The Catholic missionaries then and now are more sympathetic to local customs, traditions, music, dance, and architecture and cultural values even like respect and veneration of the dead and their ancestors.[26]

---

[21] J.B. Fuller, "Introduction," in *History of the Assam Rifles*, ed. L.W. Shakespear (London: n.p., 1928), vii.

[22] F. S. Downs, "Christianity and Cultural Change in North East India," in *Christian Faith and Multiform Culture in India*, ed. Somen Das (Bangalore: United Theological College, 1987), 97.

[23] *Foreign Political Proceedings (External A)*, 1885, September No. 37. 9.; *Bengal Judicial Proceedings*, 1873, January No. 21, cited in S. K. Barpujari, "Christianity and Its Impact on the Nagas," in *The Tribes of North East India*, ed. Sebastian Karotemprel (Shillong: Vendrame Missiological Institute, 1984), 107-8.

[24] V.C. Kanito Sema, "A Critical Assessment of Christianity Acculturation of North-East India," in *Religion and Society of North-East India*, ed. S. Miri (New Delhi: Vikas Publishing House, 1980), 78.

[25] Cited in M. M. Thomas and R.W. Taylor, eds., *Tribal Awakening* (Bangalore: Christian Institute for Study of Religion and Society, 1965), 48.

[26] George Kottupallil, "A Historical Survey of the Catholic Church in Northeast India from 1627 to 1969," in *The Catholic Church in Northeast India, 1890-1990 (A Multidimensional Study)*, ed., S. Karotemprel (Shillong/Calcutta: Vendrame/Firma KLM Pvt. Ltd., 1993), 55.

Finally, perhaps one of the most significant contributions of Christianity is "*tribal ecumenism*"[27] or "*inter-ethnic alliance.*"[28] Though the Churches were established in denominational and ethnic lines, many of the tribes who were divided into numerous small groups and living in isolation were brought together into Church organizations, associations, synods, councils, conventions, assemblies, circles and dioceses etc. One must also acknowledge that the theological education institutions have served as common platform to connect the isolated regions and people with wider world.

Nevertheless, the present societal scenario in NEI raises multiple questions with regard to the public-ness of Christianity. Like in any other world, the power of religion, no doubt, is seen playing dominant role in mobilizing the mass to achieve the political objectives. Christianity has certainly played a dominant role in political achievements particularly in the states like Mizoram, Nagaland and Meghalaya.

The present scenario of mission and witness of Church in NEI shows that the visibility and voice of Christianity in public sphere on concerns and common good of people are yet to be seen and heard. Presence is yet to be unveiled and silence towards life and death issues facing people, due to various theological and non-theological factors, is yet to be broken. The gap between what is going on out in the public sphere and the things happening within the four walls of the Church is yet to be bridged. Openness to the publicness of Christian Gospel and Christianity is yet to be unleashed by the Church.

For sure it is not that easy as ethno-political dynamic in the region as a whole is extremely complex and problematic. One must differentiate the role played by Christianity in public sphere between derivative and contributive impacts. Derivatively, Christianity has been source of inspiration for ethno-political movements for self-determination and identity among various ethnic groups. For over the past few decades, the region has undergone numerous inter-ethnic conflicts tranquilizing peace and harmony among the peace loving communities. Caught up in the throes of such a phenomenon, the ethnically diverse and culturally rich people of the region are confronted with bipolar options. On the one hand, need to safeguard the respective ethnic identities at the face of hegemonic powers and on the other hand, the necessity of promoting peaceful co-existence. How is one to maintain a balance between these two pressing necessities? Which should the

[27] Downs for the first time used the term "tribal ecumenism" in an appendix written in C.B. Firth's book, *An Introduction to Indian Church History*. He actually used the term to refer to the development of new relationships at the intra-tribal, inter-tribal and extra-tribal levels. See Appendix in C. B. Firth, *An Introduction to Indian church History* (Madras: CLS, 1976).; See also F. S. Downs, "Tribal Ecumenism in North East India : The Christian Role in Solidarity Movements" Eastern Theological College Journal 2/2 (1989): 48ff.; F. S. Downs, "Tribal Ecumenism in North East India: The Christian Role in Solidarity Movements," *ICHR* XXVIII/1 (June 1989): 23ff.

[28] S.M. Dubey, "Inter-Ethnic Alliance, Tribal Movements and Integration in Northeast India," *Tribal Movement in India, vol. I* (New Delhi: Manohar Publications, 1982), 13ff.

priority be? Ethnic identity or ethnic harmony? In all this, what is the role of Christianity and its maidservant – "Tribal Theology"?

The strategists of the peace process find their efforts repeatedly offset by unforeseen sporadic inter-ethnic tensions. The fact is that the most of the movements in NEI are predominantly based along ethnic lines, justified in the name of defending identity, ethno-cultural rights and self-determination, which, more often than not, lead to expressions of rebellion and conflict. On such conflicting ethnic voices and ethnic turmoil, perhaps, there is no public voice.

There are numerous external and internal factors underneath this issue. Externally, there are geographical isolation, racial differences, economic deprivation, political discrimination, socio-cultural and religious alienation. Internally there are crucial factors such as poverty, unemployment, rapid social changes, cultural shifts, subsequent civilization gap and various unfulfilled aspirations among the ethnic groups. It is also a fact that the plethora of ethnicity in NEI is not a merely given, but a social and political construct. The ethnic movements are generally not propelled by the common people, but it is by a few intelligentsia and developing political elites who either "politicize the ethnicity" or "ethnicize the politics" for their economic and political gain. There is also the "politicisation of culture" – an elevation of cultural identity through political force where the glorious cultural elements are hijacked by the "ethno-politicism". The few elites at times engage in fostering conflictual situations among ethnic groups by manipulating the cultural sentiments and symbols, so as to breed mutual hatred rather than mutual enrichment.

One of the ugliest sides of the scene is that many of the conflicting groups are largely Christians.[29] As the issue of ethnic identity gains the upper hand, even the Christian identity gets relegated to a secondary place among the Christians.[30] No wonder, Christianity and Christian gospel appears useless when it faces the question of ethnicity. Perhaps to a great extent it is true that "blood is thicker than baptismal water and ethnicity stronger than the bond of faith that calls for

[29] It is reported that "All the top leaders of insurgency initiated either by ATPLO (All Tripura People's Liberation Organisation) or TNV (Tripura National Volunteers) in Tripura are committed to Christianity" and "According to official sources the insurgents ranks included a large number of young boys and girls who had been converted to Christianity, although, they were of Hindu parenthood by underground Mizo rebels working in Baptist missions as evangelical teachers." (*The Statesman*. June 20, 1980). See also S.R. Bhattacharjee, *Tribal Insurgency in Tripura* (New Delhi: Inter India Publication, 1989), 151 & 152.

[30] The ethnic and tribal identity is stronger than the religious identity is proved by the fact that the ethnic strife between the groups who are predominantly Christians has often led to as much violence as any other communal conflict. See Shantanu Dutta, "Roots of Insurgency in North East India." Available from: http://shantanudutta.sulekha.com/blog/ post/2006/06/roots-of-insurgency-in-north-east-india.htm (accessed June 15, 2006).

forgiveness and reconciliation.... Christianity is only a skin deep, faith has not sunk in."[31]

One of the crucial factors for such scenario is the crisis of perception and lack of concerted and realistic academic endeavour on the part of the academicians and theologians about conceptual and notional haziness on ethnicity and proper understanding of ethnicity and its beauty. Such matters are addressed in a random fashion in various writings on Tribal Theologies, but mostly as background studies. Though the existence of "Tribal Theology" in NEI as a discipline dates back to more than two decades, it can be asserted that, hitherto no in-depth academic reflection has been done on this dimension of the ethnic issue.

To a considerable extent, the current trend of Tribal Theologies in question generally tends to be insular - mere cultural theologies of certain tribes, not primarily concerned with the flashpoints facing the Church and society. Hence, as the expressions of violence and hostility among the ethnic groups, at times are considered to be the offshoot of cultural awakenings,[32] there is also the possibility that these theologies are indirectly serving as strong ideological as well as psycho-emotional boosters for self-ethno consciousness.

Besides, what has Christianity got to do with the increasing phenomenon of individualism, corruption, misuse and misappropriation of public funds, accumulation of wealth by few rich individuals, class differentiation, chaotic electoral politics, environmental insensitiveness, alcoholism/drug addiction and the spread of HIV/AIDs, lack of social responsibility and work ethics, labourless living thereby resorting to easy or shortcut money making industry and so on?

The Church appears too weak to have public concern against such issues and remain detached as silent spectators. Even it is strange enough that one of worst social menaces – "corruption" is justified as legitimate by Christians. During elections when political parties distribute money to buy votes, acceptance of that money is seen as legitimate since it involves only "India *Toka*" [Indian money], not "amar *Toka*" [our money].[33] All these show that the Christian gospel and Christianity is completely detached from public spheres.

---

[31] L. Jeyaseelan, "Conflict Situation in North-East India: The Church's Response II," *VJTR* 63/7 (July 1999): 506-507. The ethnic situation is a kind of "survival of the fittest." It indicates that the tribal feuds and head hunting days seem to be dawning once again in the region.

[32] In 1997, twenty three Catholic Diocesan priests of NEI along with three bishops of the region who were specialised in different branches of theology met at the North East Diocesan Social Forum, Guwahati, Assam. They felt that "the positive values lurking behind the external symptoms of violence and hostility are the cultural awakening of many ethnic groups wanting to be recognised and accepted." See Peter Haokip, "Identity and Integration from the Perspective of Tribals of North East India," *Jeevadhara* XXVII/157 (1997): 11.

[33] Sanjib Baruah, *Durable Disorder: Understanding the Politics of Northeast India* (New Delhi: Oxford University Press, 2005), 74. Another justification people in general make is that since this is public's money, there is no harm in taking it; it is just coming back to the public.

Factors of Church's Detachment from Public Sphere

One of the key factors of Church's detachment from the public sphere is the sacred and secular dichotomy fed by Western philosophy and theology. In philosophical and theological interpretations, realities and attributes beyond natural realm such as transcendent, ultimate, eternal, divine, holy, purity etc. are considered of sacred domain.[34] In religion, such conceptualizations of realities beyond are considered to be at the core of existence and to have a transformative effect on lives and destinies of human beings. The Christian doctrines are framed over the overarching notion that God exists outside the time and space or realms of phenomenal realities. This has created the medieval Western idea of *secular* to indicate separation from religious affairs and involvement in temporal affairs – a complete separation between Church and State. Secularism got its meaning as religion has no place in public space and religious issues should not be the basis of non-religious institutions. All non-religious organizations or government institutions and their representatives should remain separate from religious institutions, their beliefs, and their authorities. As a result, what is called – secular society is referred to all aspects of society that are not synagogue, church and temple.

Since the public space is considered as secular space, further, the relationship of Christianity with the public space is more of conflict and confrontation rather than collaboration and cooperation. The Church has nothing to do with the State or spiritual life has nothing to do with secular public life. The Christianity and Christian mission tuned with such sacred-secular dichotomy has been a counter force against the worldviews and life-world of the natives ever since its existence in NEI soil. The Church maintained a pietistic and puritanistic belief and practices by which the believers are taught to remain detached from the so-called "worldly" things. The legacy of such uncompromising dichotomic doctrinal attachment is the theological fallacy on the part of the church in NEI that leads to detachment from the public realm. Though public sphere is an important unavoidable domain of God and Christianity, the other-world bound doctrinal and theological fundamentalism has thus far led to ignore and neglect the public sphere.

It is evident that religion is not a cup of tea for Christians and the politics is not a partner to the Church. There is hardly participation between the two publics for the cause of common public good. The possibilities of translating the gospel values into action in public life and to play a participatory role in building a society of justice, peace and harmony is at minimum. Though there is

[34] There are quite number of literatures that speak on the primacy of religion/sacred over the secular. For instance, Rudolf Otto, *The Idea of the Holy* (1923); Max F. Scheler, *On the Eternal in Man* (1960); Nathan Soderblom, "Holiness," *Encyclopedia of Religion and Ethics* (1928, reprinted 1955); W. Brede Kristensen, *The Meaning of Religion* (1960); Gerardus van der Leeuw, *Religion in Essence and Manifestation* (1963); Mircea Eliade, *The Myth of the Eternal Return* (1954), *Myth and Reality* (1963); *Patterns in Comparative Religion* (1958); *The Sacred and the Profane: The Nature of Religion* (1959).

a potential liberative social solidarity with the needy and vulnerable in Christian gospel, the over distinction made between the spiritual affairs and public affairs by the Church has made the gospel publicly irrelevance.

Christianity without doubt has lost its spiritual values and missed the mark to make impact in public sphere. Current socio-political and economic trends show that there seems a complete withdrawal of religion from the public sphere in beliefs and values. Christian spirituality is being privatized. Christianity seems to be completely an enterprise of individual and private life. It has nothing to do with life out in the public square. It is just as private experience of "alone with lone" by a few pious people. Thus, Gospel values eventually seem to be disappearing from the public scene due to the rationalization, secularization and rule of the money politics. As the process of secularization is on the rise, the non-dichotomic worldviews, life-world and religious/spiritual values are on the decrease day by day. The absence of the sense of divine in public space has made the Christian gospel meaningless and irrelevant.

III. Further Challenges and Prospects for Publicness of Christianity in NEI

No doubt Christianity has positively something special to offer in the public sphere. One may call it misuse of Christianity or negative impact of it, but the derivative use of Bible and theology in recent times in various ethno-national movements bear witness to the role of Christianity in public sphere. For instance, many of the names of camps and operations used by underground movements are taken from the Bible and history of Christianity such as Zion, Hebron, Gilgal, Hermon; operation Jericho, operation Gideon, operation Armageddon, operation Crusade etc. The cadres did not fight on Sundays unless attacked.[35] In the earlier days of the movements[36] volunteer gospel teams preached under armed guard which one might almost say "gun in one hand Bible in the other" and the conduct of the jungle camps was ordered by Christian spiritual values and activities. A puritanical life style such as abstinence from alcohol, drugs and sexual immorality are strictly followed.

Overtly Christian elements appeared in some of the official statements as well. One of the operation orders of Mizo National Army (MNA) in 1967 read: "They will be helped by the earthly soldier whereas ours will be helped by the soldier of the living God…."[37] Though no direct link between the missionaries and the rise of ethno-political insurgency could be identified, Christianity, as a contradistinctive identity marker and as an essential basis of the emerging

---

[35] M. Horam, *Naga Insurgency: The Last Thirty Years* (New Delhi: Cosmo Publications, 1988), 76-77.

[36] Phanjoubam Tarapot, *Insurgency Movement in North-Eastern India* (New Delhi: Vikas Publishing House Pvt. Ltd., 1993), 125.

[37] As cited in Nirmal Nibedon, *Mizoram: The Dagger Brigade* (New Delhi: Lancer Publishers, 1980), 39.

cultural identity, augmented Mizo ethno-nationalistic feeling. The Mizo ethno-nationalism owed part of its origin to Mizo Christianity. It was to the Mizo distinctive identity as Christians in opposition to "non-Christian India" that the MNF appealed in its claim for the sovereign independence of the Mizos.[38]

Christianity is taken as the main ideological plank of various ethno-national movements for freedom. In the case of Nagas, the slogan "Nagaland for Christ" is still a recognized rallying cry. The Constitution of the Federal Government of Nagaland, while it guaranteed free profession and practice of any religion, declared that Christianity would be the religion of the Naga State.[39] The clause on "religion" in the Manifesto of NSCN read: "We stand for the faith in God and the salvation of mankind in Jesus, the Christ, alone, that is "Nagaland for Christ"...."[40] The distinct political purpose of being united in a common Christian faith remained not only as a mark of difference with the perceived Hindu world-view of India but also an ideological and spiritual mantle to bring together various Naga tribes.[41] One of the exegeses of "Nagaland for Christ" appeared in a Church Bulletin in 1995 revealed a deep sense of commitment, confidence and faith in the Naga attachment to Christ. The Bulletin reads as follow:

> "The kingdom of Nagaland for Christ is very precious. Whoever commit themselves not wholeheartedly to Christ will perish and they will not see this Kingdom.... Nagaland's Kingdom is not only our alone but also belongs to God.... God has chosen Naga nation as the second Israel. Nagaland will be transformed to a New Jerusalem, and all nations will marvel seeing this small nation. National workers will no more be hiding in the jungles. The educated pro-Indian of the Nagas like Sanballat and Tobiah are against the sovereignty movement.... The land of the Naga is purchased by the blood of the innocent youth. Their bones are not yet decayed, and blood not yet divided. Those who died in the jungle for the nation are still shouting for Nagaland's sovereignty, and God hears these crying."[42]

---

[38] Lalsangkima, Pachuau, *Ethnic Identity and Christianity: A Socio-Historical and Missiological Study of Christianity in Northeast India with Special Reference to Mizoram* (Frankfurt am Main: Peter Laing, 2002), 175.

[39] Ibid., 61.

[40] Text as in Charles Chasie, "The Search for Peace in North East," in *Genesis of Conflict and Peace: Understanding Northeast India Views and Reviews*, ed. Anuradha Dutta and Ratna Bhuyan (Guwahati/New Delhi: Peace Studies, OKDISCD/Akansha Publications, 2007), 508.

[41] Prasenjit Biswas and Chandan Suklabaidya, *Ethnic Life-Worlds in North-East India* (New Delhi: Sage Publications, 2007), 182.

[42] *Shepoumaramth Regional Church Bulletin*, reprinted in *The Shepoumaramth in the Naga National Movement* (Shepoumaramth: Government of the People's Republic of Nagaland, 1995), 225-28.

These examples show that Christianity derivatively served as powerful means of mobilizing people for political agendas. It implies that Christianity can certainly make a difference in all spheres of public life.

Nevertheless, in turn Christianity appears to be very weak to address the resultant conflicting political situations facing peoples in public spheres. Ethnicity as the prime mover, is the fundamental cause for the bitter battle upon which Christianity is seen playing a supporting role.[43] The sharpening of ethnic identity has simultaneously sharpened the hostility of one ethnic group against the other. Whenever there is ethnic-conflict, even people sharing the same faith, but of different ethnic communities have not been spared. This shows that faith has not been able to hold the people together, not even those sharing the same faith. It fails to withstand the test when it is confronted with ethnic loyalty. The Christian faith teaches values that transcend caste, race or ethnicity. But it has found itself time and again in a helpless position *vis-a-vis* the ethnic position. And when it has taken a stand the Church has found to be a target of attack even from among the Christians. This is a dilemma which the Church has yet to resolve.[44]

Sadly, Christian response to the structural violence in NEI is almost nil. Addressing the structural violence is still not in the agenda of the life and ministry of the Church. Perhaps, the sinful situation that demands theological response is neglected by the Church due to complexities of situation. However, if the church is to have any relevance in the public sphere, she must go beyond pietism and a mere cultural theology. The must be broker of justice, peace and harmony in the region through political public theology.

Why do Christians often adopt an attitude of conscious silence when their own "tribe" makes war on another? One of the greatest challenges to the Church, therefore, is "How far has the Christianity transformed the values and attitudes of tribals or has Christianity been only a veneer of social refinement?" Attitudes of Christian leaders and local clergy during "anti-outsiders" riots and the inter-tribal riots have revealed the extent to which Christian values have or have not penetrated and transformed "tribalism" in the negative sense of the word.[45] This constitutes one of the most serious issues for Christianity *in* the public sphere.

Yet, as there is close connection between the Biblical worldview and Gospel values and the tribal worldviews and life-worlds, it may indeed be easy to break through the barriers of distance and detachment Christianity and public sphere. As justice, peace and righteousness are the key features of the Kingdom of God

---

[43] Nibedon, 30.

[44] V. Xaxa, "Sociological Impact of Evangelization in North East India," *Indian Missiological Review* 13/1 (1991): 21.

[45] Sebastian Karotemprel, "Impact of Christianity on the Tribes of North-East India," in *Tribal Situation in North-East India, ed. Sartak Sengupta* (New Delhi: Inter-India Publications, 1994), 158.

proclaimed in and through Jesus, the communitarian values of share and care in truthfulness is the principles of life and the norms of praxis.

As discussed above, the conflict of civilizations brought by western missionaries into the traditional life-world of various ethnic groups in the past had positively created a space of meeting point for Christian gospel and public sphere. The awakening of nationhood inspired by the nationalist movements among various ethnic groups has arisen sense of irrelevancy of Christian gospel to the struggles of people of nations from bellow. This context has created a sense of new thinking on the core message of gospel and its place in the public sphere. A sense of acting as a member of a religious community and acting as a citizen has emerged. Making Christianity a public religion is emerging through various tribal theologies as well. There appeared a new plurality in full force towards making gospel culturally and politically relevant. Need of translating religious ideas into a secular language and taking part in rational discourse in public sphere is felt. The widespread Tribal Theologies and emerging public theology are creating a sense of openness among the thinking public that Christianity must be open to the publicness of Christian gospel and let loose the gospel values to make impact in public spheres.

What is pressing need is that the Christianity in NEI enter into a dialogue in public sphere in order that secular world and secular ideologies be brought to an awareness of the relevance of the Gospel of Christ. The Church can any longer be merely concerned with protection of minority rights, but prophetic public voice for people's struggle for justice, freedom and peace. It must engage in raising prophetic voice against the dehumanizing policies in the political public sphere.

However, entering into public discourse should not be from the point of superiority or from a position of faith-based claims. It is possible not in the realm of ultimate truth but in the realm of public relevance. The socio-political phenomena of the day in NEI is so demanding that if the Church preach about a God who is not concerned with the social and political affairs of society, this God will mean little to many tribes. The situation people are in makes it obvious that if God cares nothing for things that virtually affects their existential lives and stair their emotions, God does not really loves and cares them. In this one can be reminded of Bonhoefer's challenge that "The hungry (person) needs bread and the homeless (person) needs a roof; the disposed needs justice and the lonely fellowship.... To allow a hungry (person) to remain hungry would be blasphemy against God and one's neighbor."[46] From the prison cell Bonhoeffer wrote: "The Church is the Church only when it exists for others. The Church must share in the secular problems of ordinary human life, not dominating, but helpful and serving."[47]

---

[46] Dietrich Bonhoeffer, *Ethics*, Second Revised Edition (London: SCM Press, 1978), 137.

[47] Dietrich Bonhoeffer, *Letters and Papers from Prison,* 3rd enlarged ed. (London: SCM, 1971), 382.

The responsibility of the church is not mere public criticism, nor it is mere a praying department for divine intervention. It is not mere critical or judgmental statements but an active participation in the struggle of the state. Neither, it is mere caring department through social work but an active participation in the society publicly. The Church's role is to be a conscience to society standing against the institutionalized evils, structural violence such as denials of basic human rights, deprivation of human dignity and freedom. She has to affirm the reality and necessity of the world of politics and demythologize and relativize its importance. In this way, instead of separatist and sectarianist attitude,[48] "the Church can be a better public social conscience...."[49]

Conclusion

Church is not just body of Christian as a conceptual and theological sense, but a public body, because the body of Christ is the body of public. Therefore, the Church based on scriptural traditions as a faith community that offers meaning and an account of human wellbeing must provide also a necessary contribution not only within the four wall of the Church but also to the wider public spheres. Though Christianity appears very weak at the face of power in operation in public spheres, Christianity in NEI has got a potential democratic civil ethos that can certainly form a public opinion and the public will. However, the greatest challenge of Christianity in NEI is that Church seems like neither the point of departure nor the arrival. It must make the public dimension of both Christianity and Christian Theology a reality by changing the self-distancing attitude and nature and move, go along and immerse in the public quest for authentic co-existing community, a community of justice and peace. To this end, Christianity and Christian Theology in NEI must hear the prophetic call of God – "Go Public!"

S.B.

[48] Such as "religion and politics do not mix"; "religion and politics are absolutely irrelevant to each other"; "racial issues and religious matters have to be kept separate' and 'all those not for us are against us so we share no part with them."

[49] Cf. Robert Benne, "The Calling of the Church in Economic Life," in *The Two Cities of God: The Church's Responsibility for the Earthly City*, ed., Carl E. Braaten and Robert W. Jensen (Grand Rapids, Michigan: William B. Eerdmans, 1997), 112.